ROOM SERVICE

ROOM

SERVICE

REPORTS FROM EASTERN EUROPE

RICHARD SWARTZ

TRANSLATED FROM THE SWEDISH
BY LINDA HAVERTY RUGG

THE NEW PRESS

NEW YORK

LIBRARY OF CONGRESS
CATALOGING-IN-PUBLICATION DATA

Swartz, Richard, 1945–
    Room service: reports from Eastern Europe/Richard Swartz; translated from the
Swedish by Linda Haverty Rugg
    p.¬   cm.
    ISBN 1-56584-418-1
    1. Europe, Eastern—Description and travel. 2. Swartz, Richard, 1945–
—Journeys—Europe, Eastern. 3. Journalist—Sweden—Biography. I. Title.
    DJKI9.S93 1998
940'.09717dc—21   97-36414

ORIGINALLY PUBLISHED IN GERMANY AS *Room Service* BY EICHBORN VERLAG.
PUBLISHED IN THE UNITED STATES BY THE NEW PRESS,
NEW YORK. DISTRIBUTED BY W. W. NORTON & COMPANY, INC., NEW YORK

Established in 1990 as a major alternative to the large,
commercial publishing houses, The New Press is the first full-scale
nonprofit American book publisher outside of the university presses.

The Press is operated editorially in the public interest,
rather than for private gain; it is committed to publishing
in innovative ways works of educational, cultural,
and community value that, despite their intellectual merits,
might not normally be commercially viable.

The New Press's editorial offices are located
at the City University of New York.

BOOK DESIGN BY BAD

PRINTED IN THE UNITED STATES OF AMERICA

9 8 7 6 5 4 3 2 1

CONTENTS

CONTENTS

ROOM SERVICE

FOREWORD

THE OTHER DAY SOMEONE TOLD ME (I'VE FORGOTTEN WHO) THAT Prague is a pleasant and lively city, full of houses in happy pastels and American students sitting in the cafés, working on *The Great American Novel*. But that's not true; everyone knows that Prague is a colorless city, full of dogs and construction sites, where, if you go out at night, the only person you'll encounter is some solitary, bewildered soul who has lost the key to his apartment building. If anybody in Prague is writing anything, it is political slogans like "Eternal Friendship with the Soviet Union."

My father visited me in Prague. He took Francis and me to a pub of a kind that I would not have believed existed in the city. But there it was. He had often eaten there before the war. My father spoke of Bohemian cuisine, of sausages, and he pointed out the places where the best ones had been served. My father pointed, and behind his back Francis and I exchanged winks. "There," said the old man who was my father, but we knew it was not true. There were no such sausages in Prague.

After two days he left for home, and that was nearly thirty years ago.

Then there was someone (it doesn't matter who) who explained to me the other day that communism had been much worse than cholera, and that was not true either, though communism was not exactly harmless, as someone (I've forgotten who) told me on the bus last week. That's how it has been going, and it will only get worse, until I finally understand that everything will soon be as it never was, and it is up to me to do something about it before somebody (anybody) says straight to my face: You must have been dreaming.

You couldn't have been there.

And so I sat down at my desk and started to write about how it had been, in any case how it had been for nearly thirty years, before even I started to forget.

How it really was; but even that was not quite true.

R. S.
Vienna, July 1996

I

FROM ASSOCIATE PROFESSOR KLÍMA I LEARNED THAT WORK DOES NOT have to be work, it only has to look like work, and that the thing that replaces the undone work is often the best thing of all, though in fact it is only an illusion.

Professor Klíma was a quiet and almost shy person, more absent than present, always on the run. With an apologetic smile and a polite, yet dismissive movement of the hand he was perpetually on his way from one place to another. His very busy-ness had become an integral part of his person. It was obvious that he had literally incorporated it, that all of this busy-ness in one and the same body had given him the short, nervous steps that would have been more appropriate in a dancer or a boxer than an economist. If you ran across him in one of the corridors, he was always on his way somewhere with a bundle of papers under his arm; just where, you never knew. His papers were like most others in the building. For the most part they were blank, and often there was a sandwich squeezed in somewhere in the middle, a sandwich, which left instead of figures or letters, spots of grease on the empty pages.

Professor Klíma was not alone in this habit. The whole city seemed occupied with the same sort of work: carrying bundles of blank paper back and forth.

Professor Klíma was my research adviser, and in his concern for my work he was guided by the same principles he applied to his own. This was generous of him, but I soon had the feeling that we might be beginning from the wrong end. As my adviser, Professor Klíma explained that it was of the greatest importance to decide which sources and archives we would *not* be using; the exclusion, dismissal, and setting aside of sources were our primary concerns when we met, once a week, when he would actually remain seated for an entire half-hour or more on his chair behind the desk in his office, where all of the windows looked out on Petřín Hill.

I asked questions. He may have found them suspicious—with some justification—and he usually dismissed them. Under *no circumstances* were we to use the institute's own archives. Never! They had not been sorted out for three or four years—in the institute's archives the greatest disorder reigned, and anyone who tried to fish something out of there in spite of that . . . Professor Klíma did not finish this sentence. In the archives we would not find anything *of value* for our work, nothing we could *depend on*. While he was killing my suggestions for research materials in this way ("reining in my topic" was his expression), as if he were dealing with an impudent request rather than a dissertation draft, he used to get up from his chair, and with longer and less nervous steps than usual walk back and forth behind his desk, ending his walk each time by standing in front of one of the windows and looking out over Petřín Hill.

Outside it was fall. The leaves were falling over Petřín; at its crown the lookout tower stood out like a solitary black insect. In the valley below large blocks of stone, which had been covered with green during the summer, were now visible. Once there had been a quarry there.

After a number of such meetings the source material for my project seemed to have shrunk to a few of the party newspaper's latest articles by the minister of economics. It was Professor Klíma's view that this represented a good beginning for us. I, on the other hand, considered it an affront. It wasn't that I was unable to understand his situation—but it had been too delicate to allude to the fact that we were working under different conditions, after all—it was that he was able to pull me down to his own level in the end; I had not quite reckoned with that. We spent a lot of time on form. Professor Klíma warmly recommended footnotes at the bottom of each page rather than a collection of notes at the end; if enough room were left at the bottom of each page we would *always* be able to add a new clarification of the text at the last minute.

Professor Klíma was not satisfied with my typewriter, either. One with a larger type would be preferable, as would broader margins and double-spacing rather than one- and-a-half spaces between lines—these features would make the reading so much easier for those who had to assess the finished work. Since the contents would already be more or less familiar to them, and therefore of less interest, it was that much more important to attach greater weight to the presentation.

Rein in. Already sliding down the slippery slope, I began to realize—a little late, but nevertheless—that my work would suffer under his care, and that it was not intended that my work would differ in any remarkable way from any other work that was carried out in this building. My work, too, was conceived as something that would only look like work, that would be written down on thin sandwich paper and bound in the same black binders as all of the other work in the building, and this insulted me, an outsider, or rather: at the moment I took up my pen to write, it proved to be impossible to stand outside. It was precisely on paper that there would no longer be any difference between us.

Even if I did not become one of them, I had been placed under the same constraints. Prague had proved to be the stronger.

The building in which Professor Klíma's institute was housed was being restored. Construction crews were at work in the inner courtyard. The professor and I used to lean out of one of the gallery windows to see how the work was progressing. The scaffolding was a confused mass of metal pipes and planks where the workers climbed up and down. They were in no great hurry, and it seemed that they had plenty of time and wanted to do a proper job. The building's walls were threatening collapse; no one had taken care of them for three hundred years. The plan was to paint them after the restoration, lion-yellow, just as they had been three hundred years ago.

The roof also had to be redone. Other workers crept around up there, a completely different group from the ones who were taking care of the walls; the roofers worked high over the courtyard and Nerudová Street. Toward the end of the day jackdaws used to settle on the roof. One night the previous winter, some of the tiles had blown away, Professor Klíma told me; it was a very stormy night. They had fallen in the street without injuring anyone—thank God it had happened late at night. Now the roof, too, was a confused mass, with tiles lying every which way. Here and there an open wound gaped.

"Luckily you can't see much from here," said Professor Klíma. But from our window he pointed out the damage that was visible from our perspective, and that was sufficient; Prague was falling apart before our eyes.

"We should not dig too much into the past," said Professor Klíma, in a tone that conjured an image of him with rolled-up sleeves, digging, getting down and dirty. "We must avoid it," he said, meaning the past. "The two of us will direct our gaze toward the future." This last phrase was said almost solemnly, though he directed his gaze not into the future, but at me, blinking behind his thick glasses in a not unkind way. What he was saying about the past seemed quite unsuited to the room where were sitting, his office, with all the gold and stucco that seemed to spill down the walls from the ceiling; in all four corners under the frescoed ceiling were golden doves with hearty appetites, busily picking at the gilded bunches of grapes, though the number of grapes did not seem to have diminished appreciably during the last three hundred years. Everything in that room was bathed in the past, even time itself seemed to stand still in self-veneration, and it was just lucky for Professor Klíma that all of this accumulated time ignored both him and his disrespectful remarks about the past, preoccupied as it was with its own eternity.

Professor Klíma seemed unaware of all of this. Behind him in the wall was an almost invisible tapestry door. On the desk there was a telephone, but I never heard it ring; Professor Klíma was not such an important person after all. In his office only the windows opening on Petřín Hill afforded a view of the world outside, two windows that were usually carefully closed.

I looked around the room. Its ornamental decoration was not

beautiful, perhaps, but it was not any more tasteless than the economic statistics that Professor Klíma was obliged to gather, designed to show that the capitalist countries, without exception, were on the decline. This was the March of History. Coffee harvests were set afire, mines were closed and filled with water; it was, as predicted, an endless misery, or in fact the opposite: the end was near. Professor Klíma had already managed to fill several volumes with this prescribed fall, sheer wastepaper which, even if it had been correct down to the last decimal point, would have remained unnoticed since no one in Prague believed or even wanted to believe in it. These apocalyptic volumes remained in the building, unread; they supported one another in the carved and gilded bookcases built into the walls.

That was the situation in this building, *our* building, as it was called when the institute's employees spoke about it, though it was not theirs and the "building" was really a palace, nationalized after the war when the last owner had been thrown out and then chose to leave the country. Professor Klíma held his ground. The past was nothing to hold on to; but we knew, at least privately, that the future was no better—it had a tendency to creep up on you indistinctly and uncertainly. Professor Klíma was taking a certain risk on that point. Despite the fact that the future was officially understood as a given (the flooded mines!), one last shred of scholarly self-respect must have kept him from encouraging me, too, to predict the future in my work.

We were left with the newspapers. "Do you like to read newspapers?" he asked, and without awaiting my answer: "that will be fine, that will be fine . . ." It would be best for our work if we stuck to what the papers said, and the latest brochures. Astonishing how much one could find of scientific value in such unassuming little publications! "That will be the best way to keep our line," Professor Klíma thought, and that "line" made me uneasy; "our" also sounded as indistinct and uncertain as the future beyond tomorrow's newspaper, which he knew from experience would be an inappropriate object of concern, at least for a researcher. But Professor Klíma held his ground. "You understand, I'm sure."

Not much remained of my original ideas. The months passed, and my position in Prague was becoming more and more untenable. Each time we met, fresh suggestions were buried, several footnotes or a whole chapter disappeared, and as autumn turned to winter, and snow began to fall on the roofs of Malá Strana, my interest in my work became more and more muted; more and more, though it made me uncomfortable, my focus started to shift from my own work to an interest in Professor's Klíma's "reining in" of my topic.

What did he fear? Or whom? But this mutilation of my work didn't seem to take place under orders from a higher authority, or even from a higher story in the building. Professor Klíma performed this task with a passion all his own, a passion that could not be discovered in any of his other occupations.

It was strange. I started to wonder whether the source of his passion might have been the secret satisfaction he derived from circling in the vicinity of the forbidden. Professor Klíma kept touching upon archives and documents that we would *not* be using in our work, but in such a way that I was given the impression that he actually felt that they were absolutely necessary to the dissertation that I now only occasionally tackled, and that it was not least for that reason that my work barely got off the ground. These forbidden documents were of great significance for him. I believe that he would even have given his sandwich for them. Most of all he would have liked to carry them under his arm, the forbidden documents in place of the sandwich, hidden among all the blank paper, right in the middle.

I left him to his secret pleasure. I had already given up, numbed by his passion. Toward the beginning of spring I had gotten to the point where I was starting to pay attention to his comments and at least appeared to let myself be convinced about why something should not be used; the lost item had fallen victim to his "reining in," and Professor Klíma was, once he had gotten started, very eloquent, especially if he were not contradicted. I no longer interrupted him. I even took part in the conversation, which was actually a monologue, though I harbored no expectations. But even Professor Klíma's passion for the forbidden was not strong enough to overcome the mild and jaded aspect of his personality. He remained true to character, as if clipped out of one of his own blank and almost transparent papers.

But still, he existed. There was a Professor Klíma, despite the fact that the porter at the front door did not think it worth the effort to distinguish him from all the others in the institute in order to give him an individual existence; he just spoke of the "high and mighty." The heavy wooden door creaked open on its iron hinges. I stepped inside and started to sign the visitors' book.

"Comrade Klíma is not here."

"But I have an appointment for one o'clock. It's already three past one."

"Well, he's not here, anyway."

"Didn't he leave a message?"

"I don't have one here."

"Could we maybe call the department and ask?"

"He left here with some people from the Party."

"Is he coming back today?"

"If he comes I'll tell him that someone was looking for him. I'd advise you to stick around. They could come back any minute. You can never tell, they just come and go, and I'm supposed to keep track of them all."

"Well, I guess I'll go to lunch."

"Come back in an hour or two."

"It will probably just take one."

"Fine, just cross your name off in the book! You haven't met with him, so I can't have your name in the book. He's not here. Cross off your name if you wrote in ink. Why didn't you write with a pencil? What do you think this pencil here is for?"

I had to wait with the porter every week while he sought the "high and mighty" via telephone. It was a difficult task, not so much dependent on whether Professor Klíma was there or not, but on the telephone connection and the porter's mood. He didn't waste all too much of his time on the phone in search of the "high and mighty," who transformed into "comrades" as soon as he got hold of them. They weren't particularly "high" either, and the porter was well aware of that, too; just by calling them "high and mighty" and placing them far above the rest of us, he was showing more scorn than respect, and it was the same with his habit of speaking of them only as a collective, an ill-defined mass of academic doctors, people who came and went; it wasn't worth his trouble to remember any of them particularly.

"Now you're in luck," bellowed the porter, leaning out of his box. "Incredible luck! The comrade just came back, that's what I call luck."

"Is he alone?"

"There was no one with him. I'll call up and announce you."

"Thanks."

"Sign in under the hour, on the right line. We have to keep some kind of order around here."

I wrote my name, passport number, whom I was going to visit and the time of my arrival, all in pencil.

My encounters with the porter should have taught me who had the real power in Prague. It was neither the porter nor the comrades. The real power was somewhere else; there is in any case a difference between the "high and mighty" and the high and mighty, and if Count S.—or one of his ancestors—had risen from the grave and decided upon a Bohemian excursion from Vienna or Passau in order to inspect the family's former palace in Prague, the institute's porter would have flown from his chair, overcome by a servility that lay dormant in his being like an incurable cancer. Though his parents had kept silence about it, it would break out with such power that, confronted with the real thing, he would instantly have renounced the "high and mighty"; he would betray all of them and everything they stood for, without exception.

His Excellency would not imagine that he—*he, of all people!*—

would let someone in (for the first time, the "high and mighty" would be not just a meaningless mass in the porter's eyes, but meaningless individuals) who didn't belong here; His Excellency could not believe that, not of *him*, in any case? And the porter would go on in that vein for a while. The Count would already have cleared his throat several times, but the porter would not allow himself to be interrupted until he was quite finished and had denied the very existence of the "high and mighty": it would not even matter if at just that moment Professor Klíma had shown up, with a bundle of papers under his arm, as usual.

He would no longer have existed.

Spring comes early to Prague. The linden trees bloom in April, and like cotton from a morning dream the trees' flowers float through the streets for three, four, five days, until the miracle is over. This period of blooming held sway over the professor. For the first time in more than half a year I saw him lose control over himself. He became restless, something inside him must have changed, the way the full moon calls forth in certain people aspects of their natures we haven't seen before. First I thought that his restlessness had to do with our work, which wasn't getting off the ground. But I was wrong, and I realized I was wrong when Professor Klíma more and more often opened one of the two windows that looked out on Petřín Hill, leaned out to breathe in the outside air, and then began to speak of spring fever and gypsies.

He combined these two topics, spring fever and gypsies, so sensuously that it was obvious that this alloy had special meaning for him, and that he had decided to initiate me into an extremely private ideology in the place of the official one, which he had never wasted a word on. So we spoke of gypsies; about how back east, in Slovakia, with the help of quite a different alloy, consisting of threats and bribes, they had tried to get the gypsies to give up their wandering existence and become settled. "Can you imagine," said Professor Klíma, who had a good heart. The state provided houses where they were meant to live, but the gypsies destroyed them immediately, out of an instinct of sheer self-preservation, as they were prepared to destroy anything intended to fix them in one place. It was clear that Professor Klíma wished the gypsies well, that running water and taxes were among the blessings he wished them, but that his feelings and heart were more taken by the escapist and incalculable aspects of their existence. The gypsies preferred an existence under the open sky, and he sympathized with them.

Was it their freedom he was drawn to? No, he was much too sober and clean-shaven for that kind of sentimentality. He wanted no gypsy freedom for himself, nor for them, actually. Instead I think it was their defiance he admired, the unreinable and indestructible defiance that led them to destroy the apartments that had been set up for them to live all year long, the apartments that they left for good, with the precision of a chronometer, at the first sign of spring. Even if it was raining! He envied them that defiance, which also could be called courage, and in his envy he went so far as to reconcile himself to those things that must have gone against his sense of propriety—the torn-up parquet floors, the pigs in the bathtub, and so on—because of that one fact, the fact that they *disappeared* every year, so completely that not even the police could find them. For him, the housebound economist, it presented itself as a solution that he had neither the strength nor the courage for; and in that impossible solution lay dignity.

In the spring he envied the gypsies.

"They take off," he said, distressed, and shut the window. "They just disappear."

But his eyes glowed with enchantment. A consuming spring flame burned within them, threatening to ignite the professor, and the message of his eyes was meant for me. He was shaking his head as well, but his head's message was meant for others, though we were alone in the room. Professor Klíma was shaking his head in resignation and submission to the same constraining force that did not allow him to take a single step in the corridor without a bundle of papers under his arm.

How many times he had wished to be able to disappear I could only guess. But instead he had stayed, every morning he took the old elevator up to his office on the third floor in order to take part in a destruction that entailed more than parquet floors and bathrooms.

At the onset of spring he was afflicted with a heavy melancholy. He opened his windows out onto Petřín Hill, not so much for the sake of the warmth and birdsong, but in order to air out the room, as if the whole thing were a question of bad air.

So Professor Klíma tried, in this palace that was not his, but a place where he did not belong, to come to terms with his two existences: his private, which had the drawback of not letting itself be taken off and hung like a coat in the hall, and his public, which did let itself be hung up or put on as needed, but every time he squeezed into it again, it must have seemed ever heavier and more worn, harder to close over the chest.

And it happened that Professor Klíma did not always remember what was demanded of him or that he just didn't have the heart for it anymore; and on those rare occasions he confused the two coats and was caught with the wrong one, for everyone to see.

Actually these were his finest hours, perhaps the only times he allowed himself to be honest with himself. On such occasions he left the palace head over heels. With even quicker steps than usual, and without a greeting to the porter, he hurried down to the pub U Schnellů at the bottom of the hill on Nerudová to drink himself into a stupor.

It happened then that he managed to lose his hat. The hat was suddenly gone. Disappeared in the pub or left on its hook in the office; later it was not so easy to know.

II

Of course Doctor Burian knew the count whose palace had been nationalized, where I came and went; he had even been, as one might imagine, an intimate of his, though when asked, he contented himself with saying that their intimacy extended "to a certain degree, to a certain degree," an answer which I however took as an expression of that circle's customary discretion. Not himself by birth a member of the nobility, Doctor Burian embraced their discretion with that much more devotion.

I had fallen into Doctor Burian's company by chance: someone I knew knew someone whom I did not know, and that person in turn knew a third who was a stranger to the first two of us, who was a good friend of Doctor Burian. It could all have been a conspiracy. And so I was invited to bridge. If Prague's grapevine had been a chain letter, the city would have been full of millionaires.

It did not take long for me to find out that Doctor Burian's friendship with Count S. was not as intimate as I had imagined it. In fact they probably did not know one another at all, or only in the way that Doctor Burian knew everyone worth knowing: he simply laid claim to them, and to third parties he presented such kidnappings as *faits accomplis*; in this way his circle of acquaintances grew steadily in the most unexpected directions. I should have realized that the greedy heedlessness with which he had fallen upon me did not concur with his "to a certain degree, to a certain degree," which, already at our second or third bridge party, I no longer remember exactly, would be unveiled as a boldfaced lie.

On the other hand, it took Doctor Burian even less time to discover that I did not play bridge. Really, not at all: my conception of bidding was vague, I did not know much about suits and wanted to hold on to my queens, any one of the four, though the game was constructed in such a way that I should have torn myself from one of them in order to allow someone else at the table the pleasure of taking her over (after all, our host, Doctor Burian, sank to even more inappropriate appropriations). But it did not matter so much, my ignorance of bridge. I had not really been invited to play cards. The ceremony around the card table was just a cover. Instead I was there *to be seen,* and since I myself was there for the same reason, only inverted, *to study them,* the sides of the equation were, astonishingly enough, equal, while every bridge game in this world must in the end have a losing side.

"Three no-trump," I said.

This was courageous of me, and Doctor Burian sank in thought behind his cards. The other players around the table (or tables; sometimes there were three tables in play at the same time, and we moved around them according to low cards and an order of turn-taking that I did not grasp) were all Doctor Burian's age. They had their best years behind them, and I did not learn anything more about their prime than that it had been great and that it was now past, and that, at best, it had ended right after the war.

We continued to play cards while they spoke of their past as *the good old days*. The nonchalance with which they treated the topic surprised me. This time was an unknown for me, but it seemed to suit Doctor Burian's apartment well; the place was dark and quiet, perhaps not much larger than other apartments in Prague, but it gave me the sense that there were more rooms than the one in which I was invited to sit every Wednesday, a room shadowed by the trees outside on the street, where the tracery of leaves threw uneasy shadows onto the worn Oriental rugs on the floor. The people who customarily assembled there on Wednesdays all belonged to the *good old days*, though they would not have been able to remember them through Proust's simple trick of popping a *madeleine* in his mouth. There were no *madeleines*, or any other cakes.

Cakes were missing like so much else; there was a shortage of things that ruled over Prague and had also taken over their memories. There were no longer any flowers or butter for sale of the kind they remembered from *the good old days*; their family photographs had been lost in the war and the occupation; their suits and dresses had been patched and altered until unrecognizable, so that not even they could bring back the memory of who had once worn them. And so their time, along with a great number of things, had abandoned them, making any search for the past more or less impossible. Memory itself had become an album without pictures, and perhaps it was for that very reason that they had decided to remain in their *good old days*—to fill that empty space with themselves.

But the emptiness around them was confusing. What did they have to hold on to there? Often it seemed to me that they had no idea of what they were talking about. Especially the ladies of the company, who had an enchanting way of confusing decades and could summon up as little interest for the day's political leaders in Prague as they once had for their own servants, so that they mixed up the politicians in the same way they had confused the names of their maids.

The gentlemen spoke of places with names that had long ago been replaced by other names, about products and spas that had gone out of fashion. Sultan was not a horse, but a cigarette. But what was a Trafalgar? Biarritz and Ostende were revived; Vichy was a place where one took the waters and played roulette. They relived the political arguments of their youth, despite the fact that the newspapers had long since written them off and explained that they had been definitively resolved; the newspapers wrote that the March of History could not go into retreat. But the gentlemen who met in Doctor Burian's salon did not care about the March, and the image that they had made of the past for themselves did not allow for issues and objects to end up in the wrong place; too few of them had survived for that. They knew what they were about, and if their memories failed them, they fought against that weakness in themselves with the same stubbornness they exerted against their enemies. They improved their image of the past, their *good old days,* to satisfy their purposes, so that in retrospect they overthrew entire governments, rewrote historical tracts or at least cut out the fine print at the bottom, they left out persons who displeased them or invented quite new ones, and at the same time they allowed themselves to forget or not hear my questions when they suspected that I was trying to touch on their despair by some roundabout route.

For sometimes they did really despair.

When I secretly studied them over the edge of my cards I saw how they stroked their faces with their hands, sunk in brooding and uncertainty.

With the ladies everything was more like a coquettish, lighthearted game. This made them younger than they were, and when they returned from one of their excursions to *the good old days*, it was with trembling red lips, as if the only thing that really concerned them about the past was their own youth, when they were courted by various cavaliers (none of whom played cards at Doctor Burian's). Of a particular government-crisis, which they remembered only vaguely as a background to their own gallant adventure, they unfailingly conjured up only a lieutenant in a brightly colored uniform. The lieutenants were important; *the good old days* seemed to have been teeming with them. The abundant presence of officers in the old ladies' memories gave them a more martial coloring than those of younger women. But perhaps the number of lieutenants had been exaggerated, perhaps their uniforms had tended more toward field gray, and the ladies took their lipsticks from their petit point handbags to redraw their faces, quite unembarrassed, while the gentlemen became engrossed in their cards.

"Has he already done his military service?" asked the ladies.

"You do have a military service?"

"The boy is too short." One of them lashed out before I had a chance to answer, her retort snapping like a riding whip.

To have gotten through these Wednesday afternoons with my honor intact I would have needed not only a rule book for bridge, but also an *Almanach de Gotha*. I missed having both. They got along without them.

"How is His Majesty?" they asked, and I had no answer.

The only thing they lacked in the way of printed matter was travel documents. They discussed different passports as if they were horses at a racecourse. The British was praised, the French was placed ahead of the Italian, and they were unanimous in their assessment of the Swiss passport's robust qualities, but in such a way that I understood that their own stalls were empty. This did not trouble them, just as a bettor feels it is unnecessary to ride the horse before he puts his money on it.

The passports were of course better before the war. This did not surprise me as much as their choice for the very best passport: the one with the cross, the Maltese Order's passport, was the very finest, unbeaten in its field.

"But who acknowledges it?" I asked. They looked at me in amazement, then at each other.

"No one," said Doctor Burian. And once again, silently, they all looked at me.

Such silences were of short duration, but they were not to my advantage. What were they to do with me? And if my awkwardness were in fact something worse than simply youth and ignorance, if it were indifference to the things that were important to them, just as my bridge bids were perhaps not signs of originality, but proof that I did not take the game quite seriously, then I was in trouble: then my position at Doctor Burian's house was on its way to be undermined. In matters of honor they were not to be trifled with. With large white hands, which seemed more important and more personal than their faces, they emphasized with gestures what they wanted to say. Such a hand could seem to be lifted in order to grip a weapon hidden somewhere in Doctor Burian's apartment; preferably a saber. Even at the bridge table they sat as if mounted on horseback, they fumbled for their sabers, and even without the saber would ride to engage the enemy. The bloodthirstiness of these fragile men was terrible, and they saw it as their responsibility to warn me; with the best of intentions, they said.

An ex-legionnaire gave himself special pains. This "ex-" he wore like a medal he had earned, but not aimed for; a tall, skeletally thin man in suits that hung fluttering at half-mast around his person in a sort of undefined, uninterrupted mourning. With the Czech legion he had shot his way home to Prague across revolutionary Russia. His concern for me was touching. I was young, though not so young that I needed to be educated on love's clinical side, but what concerned the legionnaire and the others proved to be my mind, or more particularly, my powers of political discernment, and not only mine, but those of the entire Western world. They saw themselves as having a mission. At their age it was an admirable ambition, especially since it seemed that the entire project was to be spearheaded from Doctor Burian's apartment.

Each time, the ex-legionnaire took me out into the hall. The hall lay in half-darkness and was well suited to warnings.

"You don't know whom you are dealing with," he whispered. His suit fluttered around him more fatefully than usual, and with "you" he meant the entire Western world. I also knew that spiritualist seances used to take place in Doctor Burian's apartment every other week as a change from bridge, when Egyptian pharaohs and various shady abortionists from the distant past showed up to visit, and I was not invited. On the other hand, where political discernment was concerned, one turned to me and no other, in my capacity as medium, so to speak, and representative for the entire Western world.

We stood at the farthest end of the hall, almost out in the little entry hall where the light scarcely reached. Together we stood before the great hall mirror; the gold in the frame was flaking, its corners shone white. The legionnaire looked around, but mostly he looked in the mirror. He sighed deeply, theatrically, it seemed to me, though he must have known that the mirror could not do his sigh justice.

"They wrote Stalin into our folk songs," he said, and looked into the mirror before he sighed again. "Even into the Moravian ones."

"The Moravian ones," I said.

"Yes," he answered, with another sigh. "The very oldest we have," and when he once again turned his profile to me in order to look once more, not without satisfaction, at himself in the mirror, we found ourselves no longer in the hallway at Doctor Burian's, but in the diplomatic theater, I a messenger from Ignorantia and he himself a governor of the United Kingdoms of Great Suffering, and with a short, "Yes, that will be all," he closed our conference; the audience was over.

I had fulfilled my charge. Once more he regarded himself in the mirror so that I understood that it was, in fact, not a mirror, but a camera, and that we two, the governor and the messenger, would appear already the next morning on the front page of a long-since discontinued or even nonexistent newspaper; a touch underexposed thanks to the lighting in Doctor Burian's hallway, but *quand même,* unmistakably just we two.

"Electricity," the legionnaire whispered, and made a contemptuous gesture with his large, white hand.

"Electricity and folk dancing."

We returned to bridge.

"Three no-trump," I said.

This was courageous of me, and Doctor Burian sank in thought behind his cards.

"Original, original," he mumbled, and stroked his white mustache, meditating on my bid, and the mumbling gave him the time he needed to decide whether it was a question of a *faux pas* or a revolution in the art of bridge.

Everyone sat silently.

"One really could not have expected that," said Doctor Burian.

So, a *faux pas.*

For *One* was their supreme court, and though *One* had no jurisdiction outside Doctor Burian's apartment, within these four walls it was impossible to appeal. "This is how *One* does," or even more often, "this is *not* how *One* does," was their final argument against the present day, and it was pronounced abruptly, almost yapped. Elsewhere in Prague a word like "One" had no meaning. That there could be anything to define behind a term so inconspicuous, even anonymous, did not belong to the city's conceptual universe, where "we" and "they" were the pronouns that grounded the poles in the force field of existence. "We" and "they" appeared at the bridge table, as well. "*Chez nous,*" Doctor Burian and his friends could say, without specifying where this place was located; it was not charted on any map. Other words they used like spikes. They hung everything that was right and proper on *before,* while *nowadays* was produced in order to nail down anything that was particularly repellent. Most of the time they were charming, but toward absent strangers who did not please them, they could be malicious in a way that allowed for an exquisite, but, I fear, almost extinct, elegance. Most particularly this disgust was directed at those of their own circle who no longer belonged.

Count Auersperg was one such detested person. I suspected that this was because he was a good bridge player who nevertheless had decided to work to change a world that the circle around Doctor Burian's bridge table understood as being held together by tricks and trump suits. Count Auersperg had wanted to change this world. And what was worse in their eyes, he had done it, so that they no longer recognized themselves in it, and God knows if he might not also have betrayed some of bidding's most carefully protected secrets.

Count Auersperg had joined the Party. Was bridge played there? That he was an initiate of their circle made the matter that much worse; one had no contact with the other commisars, but it was different with the Count. His name was usually pronounced at the tables in a high voice and with an accent on each of the three syllables, AU-ER-SPERG, and when his name had turned up in the conversation (one did not have to wait long) I knew what would happen next; the exorcism would continue until each and every one of those present had taken AU-ER-SPERG into his mouth, so that the Count had to be sent two or three rounds around the table, and the expulsion was not complete until the Count finally disappeared into Doctor Burian's mouth, so that our host could append his SCOUNDREL loudly, as if on a parade field, immediately followed by—in a completely different tone—"three hearts" or "two clubs."

Doctor Burian did not want to change the world. He was occupied with preserving what was left of it.

The problem was that what was left of the good old days had been dealt out somewhat like playing cards. Chance had replaced God and the general staff, and it did not pay to complain about the cards one had failed to get. That was the way of the game nowadays. In order to change the world, a person like Count Auersperg needed only a plan, a doctrine, while Doctor Burian, in order to preserve the remnants of his world, needed both luck and a good memory. A joker in the deck would have been of great use to him. But Doctor Burian was no gambler. He stuck to bridge, he tried to preserve his world without the aid of a joker. Cautiously I peeked (around the room, not over his shoulder) to see which trumps he was holding: a rack for walking sticks, mineral collections in glass cases, a magnifying glass, empty liqueur bottles made into lamps, various letter openers, a porcelain parrot, dance programes, Meyers's *Conversationslexikon,* two desiccated seahorses with sad expressions (in cotton), a Japanese radio for foreign shortwave programs, a number of blurry oil paintings, a billiard cue, two pairs of galoshes, copper etchings of countries that now existed only in that form, and some large seashells containing the roar of distant oceans.

Most of all I admired the old paintings on the walls. They portrayed landscapes from such unknown places that it was quite appropriate that they had blackened with time and now seemed to be painted in a single, dark color; only at close range, where I could see how the canvas had taken on the form of waves (though the landscapes mostly consisted of mountains and woods), was it possible to make out one or two grayish clouds in one of the corners.

Once, it was certain, the clouds had been quite white.

In the world Doctor Burian tried to preserve, everything had already happened. The rest was repetition. The only event, aside from the bridge parties, that he and his friends had to look forward to, was their meeting with death, and it was true—they died: during my time at the bridge tables two of the gentlemen did, one right after the other, as if they had agreed to accompany one another over to the other side. Someone died behind drawn curtains, the candle burned out, someone sat down or rose from an armchair, and despite their views, this very repetition revealed the obstinacy and mechanical nature of their world. This must have irritated them, since they knew that the step from repetition to the purely ridiculous is short. And attracting ridicule was not to be considered, they were panicky about that; to be ridiculous was inconsistent with their *contenance*.

I admired their arrogance, which was directed more at circumstances than at people. With the help of their grace and unwillingness to compromise, they tried to hold out. But there was something else there—and it was fear. Several decades ago they had already stiffened with fear, and the spasm had not yet loosened its grip on them. All of their obstinance, their appeals to a mute *One,* were not only the remains of their upbringing, but signs of the terror that had entered their bloodstream.

And so they played their cards. They had tried to arrest time and they had succeeded, all too well.

But when their falsification of history became too obvious, I started to disagree with them. I corrected them. Why? Out of youthful overconfidence, out of insensitivity, but also because America's president really is not paid by the Kremlin. Still, I should not have done it. They were not used to being contradicted, least of all in Doctor Burian's apartment. In the beginning they pretended to have misheard, just as they had misheard my more adventurous bids in bridge, and instead politely gave me the chance to correct them. But to be corrected themselves was not to their taste. Who was I to make pronouncements about things that had happened long before the war? Or about how it was to live in Prague, on *the wrong side of the iron curtain?* They did not want to be treated like relics from the past, and they did not want to be interrupted, accustomed as they were to telling their life stories; in me they wanted only a listener, someone who would assure them that everything on *the right side of the iron curtain* was precisely as it was before. For their very last hope (they never told me this, but there was no need) was based on the world I came from; that was why I was there, invited to Doctor Burian's, in order to assure them with my presence that this world was still there. My mission was to set up this world for them. But precisely as they remembered it, with everything in its place, as they wanted it and always would want it, and no other way.

"What I still cannot quite understand is your last bid," said Doctor Burian as he clipped his cigar, a Cuban. "Yes, excuse me," he added, "I am changing the subject now, of course. But I thought that it could be of interest for all of us here if you would be kind enough to explain it. Your bid, that is."

There was that silence again; from the sofa and the armchairs everyone regarded me, and at that moment they seemed to me something more than old folks and bridge players.

"Three no-trump?" I asked.

Doctor Burian was silent.

"Yes," I said, unable to make my voice as steady as I had hoped, "I knew what was in my hand, and since Mr. Stoklasa had bid . . ."

I couldn't remember anymore what he had bid and I fell silent, as the others had before. In the room one could hear only the ticking of the pendulum clock on the bureau between the windows. With a quick glance I saw that it was slow, at least a quarter of an hour. Blue smoke from Doctor Burian's cigar drifted through the room. The pendulum kept ticking.

"Two diamonds," said Doctor Burian. "Two diamonds. And you bid three no-trump to that."

"Yes," I answered, "that's right," and Doctor Burian drew on his cigar and nodded.

"That's right," he repeated, and at that moment the telephone rang, Doctor Burian got up to answer, and around the table everyone began to speak at once, nervous and yet relieved, it seemed to me. The legionnaire looked at his watch and said that it really was time to go home, high time, and Mr. Stoklasa was of quite the same opinion and shook my hand several times, loudly repeating "quite right, two diamonds, two diamonds," but in a not at all unkind tone. When Doctor Burian came back, the entire party was on its way out into the hall to take their leave and go home.

The time for departure seemed to depend on the placement of the king of diamonds. If West had it, South would take the ace of spades in the first trick and continue with the ace of diamonds and low card. The jack of spades is an effective defense and brakes West's progress in that suit. But if the king of diamonds is held by the East, South must lose the first spade trick and take the ace the second time the suit is played. Then East has no spades to play when he is confronted with the king of diamonds.

Pardon! Diamonds all too easily become spades, especially in the hands of a player who does not know much about the rules or what one expects of him. Who was I to take from them the last thing they owned, and we are not talking about the billiard cue in the hall or the porcelain parrot, or even about the letter openers, but pain itself? Worse than all of their material losses was the horror of the lukewarm apologist, the bad conscience that I had introduced into Doctor Burian's apartment. They knew of course how little we, that is, I, that is, the Western World, had done for our common cause, and now this young upstart was sitting in their midst, trying to ease a bad conscience (that is, his own, or rather, the Western World's) by smoothing things over and saying that they might be exaggerating—even a Count Auersperg was nothing more than a human being.

"Three no-trump!"

That was courageous of me.

What had happened, actually?

Doctor Burian had looked up from his cards and directed his gaze at me.

"Did I hear correctly? Was that three no-trump you said?"

I had humiliated them, and in Doctor Burian's world, humiliation was a deadly serious thing. There were no mitigating circumstances.

A little more than a month had passed since I crossed Doctor Burian's threshold for the first time. Since I was not sufficiently significant, a subaltern from the circle was delegated to tell me by telephone that Doctor Burian had decided to call off his afternoon bridge parties "until further notice." That no reason was given only emphasized the disappointment with which the subaltern assured me that *he too* had received Doctor Burian's decision, but this was said into the receiver with an abominable politeness that could only be intended—on the surface—to hide that *I* was the source of the disappointment.

From an acquaintance who knew someone whom I did not know, but who was in turn informed about Doctor Burian's movements, I found out that nothing that was said in that telephone conversation was true.

One continued to play. Precisely as *before*.

But without me.

III

For such a short, rather stout, yet still inconspicuous person, Mr. Clementis was unusually full of history, as if a sausage casing had been drawn over some of the greatest European catastrophes of our century and everything was squeezed in against all odds, so that in Mr. Clementis's figure we had a piece of *living* history as well as a walking advertisement for the butcher's profession, which in Prague is so important that it, too, is of historic significance.

Mr. Clementis would not have objected to this description. He himself imagined history more as a question of flesh than of spirit.

Actually he was a Slovak. During the end of the war he had taken part in what schoolbooks would later proclaim the Slovak National Uprising. After he had shot at the Germans, their response forced him to flee head over heels into the Tatry Mountains, where for months he lived on melted snow, horse cadavers, and whatever the Russians, despite the darkness, managed to throw down to them during one of their night flights.

The Russian pilots were afraid of moonlit nights. "The Russian will give you the shirt off his back," Mr. Clementis used to say, "and then shoot you dead in order to take it back." The greater part of the time up there in the mountains was spent by Mr. Clementis and the other national heroes in a squatting position, bare-assed in the snow, victims of chronic diarrhea.

Soldiers do not see much of the world, but they do learn a thing or two about life. Mr. Clementis had learned to fall asleep as soon as he got the chance, with open eyes if necessary, and he had some use for this skill after the war, as well. He had learned to wait and to live with his own fear. The first to die were the terrified or the too courageous, those who did not realize that controlled fear was a better life insurance than the carbine. All of this the war had taught him, and also about boots, of course—the significance of a pair of water-proof boots, not too tight, made of real leather.

Mr. Clementis had survived. After the war he had fattened himself up on canned American food, become himself again, and he began to look for something to do in civilian life. The Party needed people, so he joined the Party. That's the way it was then; that is, different from the way it had been. But the Russians had been his allies, and he trusted their accuracy and decisiveness on land more than from the air. In any case there was no more darkness to keep them from doing what they had promised, and what the Russians promised could now be found in black and white in every party brochure. With their friendship, the future would be bright.

After the invasion of 1968—Mr. Clementis usually made that leap in his biography, a strikingly elegant leap if one considered his corpulence—he had turned in his Party book. This was not how he had imagined either the bright future or the Russians' aid, and he was immediately forced to leave his position as director of a large iron and steel factory. That put an end to his business trips to inspect rolling mills and foundries. He was offered the choice between public self-criticism and taking a job as a hotel bellhop and night porter. Despite his bad heart he decided on the suitcases. Hotel Esplanade, on the City Park.

Such career moves were not uncommon in Prague at that time. During my nightly rambles through the city I used to look in on him, usually after midnight. We drank a beer or two while we talked away an hour. Mr. Clementis wore a comical little uniform with a cap; over the cap's bill stood the name of the hotel in brass letters. Only his compact little head and the topmost two or three brass buttons of his uniform stuck up over the porter's desk. The uniform strained over his stomach and thighs; it had not been sewn for so much history at once. He cocked his head a bit; there was not much that could concern him anymore. But his expression was still mocking and cheeky, because the Party had been wrong on one point—they had thought of his hotel posting as a humiliation, but people do not always move to the beat of the march of history, and a hotel in Prague is still a long way from Siberia.

In fact I think he was pleased with what had happened to him. The Party had not counted on that, either. But for a person who has experienced mortal danger and perhaps already had the opportunity to reconcile himself to the very worst, imagining himself dead and then suddenly by chance getting his life back as a gift, there are probably a few things that he does not take quite seriously anymore. Mr. Clementis was such a person. Full of anticipation, he seemed to look forward to what fate held in store for him this time, though he himself preferred to speak of *theatrum mundi* rather than fate. As a child he had danced and sung *couplettes* on a real stage under the eyes of his parents, in Piešťany, and even as far away as Košice, where his father's sisters lived.

Fate? That sounded like a bank of dark clouds on the horizon, and he preferred to tread the boards. A stage instead of dark clouds.

The advantage of the porter's desk was that Mr. Clementis could observe from that station how all the rest of us came to grips with our roles. Not only was he an actor, but an audience, too. And in the front row; a hotel is almost a real theater. So what did the rest of us make of our parts? Some roles were perhaps better than others, but as his theater-loving parents and his life had taught him, he knew that everything depends on how a part is played. It is all a question of style. A talented actor can make something of almost anything. Mr. Clementis had style, and it would never occur to him to despise even a minor part.

The play? It could have been better. But just before his retirement they had thought of him and given him a new role, which he now took pains to learn, firmly determined to do the best he could when his cue came.

Actually he had been lucky. The Esplanade was, despite its decline, one of Prague's very best hotels, with its back genteelly turned to Wenceslas Square, and sufficiently remote so that Mr. Clementis did not have to wear himself out with too many bags. Nothing much happened at night. Greedily he observed everything that played itself out in the hotel foyer. "Today we have guests from Italy," he told me on one of my visits. "From Mestre. One of the ladies was eating chocolate right out of the box." Then he wanted to hear my reports of what was going on in the city at night. He listened attentively, but of course a bit skeptically; just like the stories I told him, Prague was not quite to be trusted.

"Imagine that," he said, cocking his head. "And they would not even let you in?" As usual he was good humor personified. Not even his former Party was worth getting worked up about. He just smiled knowingly.

He had decided to sit this dance out.

"Dance?" I asked.

I liked that use of "dance," even if it was difficult to imagine such a corpulent person as Mr. Clementis in a waltz, or even a slow fox-trot, and therefore it was quite understandable that he would rather sit one or two out, while at the same time his interest in shaking a leg betrayed a musical bent that I would liked to have seen passed down in his family. It was actually Kateřina, rather than the whole family, that I had in mind. Mr. Clementis's daughter looked on me and the world with great, sad eyes, so sadly unfathomable that I decided that they must stand in the same relation to her soul that a mountain lake does to the sea. With the help of music I was going to obtain direct access to that soul. I had settled my hopes on Károly Goldmark, the Hungarian composer: his violin Concerto in A Minor.

Kateřina came for a visit. She sat on my only chair. Her hands rested in her lap, and I, squatting by the portable record-player on the floor, lifted the needle from the record and tried to drop it right into the silence between the first and second movements, a silence visible to the bare eye as a deeper and smoother black in all of that black, and often I did not hit the silence but instead the last timpani rolls from the first movement, or else I plunged too precipitously into the slow introduction to the second, which sounded suspiciously like the overture to Goldmark's opera *The Queen of Saba*. To Kateřina I said "listen," and lifted my right hand, extending my index finger, as if I believed that without a conductor's baton, here in my dormitory room, I could direct music that had already been rolled out into a black vinyl pancake and only gave up its sound with the aid of a diamond or sapphire needle, not a conductor's baton and absolutely not an outstretched index finger. "Listen," I said to Kateřina who was sitting on the room's only chair with her hands folded in her lap, but Kateřina looked as if she were listening to her own soul, not to Goldmark.

But one cannot give up so easily.

Not everyone takes to music as a pure revelation. Many people have to have the music ground in through repetition, and I lifted the needle from the record in order to play once more the piece of music I thought would help me find the way into Kateřina's soul, the strings from the second movement's *andante,* always the second movement, and almost every time I got a bit of the rest of the orchestra, though my intention was to have her listen to the violin solo. Or I set the arm down so clumsily that it dragged with a screech over the record and stopped somewhere in the third movement, and there were the timpani again, the timpani that I wanted to avoid because the rolls sounded like thunder, which I knew would not awaken an echo in a soul like Kateřina's, that still water, and it was all because my hand was shaking, a trembling that revealed that my intentions were not entirely pure, not solely devoted to the service of art. With timpani and brass my siege would fail. I needed something more romantic. She would be deaf to all other kinds of music; only the solitary violin from the second movement, *solo*, would open the way to her soul to me.

I looked at her, full of expectation. "Isn't it beautiful?" I asked. She nodded, and encouraged by this success I started to play the second movement's *andante* once again. I lifted the needle from the record and Kateřina rose suddenly from her chair and said that she had to go; there was an iron that had been left in for repair that needed to be picked up.

"Must you really go?" I, too, had stood, so that only the music was left down there. Goldmark kept turning again and again, but without making a sound, though now the silence was a different one from the silence stored in the smooth blackness of the space between movements.

"They close at five," said Kateřina.

"Will I see you tomorrow?" I asked, and she turned away and answered, "Maybe."

"Did you like it?" I asked.

"What?" she said.

"The music I played for you," I said, and she nodded.

She liked Goldmark. She liked what I had played for her in about the same way that she liked it when I bought her a chocolate bar with hazelnuts from Tuzex, or the way she liked chocolate even without hazelnuts. So she liked the music. But she didn't *hear* it; not even the repetition held any sway over her. If I had been able to lock her into my room and bombard her day and night with Goldmark, it still would have been in vain. Kateřina would have stayed the same—a mute soul with two black eyes directed at the world, two eyes that saw God only knows what of it.

My dormitory, the Rooseveltová, lay in Holešovice, the part of Prague where the last of the resistance radio transmitters had been silenced after the invasion. Outside at night the freight trains rolled past on their way to Dresden and East Berlin, and we always kept our windows shut, as much against the locomotive smoke as the noise. Sometimes at night we were awakened by the crash when sections of trains were attached at the shunting yard at the central freight station, or by the screech from the car wheels around the curve at the exhibition pavilion in Julius-Fučík Park, a screaming of metal, as if enormous primitive armored creatures were being whipped in the convention halls, and the soot from the locomotive got into my room through the closed window; it lay over everything, a fine dust that could be seen by the light of my reading lamp when I lay on my back in bed at night and looked up from my book.

What should I do with Károly Goldmark?

I wiped the record and realized that the two of us had failed. This composer with his ingratiating violin had not been of the slightest help to me. His artistry had not been able to break down Kateřina's last line of resistance so that she would give up, as everyone else in Prague had already given up, and give herself over to the one who wanted to have her in his power. Goldmark had let me down. There I stood with his music in my hand, alone in a room where only the soot came in, and the room was too little for me to be able to hide from the suspicion which, as soon as it arose, became a certainty: Goldmark had let me down because I had let him down first. I had tried to use him, and that is why he, out of wounded pride, had withdrawn the support of his music, in protest against the fact that no longer could be hidden when we two, Goldmark and I, were left quite alone in the room—the fact that in my heart and soul, I had considered his music, even the violin concerto's second movement and its *andante,* kitsch.

Beautiful, dreamy music. But pure kitsch, just the same.

Not even a dead composer should have to accept treatment like that, especially not one who, like Károly Goldmark, had enjoyed a reputation in his day.

And Kateřina? It is difficult and painful to imagine such people, but I was forced to realize that she was completely unmusical. Kateřina was one of those fellow human beings who lives her life without music. Silence itself was her element, and if there had been more of that black smoothness between all the music on my record, she might have stayed with me in my room. But the depth that I had first imagined in her sad eyes had now changed into the same smooth surface as on the record, a black and rejecting surface with a connection neither to soul nor water, a monotonous silence which, if I had not happened to be in love, would have bored me and soon gotten on my nerves.

Kateřina's visits grew rare, so rare that her father began to look searchingly at me when I visited him at night at the Esplanade. But he did not say anything, either. The record with its solitary violin was stowed away at the bottom of my closet, so that the only music remaining in my room was Bedřich Smetana's first harp chords from *Má Vlast* (*My Country*).

Smetana's chords were at first a mystery. For a long time I did not know that they awoke every morning in my room along with the radio. And so in the beginning I imagined the harp music as something performed inside my head, heavenly notes that could only be heard in a half-waking state, but did not keep me from falling asleep again, so that when I woke up again several hours later and actually got up, the heavenly music had, of course, vanished. But every morning at dawn, the harp sounded again. I did not know where the music came from, and therefore I decided that it must be heavenly and could have no other origin. It had nothing to do with our world. But I was not particularly satisfied with that explanation, and one day when I was sitting over my papers and books as usual, my glance fell on the radio, the same kind of radio that was in every room in the dormitory, a radio I had never turned on, but from which I now thought I could hear a soft murmuring, a whisper so soft it seemed designed for only the finest sense of hearing. I got up from my desk and turned up the volume. The room was filled with a man's voice— one other than my own.

On the radio the latest statistics on coal production were being read. Perhaps Professsor Klíma was at work here, but when I tired of the numbers and wanted to get rid of the strange voice, I found it to be impossible. The radio could not be turned off. One could turn down the volume, but a soft whisper always remained.

Finally I understood. This radio was constructed so that whatever was being broadcast was *always there,* so that—even if no one were listening—it would not be possible to replace the transmitted message with anything else, not even with silence.

Even silence had to be suppressed in Prague, the silence from which new sounds could all too easily arise. But the sounds were all *theirs*; as soon as it began to crackle from a loudspeaker or megaphone one could be sure that a sound was on its way that belonged to *them,* which they wanted to have heard because it was a sound that substantiated that everything was as it should be, the screech of overcrowded streetcars, the slam of trays at the canteen, factory whistles, the stamping of demonstrators forced to march, hammers striking steel, the coal that rushed into the cellars of buildings, and every morning at the same time, at dawn, the sound of those first harp chords from Smetana's *Má Vlast,* which introduced the radio's daily program and reminded us that there was and could not be any other radio station.

It was that kind of music. A limitless and predictable one, at war with every other music and even with silence itself, so that in the end I did not hear it, either, not even at dawn.

Instead I began to listen for the sounds that their sounds had been made to drown out, and it was probably for that reason that early one October morning I perceived another sound, a knock at my door, instead of Smetana; not even a real knock, more like a scratching, as if a cat had scratched the door with its claws.

A strange sound! Something must have happened. With a jerk I sat up in bed. I looked at the clock. It was not yet even six.

Out in the corridor stood Kateřina.

How had she gotten past the porter was my first thought, the flabby one in the flowered cleaning gown who did not even let in any girls during the day, as if she wanted to keep us for herself, a whole building full of the opposite sex. Without making a single sound,

Kateřina sat for the first time on the bed that, despite the music now hidden in my closet, she had managed to avoid with such skill for months. It struck me that even the porter had to sleep behind the window in her glass cage, as everyone else was still sleeping and as even I had slept until a strange noise had awakened me. But what Kateřina was doing here and at this hour of the day I did not understand, and it was making me nervous.

What could have happened? Not a word passed her lips; they just moved like those of a fish, as if my room had been filled with water instead of the first morning light that sifted in through the curtains and now lay over the coal dust in the room which, despite my closed windows, was always there, just like *their* sound from the radio was always there and would not let itself be turned off or shut out, even if it were only sound for the most sensitive ears; and I asked her what had happened, why she had come, but I got no answer.

Instead of answering she lay down at the outer edge of my bed and drew her legs up under herself. Then she rolled into a ball as if she had just come here to sleep. She held her hands in front of her face. Carefully I sat down beside her on the bed and wished that Goldmark had been able to see me at that moment, see that what I had desired for so long could happen so easily, without the help of his awful music, in this perfect silence.

Neither of us said anything, and when I carefully stroked her legs, her pantyhose crackled. She lay completely still, and that was not how it was supposed to be; I had imagined that she would move, that the music would take control of her and loosen all her stiffness and immobility, that the solitary violin would get her to lose control of herself and her limbs, but none of that happened, and so Kateřina must have come with the intention of torturing me, to show how little I meant to her. Now silence ruled my room. When she took her hands from her face her mouth was still opening and closing like that of a fish. Not the tiniest sound passed her lips.

I had imagined things differently, but without Goldmark nothing was quite the same. Her silence did not seem like consent, as if she finally wanted to give up, but instead like a mute counterpoint that emphasized precisely the absence of music and how impossible my desire had become without the slightest sound from her, from my own Kateřina, so that I actually was relieved when she finally sat up and went to my desk. As usual my papers and books were lying there, among them Professor Poldauf's big Czech–English dictionary. Kateřina opened it and nervously paged back and forth, until she found the word she was seeking and was not able to utter.

Her finger had stopped in a column on the right. With relief she pointed at the word: *zaknout,* to arrest.

O Prague, you city of half-eaten angels and dead telephones, my Prague with beer scum around the mouths of informers!

Sometime during the night, two unknown men had visited her father at the Hotel Esplanade, and after a short conversation they had taken him away. The hotel operator had not dared to call the family, they did not have a telephone anyway, but she sent her son, and then Kateřina had hurried to me. I was a friend of the family, in any case, and a foreigner, besides. Maybe a foreign embassy could do something for her father, but all of this did not pour out of her until we had left my dorm room in Rooseveltová and I had taken her to the canteen by Julius-Fučík Park, outside the exhibition halls, where the proletariat could already eat its early morning breakfast standing, even at this hour.

When she had told me what had happened and calmed herself, I asked her to go home and promised to speak to someone at the embassy later in the day. It proved to be superfluous; late in the afternoon Mr. Clementis was back home. That same evening I visited the family. Mr. Clementis was his usual good-humored self. They probably just wanted to scare him with the interrogation and twelve hours in a cell, remind him that while *they* could close him out of the Party any time they wanted, that did not mean that he could step out whenever it happened to suit him. For Mr. Clementis the whole thing was just bad theater, and he waved it away like a bagatelle.

For the sake of appearances they had accused him of using his position as hotel porter to procure prostitutes for foreign hotel guests. Two such ladies were supposed to have been let up to the room of a West German businessman at the same time, and at the police station at Bartolomějská 9 they had managed to scare up two whores to commit perjury against him; Mr. Clementis was elated that both of them had been really seductive and had lied with so many daring details that he himself became completely fascinated.

"You probably know that Bartolomějská was a Jesuit cloister before the police took it over?" he asked.

"That must have been long before the war," said Kateřina. I had seldom heard her complete such a long and coherent sentence.

"Yes, yes, before the war," said her father, but so distracted and distant that we understood that as far as he was concerned the matter was no longer of this world, something like when one opens a window again which one had hurried to close during a sudden storm.

And indeed! A thunder storm had passed over Prague the night Mr. Clementis had been arrested. None of the rest of us had heard it, it had not even rained, but as he was led away a storm had broken. The big trees in the City Park outside the Hotel Esplanade had bent back and forth in the wind, and the two strange men had taken him to a car in the hotel's parking lot. Later they parked the car down by the river, only a few blocks from Bartolomějská 9. Perhaps it was prescribed that the last bit of the way had to be done on foot, and right there down by the river it had happened—a sudden gust of wind had taken Mr. Clementis's uniform cap and tossed it into the river.

One of the plainclothes policemen had screamed. Could that be heard in the wind? A scream of wrath, perhaps a policeman's reflex against all forms of insubordination. That his wrath was in this case actually directed against the wind and not the suspect did not make any difference; it only made his scream meaningless.

So the Hotel Esplanade ended up in the Moldau. The cap disappeared into the waves. On foot the three continued together toward the jail, and as I write this I am certain that this scene—which I did not witness with my own eyes, only heard about secondhand—is even more clear and in a crucial way more real than all of my own memories from Prague.

How two men in the night lead a third one between them.

A corpulent little man in uniform, in white bellhop gloves, yellowed after too many washings and already beginning to split down the seams.

BEFORE THE WASPS IN SIBIU DIE IN THE AUTUMN, THEY BECOME contrary and seek out even things that are not sweet. They become interested in the already-dead carp in the pails on the street in front of the Protestant church, in the dark blue grapes with skins like leather, and in my room they creep over the bedspread, although there is not a trace of the scent of soap there; it is as if the wasps wanted to take a catnap in the middle of day, little suspecting that what awaits them is a much longer and deeper sleep.

On the table between us, too, a lone wasp crawls over the cloth, and when the prince looks at it, it is through brown and sleepy eyes, with heavy lids over the sleepy eyes, and when he lifts the empty water glass from the table and turns it upside down over the wasp, it is a slow movement that belongs to autumn, precisely autumn and no other season.

The sky lowers over the wasp, an autumn sky of glass from the underworld of the insects.

"You have come to meet my father," says the prince.

It sounds more like a statement than a question. The prince is wearing a light brown leather jacket with shiny rivets. The rivets are a touch rusty, as if they were dusted with a fine layer of pollen. Instead of looking at me, he looks through his brown eyes at the insect under the overturned glass. The wasp is not moving any longer. It lies suddenly still, as if lifeless.

That is correct. I nod. It is the prince's father I want to meet, and for this very morning, I have been granted an audience at the stroke of ten. I look at my watch; it is three minutes past ten.

But his majesty is not here.

"My father," continues the prince, without looking at me, "is in Bucharest meeting Michael Jackson."

"Michael Jackson," I say.

"He is meeting Michael Jackson in Bucharest," says the prince.

For that reason there can be no question of an audience today. Perhaps tomorrow. Perhaps on Sunday. But under no circumstances today.

"You do of course understand," says the prince.

He makes a gesture with his right hand as if he wants to indicate how few days a week actually contains, especially if one thinks of how many people there are who would like nothing better than to meet his father.

The room where we sit is narrow and dark, with thin, white, tattered curtains, which close out the view to the street. If there had been two rows of little desks in here, we would have had a schoolroom. The prince sits behind a large desk; his right hand flashes, and I rise and thank him for the information. I really do not wish to disturb him any longer. I thank him for the audience in advance, and the prince promises that I will be contacted.

"Someone will call you soon enough," he says.

WAITING TIME IS DIFFERENT FROM THE TIME IT TAKES TO GET SOMEthing done. Waiting time is like an empty glass placed over the person waiting like a glass over a wasp, and imprisoned under the glass, the movements of the person waiting become heavy and slow; sometimes he falls asleep. In times of great tension or waiting, sleep is never far away.

Through the window I look out over the tile roofs and beyond them black smoke rises into the sky; a field is burning. No church bells ring in Sibiu.

How does one kill time while waiting for a royal audience? For lack of experience I can think of nothing better than to lie on my back on the bed and give the matter some thought. The morning's wasps have disappeared. My only company in the room is a fly. On the ceiling above the bed it sits, completely still, with its feet glued to the ceiling, as if on its back in space. The fly might have been surprised in that position by the moment that summer changed to autumn, and since every autumn is followed by a winter, it is not out of the question that the fly will still be there, on the very same spot on the ceiling, much longer than I lie on my back on the bed.

But this is not certain.

As I am lying there it strikes me that this is precisely the way that people have always had to wait for the masters and czars of Eastern Europe: half asleep in their clothes, hungry and with flies flying in and out of their open mouths, lying or slumping, day in and day out, with flies stuck like glue to the ceiling and minds so befuddled that they can no longer distinguish Wednesdays from Mondays and would in any case mistake a gold-braided doorkeeper for the Majesty himself.

Is that a knock at the door? With a start I awake from my doze. The telephone is covered with a sticky layer of dirt, the cord has been pulled from the wall so that green and red wires, the wallpaper, and mortar have followed. The fly is still there in his place on the ceiling. When I open the door a thin little girl is standing out in the corridor; she asks to speak with Gabriella.

During the night I am awakened by a nightmare that contains ingredients like "castle," "irons," and "dungeon." With a laugh at such silliness I awake from my own dream. When I turn on the light and try to get out of bed I notice that in my sleep I have pushed my left foot straight through a hole in the sheet, then wound it several times around my body like a rope.

In the morning as I am standing in front of the bathroom mirror the telephone rings.

It is Princess Luminiţa, the Little Light, who says that her father is back from Bucharest and will receive me at half-past ten.

"It is so hard for me to hear you on this line," I say.

"Bring coffee," says the princess.

They are out of it at the royal palace, and her father forgot to buy some while he was in Bucharest.

THE KING DOES NOT ARRIVE IN TIME FOR THE AUDIENCE, AND I HAVE plenty of time to get reacquainted with the audience hall. In the vases there are plastic flowers; the pink flowers are much too pink, and the green leaves are much too green to be considered green, though they could not be taken for any other color. The royal palace, too, is green. It lies on the opposite side of the street, and when I look out the window, which is veiled with its thin, transparent curtain, I discover a man in a light brown leather jacket standing outside the gate to the palace. It is the prince.

On the oblong audience table in front of me there is a car radio. The package of coffee, a West German brand, had been commandeered with a bow by a friendly person from the court administration even before I stepped into the audience hall.

I am sitting alone at the table waiting for the king.

When the king does suddenly enter the hall through a door at the other end of the room, he does not sit at the large desk where the prince had sat the day before, but right across from me, at the oblong table with the car radio. The king is wearing a suit jacket. It is of no particular color at all, and his tie is more discreet than the pink and gray one I had seen on his official portrait; his cheeks are not as rosy, his hair is not as black, and without saying anything he lays his calling card in front of me on the table.

"Obligations in Bucharest detained me," says the king.

The royal crest on the calling card is a blue oblong field, symbolizing the sky, with a green field below, which stands for the earth. Between the sky and the earth there is a drawing of a wagon wheel. On the calling card the wheel stands still, but only on the calling card, because Ion Cioabă is not only the king of the coppersmith gypsies, but also king of the journeying gypsies, and on his hands he wears four gold rings, two on each hand, so large and with so much gold that his fingers are splayed.

Even in his mouth the king has gold, but not just here and there among his back teeth; he has it in the very front of his upper jaw, four teeth in a row, solid gold. Now and then he touches them with the tip of his tongue; in this country people steal even in broad daylight, and if you don't watch out you could be robbed of your very teeth.

The tip of the king's tongue is gray. Instantly it disappears again. During a large portion of the audience he keeps his mouth closed.

The king is taciturn. He speaks in short sentences. Each word seems as valuable as his time, and since his face is motionless when he speaks, it is difficult to grasp what he is saying. The king speaks very slowly. When he speaks, no part of his face moves, and his hands rest motionlessly on the table in front of him, so that it is hard to understand why these words require a body. Each word is easiest to hear singly, as if all by itself, so that it is difficult to understand what any one word has to do with any of the king's other words. And thus he demands the entire attention of his listener, but in such a way that it is not a question of his words but of what there is behind them, that is, the monotonous royal voice that pronounces them, which is much more his message than anything that happens to be said— a voice that seems to fill the king himself with satisfaction.

"How is the autumn weather in Vienna?" asks the king. "Does it rain much?"

Just like his tongue, his face is gray. But as soon as he opens his mouth, the gold glimmers faintly within, while nothing glimmers from a poor man's mouth, no matter how widely he opens it, and I am certain that the king knows this, too.

I ask him about his family tree and whether the crown is inherited. I have only seen the crown in a newspaper photograph. The picture shows Ion Cioabă on the eighth of September in Horezu in southern Romania, where he was crowned king of the Roma people in all of Europe and both American continents.

"Were you at my coronation?" he asks.

"No," I answer. "I didn't know about it."

"The coronation was covered by all of the newspapers."

"Unfortunately I didn't read about it until it was too late."

The king looks at me.

"Such an opportunity will not come again so soon," he says.

"No," I say. "I realize that."

But I would like to see the crown.

The king informs me that he has been king since he was twenty-two years old and that the royal crown is kept in a safe at the bank. One cannot keep a crown like that lying around at home. Not in this country. His family has ruled over all the Roma for five generations, but the crown is completely new. He had it made especially for his coronation with his own gold and diamonds, the family's very best diamonds.

"For four hundred years we have been kings in my family," he says, and in my head I count and recount without being able to stretch five generations over four hundred years. Finally I have to ask (though I have already realized that the king does not like questions) as I am convinced that I must be on to some secret gypsy theory of numbers.

The king looks at me, but without changing his expression. He looks at me with eyes which were brown when he entered the hall and sat down across the table from me, but which now have become two almost black lines. Throughout the entire audience his face has remained otherwise unchanged, stiffened in a watchful arrogance which could also be interpreted as indifference. But now his eyes have darkened—though only a touch.

"In my family," says the king, "it is not unusual for a person to reach one hundred and twenty years of age. Sometimes we get even older. My father reached ninety-seven.

"So, you were not at the coronation," says the king, and I can see that this must now be a serious mistake in his black eyes, a mistake that can no longer be so easily excused, for had I been there, the king doesn't even need to say this, my questions to him would certainly have been completely different.

The Gipsy Kings had been invited to play at the coronation in Horezu, but they never came.

This still irritates the king.

"If I had known how talented Michael Jackson is, I would have had him appear at my celebration," says the king.

Instead of those Gipsy Kings.

With the Gipsy Kings both the coronation and music have been exhausted as topics of conversation, and the king now turns to speaking about his people. The words start to flow. He has a warm place in his heart for his people, but they also cause him much concern. Almost all of his subjects are poor, unemployed, and downtrodden. For years he has traveled around the world to speak on their behalf, even as far away as America, and he tells me expansively about his great journey to America without my asking. Names of American cities bob up in the stream of the king's monologue, but as if by chance—a long list of American places which he only mentions before abandoning them and leaving them to their fate, as if the actual time spent in them were irrelevant, something that only impeded the much more important task, which was his movement from one side of the American continent to the other.

I do what I can to try to pin him down to one place, so that he cannot take off again. But it is difficult, and it does not entirely please him.

"Of course," he admits. All the evil things that are said about his people are not necessarily untrue. In every forest there are more than enough dead trees, and it is probably true that there are also Roma who steal. But why don't the police come to him, the master of all the Roma? Then things could be cleared up. The Roma have their own laws that the police don't know and these are different from the laws the police must enforce. As king he knows his people's laws better than others do—and the king lifts his right hand from the table.

If the police were to come to him, they would not need to waste their time on something as pointless as trying to capture the guilty party on their own.

"It is like trying to find a needle in a haystack," he says. "Have you heard that expression before?"

In order to stress how impossible it would be for the Romanian police to find what they are seeking in the haystack on their own, he shakes his head; and with that the king's gaze happens to fall on the car radio in the middle of the audience table. Silently we look at the car radio.

He sighs, and when he breaks his silence it is to remind me of a theft of an entirely different order, perhaps the greatest that has ever afflicted his people. A German theft. In 1941 Romania's Roma were deported to the East; more than 35,000 of them never returned. Only once he names their destination, but not a particular town, only the larger and vaguer area of Transnistria. After that he speaks of "there" and "over there," and finally this place receives no name at all, just a gesture with his hand toward the window that opens onto the street must suffice.

The king himself was one of those who survived. It is certainly true that nothing can bring the others back to life, but the king believes that Germany still owes his people what it stole. According to his calculations, it is a matter of twenty tons of gold and forty tons of silver, and he wants it all back.

"During the Leader's time, the Conducător's time," says the king, "everything was much better. My people were not happy, perhaps, but we were safe. When Ceauşescu was here no one touched our gold, and now that he is gone"—the king says "gone" as if the Conducător had just left through the door of the audience hall— "they are trying to steal our gold from us again, because they believe that we have gold in abundance, buried or hidden, it doesn't matter. Gold is what people think of when they hear the word gypsy, and that's why we miss the Conducător. We are the only ones who mourn him."

"When he was alive, no one could attack my people," says the king. "If someone had dared to strike or burn one of my people alive, he would have been punished by the law, the same laws that have been used against us since the Conducător is gone."

"Do you see the smoke," says the king, pointing out the window. "There's a fire out there, and the police just stand by and watch. It is almost like the German time."

"A few of us are rich," he says. "But all of the others are very poor."

The king also says that he has respect for the Germans of today, but it is not enough that they apologize, and it worries him to hear that the Germans have decided to send all the Roma from Germany back to Romania. Haven't I heard about that? But here in Romania there is no work for so many people. And no homes; bulldozers tore down the shacks where they used to live—as soon as they left for Germany, their homes were destroyed. And now they are being sent back. His people are going to starve or freeze to death.

"It is already autumn, and soon winter will be here," says the king. And yet the Germans have decided to send everyone back to Romania.

When I suggest that I believe that this concerns only those who have asked for asylum, and not Roma who already have German passports, the king gives me a little smile, so that for a moment I can see the four gold teeth in his upper jaw, all of them at once, a superior smile, the kind a person smiles who happens to be better informed.

It would be best if he, a crowned king, personally took care of the money that the Germans have promised Romania so that his people will not take off for Germany. It is a matter of thirty-one million German marks. That is a lot of money, and it would be best to turn it over to him, so that it won't end up in the pocket of the army or the police. The army and the police are trying to convince the Germans that they can hold his subjects in the country by watching the borders.

"Have you ever heard of anything so stupid?" asks the king.

His Roma think that the money should be used instead to build houses, not for putting bells around their necks.

"We are not sheep," says the king. "Give me the money and I will vouch for the family."

When the king says "my Roma," it sounds like one big family and as if the family were his, but still it is not just anyone who can call himself king; in most cases one has to be born a king. In Romania it is only a member of the Cioabă family who has claim to the throne, says the king, and I take this opportunity to say that that is why it astonishes me that the Romanian press sometimes describes the coronation in Horezu as an "election." Ion Cioabă is supposed to have been elected king. In some papers one can even read that he himself, like Napoleon, is supposed to have set the crown on his own head before letting himself be blessed by an Orthodox priest.

The king looks as if this is not the first time he has heard that question.

"There is no royal family other than mine in this country," he says.

Once again he shakes his head, as if the subject of new thefts had come up, this time a thief who had reached for the very crown on his head.

"But once one has been crowned one must prove oneself worthy," says the king.

It is all a question of character, that one achieve a reputation as an honorable man. Neither a smoker nor a drinker.

When he says "drinker" it occurs to me for the first time that nothing has been served during the entire audience. On the table there are no glasses, no cups, not even an ashtray—only a car radio. No ashtray and no coffee cup; and the absence of coffee is actually the most surprising, since the king does not look as if he smoked, not even privately or secretly.

The king looks at his watch, and at almost the same moment the door to the audience hall is opened; Princess Luminiţa, the Little Light, stands in the open door. The king has looked at his watch, a shiny steel watch rather than a gold one, and that must mean that the audience is over.

The princess holds a little girl by the hand. The girl is two years old and her name is Tiffany, and even before they enter the hall, hand in hand, I know that this cannot be the princess's own daughter. In Sibiu people have told me that Princess Luminiţa cannot have any children of her own. Tiffany is her niece, the prince's daughter. The Little Light's husband has divorced her, something very rare among the Roma, but the princess has kept her ex-husband's surname; as Luminiţa Mihai she publishes a literary magazine. The princess fills it with her own short stories and occasionally some prose poetry, and now she wants to give their guest proof of the existence of Romany culture. In the corridor outside the audience hall she has set forth a selection of copper tubs, colorful shawls and dresses.

The king gives me his hand in parting, a powerful and broad hand with splayed fingers. In our handshake he stretches his hand toward mine with peculiar energy, as if he wanted to make his fingers longer than they are. He leaves Culture to the Little Light. The princess smiles at me. She smooths both of her hands over the shawls to show me how soft they are.

The copper tubs are produced in the little pewter and copper workshop that adjoins the audience hall. Luminiţa explains that her brother, the prince, supervises the work full time as director. While I am lifting up the copper tubs to inspect them and running my hands over the shawls, precisely as the princess did, I get the feeling that this culture is not just being exhibited, but that it is also for sale, and that the guest, after a concluded audience, is expected to buy a souvenir.

The princess has discreetly taken a few steps back as if she did not want to influence my choice. I decide on a little copper vessel for making Turkish coffee. The princess observes me with interest as I fumble back and forth in my wallet, and I imagine an almost invisible, gracious princessly nod as my hand thumbs past some wrinkled domestic bills and instead begins to root among shillings and marks.

Afterward I stand outside on the street with my copper vessel and two volumes of the princess's *Divano Romano* under my arm. On the other side of the street lies the palace, and I see the prince standing outside; he is wearing his light brown leather jacket. Dust rises on the road between us as heavy trucks drive past, the prince is standing on the shoulder of the road, in both directions traffic rolls past the palace, almost only heavy trucks, and in the gap between two of them the prince waves to me from the other side, and dust whirls from the wheels of the trucks.

The road ends in a field. There are fires burning in the field, smoke rises straight into the sky. None of the king's subjects can be seen.

I think about crossing the street to drink a cup of coffee at the King Gypsy Non Stop, the king's own snack bar, but I pass it up.

Instead I go home. Outside the Hotel Impăratul Roman a man in worn boots digs in the black flower beds. At this time of autumn it is hard to find flowers in the wasps' world. They creep so far into the very last ones that they have a hard time finding their way out again, but everything has its order here in the world; finally they find their way out, and the plastic flowers in the pots outside the hotel windows do not tempt them. There is too much green that is not green, too much red that is not red; there is not a single color that the wasps recognize.

While drinking a cup of cold instant coffee I leaf through the princess's magazine and light upon a couple lines from her poem "Destiny":

> *someone is playing with me*
> *an accursed game*
> *a princess for eternity*
> *and each day*
> *a poor woman*

IT WAS MY HUNGARIAN FRIEND PÉTER NÁDAS WHO GOT ME TO reconsider. He turned pale and asked me if I had lost my mind when I said I didn't care what kind of information the Stasi had about me in their papers.

Why should I care about my file?

"Because you don't know what's in it," said Péter.

This seemed to me a peculiar argument, since it was precisely what the files probably contained that I didn't want to know. It didn't interest me. East Germany is gone, the Stasi is no longer with us, there's no little gnome making entries in those files anymore. And whoever it was among my circle of friends and acquaintances that had informed on me would have it on his or her own conscience; besides, I've never been the type to go snooping through other people's drawers, I told Péter, who wasn't listening. He interrupted me to tell his own story.

Through pure chance he had recently found out that the Hungarian writers' union had entered him as a member of the Communist youth organization for several years during the seventies. Péter's name appeared in the Party's papers; even his membership dues had been kept up, despite the fact that he'd never been a member of the Communist Party. But there in the party's files was a completely different version of Péter, incomprehensible until another author, a contemporary of his, took pity on him and explained how the whole thing had happened.

The chairman of the party cell, an older author, had taken it upon himself to improve their statistics. It was during the seventies in Budapest, and there was an acute shortage of Communist authors. But with the help of his creative bookkeeping, at least a few young talents were enrolled without their having to know about it.

The membership dues? The old man must have paid them himself. Or taken the money from one of the Party's accounts. Maybe he even arranged the whole thing because he was embarrassed at the ever-smaller size of the cell, since he was after all the chair, or because deep in his heart he believed in artistic freedom and wanted the writers' union to be left in peace, wanted to avoid the unnecessary risk of being criticized for lack of ideological consciousness.

Or had he done it out of purely personal concern? With the thought of helping some young and careless colleagues, to save them future grief?

We'll never know; Istvan Gáll died a couple of years ago.

"They may have handed you a biography like that, too," said Péter. "And one day you won't be around to defend your real life. You'll be gone. Just the files will be left, and they'll have the last word."

LATE THAT FALL I FILLED IN VARIOUS FORMS AND SENT THEM TO Berlin, actually without much hope of seeing my files for quite some time. But I must have been lucky; already during the first week of March a clerk called me in Vienna and notified me that my file had been found, five hundred and twelve pages in total, and that I was welcome to come to Berlin and read it.

Shortly after nine o'clock in the morning on the eighth of March I was received by Herr Schwalm at the Rusche Street building. He was a soft-spoken and almost shy person, who would have been easier to imagine in a greenhouse, surrounded by tomatoes and cucumbers, than as a caretaker of reports by the secret police. Herr Schwalm is one of the clerks in charge of the files housed in Building 7, and Building 7 is just one small part of the complex of buildings, a whole neighborhood, in fact, where Erich Mielke's Ministry for State Security used to be located. Herr Schwalm accompanied me to the reading room where my file was already laid out on a table. The walls and furnishings were painted a yellowish white and a kind of weak-cappuccino brown. Total silence reigned in the reading room. Around the room at tables like mine there were people I didn't know, already immersed in their reading.

"If you're lucky you might consider this a companion piece to your journal," whispered Herr Schwalm with a friendly smile, and he left me to my reading.

My feelings were mixed as I sat down at the table. In front of me lay a thick binder along with three folders in different colors. Uneasiness? Yes, I was uneasy. The papers might contain some unpleasant surprises, surprises I had no way of anticipating, and I was also uneasy that now, despite my better instincts, I was getting drawn into these police documents.

Curiosity? Yes, I was curious, too. What had Mielke's people been up to for all those years? What were their interests, what had they actually known? And then there was a peculiar feeling of solemnity, almost of triumph, as I opened the first folder that lay under my hand, the one on top, the pink one—turning the first page was like a ritual act that finally confirmed once and for all that the socialism of the Soviet bloc had died, that it no longer existed, that all that was left was nothing more than piles of paper and more paper, at best material for some future historian.

I turned the first page. My hand trembled, a hand that suddenly felt heavy and alien, a hand that belonged to a body other than my own.

I did not have to read many pages before I discovered that the Stasi had had me under surveillance since my first visit as a journalist in 1974. This hardly came as a surprise, but here it was, all documented in black and white, with official stamps and signatures that set forth information with a brutality that did not seem to belong on ordinary typing paper. My telephone had been tapped, I had been shadowed, my baggage had been searched every time I came through the Schönefeld airport, they had gone into my hotel room when I wasn't there, and they received reports on everything I had said to East German diplomats at luncheons, at embassies, or at the Ministry of Foreign Affairs.

In my file, the big binder, tucked in here and there, were small gray envelopes made of nappy, inferior paper. They awakened in me for the first time a kind of quiet melancholy. When I opened them they proved to contain yard-long strips of microfilm. I took one filmstrip out of its envelope; it fell from the table and curled up like a snake on the floor. Carefully I rose from the table, went to one of the windows in the reading room, and held the strip up to the light: just clippings, newspaper clippings of the sort that journalists usually have in their baggage, brochures, magazines, everything photographed secretly, books, too, at least their covers, and soon I gave up. Once I had inspected a half-dozen envelopes like that, I didn't bother to open any more.

After hours of reading my head felt heavy. I took a break and walked out into the hall to eat an apple. Other readers trudged back and forth out there, like prisoners who had been chained together for a walk in the yard.

IN AUGUST OF 1977, THE SURVEILLANCE OF MY PERSON HAD apparently produced results that prompted the secret police to set up a special dossier; up until the fall of the Wall it was kept up continuously under the rather unimaginative code name "Black," the English translation of my real name, Swartz. From that point on I appeared as "Black" or "the subject" in the files. Just a few months before I became "Black," the Main Department for Counter-Intelligence (Hauptabteilung II, HA II) under the leadership of Lieutenant General G. Kratsch (G. stands for Günter), entered me into their card index as investigation number 500 087. At the same time a special "plan of action" (*Maßnahmeplan*) concerning Black was conceived.

One of their strategies was to gather information from the Stasi's colleagues in their fellow socialist countries. Among these, only the countries of Central Europe counted. East Berlin wanted nothing to do with the Balkans. They did not turn to their colleagues in Romania or Bulgaria; it is Prague, Budapest, and Warsaw that receive inquiries about my person, and who in turn ask East Berlin for help.

What would be more natural than beginning with Prague? Mielke's people knew quite well of course that I had once studied there for several years, especially since I had never thought to conceal that fact. East Berlin does not have to wait long for an answer. Prague informs them that from 1975 to 1977, I participated actively in the "campaign against Czechoslovakia," and that they suspect me of having smuggled out messages from Alexander Dubček to the west. In addition, I was supposed to have continued to supply documents and information directly from Czechoslovakia to the Czech opposition in exile.

This last piece of information was formulated as an assertion. The police have very little to say about my years as a student in Prague. They limit themselves to stating that now, as a foreign correspondent, I am particularly concerned with re-establishing ties with my old friends from that time.

Warsaw confirms that they, too, have reason to show "operational interest" in my person, that since 1972 I have often visited Poland, where I have a large circle of acquaintances among "Polish citizens," chiefly drawn from "the so-called political opposition." According to Warsaw I can speak both Polish and Czech, do not report objectively about Poland, and my "homosexual leanings are well known," as well.

These leanings seem to confuse East Berlin. According to my file, at that time they had been wondering if it might be useful to propel me into the arms of one of Mielke's female agents. But this Mata Hari never turned up, and perhaps I have to thank those lines from Warsaw, signed W. Pawelec, for robbing me of that delight.

The thing that really astonishes me is the report from Budapest, which asserts that I am strongly suspected of espionage. Espionage! This is the first time the word shows up in my file; there it is, in the middle of the page, faded a little with time, but though the word has been there for fifteen years, it has yet to take on the patina of age that would render it inoffensive. A large portion of the official police correspondence between Budapest and East Berlin takes place in Russian. The Cyrillic letters, it seems to me, lend this exchange an especially threatening aspect. Budapest writes to East Berlin that my "intensive contacts with the inner opposition" have been observed, and they surmise that I must be the one who put Péter Nádas in contact with Western intelligence.

My dear Péter—to think that you and I would run across one another like this in this pile of paper! And yet our meeting astounds me far less than the aggressive tone in Dr. László Eperjesi's classified documents—Budapest, where we correspondents used to go with a sigh of relief upon leaving Stalinist Prague or Bucharest, Hungary with its melancholy cadres, its *apparatchiks* who would rather play the asthmatic chain-smoker than the ideologue, who used to shake their heads as soon as the topic of Moscow came up, suggesting a cup of coffee or a glass of wine to avoid talking politics . . .

For years East Berlin, Warsaw, Prague, and Budapest continue to exchange information, not least about my so-called contacts. A list of names is established. It gets longer with each report, and soon it reads like a fairly complete edition of Who's Who in Eastern Europe's opposition. These are names fished out of my baggage or notebooks by the secret police, names of people who would never have been there had their oppositional positions not been both open and known by the police for a long time. Wolf Biermann, Paul Goma, Miklós Haraszti, Jacek Kuroń, Adam Michnik, Václav Havel, György Konrád. Or people who were protected by their names: Christa Wolf, Stephan Hermlin, Bohumil Hrabal, Jacek Bocheński.

But all of these names might have strengthened the Stasi's conviction that I really acted as a courier, spinning a web of conspiracy right in front of their noses. From the beginning of the eighties, East Berlin seems to go on the assumption that I am on assignment with foreign intelligence, doing what I can to support an inimical opposition within Socialist Europe, "even though Black's instigating role has not yet been completely confirmed."

It is around this time that the Black of the Stasi's reports becomes ever more diabolical. His polite manner is a disguise; a disguise put on to conceal his actual activity. Part of his cunning is a pretended candor. Of course Black is an anticommunist, but he is one of that malignant type who are in fact ready "to risk something in order to strengthen Western democracy." My articles are taken as sufficient proof that I stand on the same side as Charter 77 in Czechoslovakia and Solidarność in Poland. When a report in 1980 remarks that I have "excellent knowledge of the socialist world," it is not meant as a reluctant compliment. The idea is to underscore what a very dangerous person the Socialist camp is dealing with here.

BUT THERE IS STILL SOMETHING MISSING. MY WORK AS A SPY REQUIRES an employer, and here is where Radio Free Europe comes in. Already in 1976, during an autumn fair in Leipzig, the Stasi had found printed reports in my baggage from the radio station in Munich. In my file it says that I have access to the American "propaganda network's" internal reports, intended solely for the station's script editors. "Internal" and "intended for the editors" are East Berlin's words, assertions that they fail to back up. But from one report to the next these formulations grow in authority; they even appear underscored or in boldface, as if to refute their dubious origins. Whoever reads them must feel a strengthened suspicion that I am, in fact, a spy.

It looks rather dismal for Black, even though Lieutenant General Kratsch could have done precisely as I had done: he could have deposited some of his own or the Stasi's money into a bank account in Munich and used the funds to have these same reports sent to him on subscription to his mailbox in East Berlin.

Didn't he know that? And if he didn't know—did he believe, professional that he was, that spies travel around with their secrets in their suitcases? In Black's case, in a suitcase that couldn't be locked, because Black had long ago lost the two keys that opened it?

Of course he didn't believe it—the Lieutenant General knew better than that. But it was in his best interest for Hauptabteilung II to show that they were really doing something, and producing reports about what they did. On this point, Mielke's dismal empire did not differ materially from any other sector of the socialist—it was the plan that determined all of their lives. A quota filled beyond expectation brought reward; one that wasn't filled invited punishment. The plan must be satisfied, and it was the Lieutenant General's business to choose the simplest way to do so, just like the boot factory that decided to produce boots for only the left foot because it was simpler, never mind that people happen to have right feet, too. But the quota, the plan, superseded reality, and so the Stasi, too, determined to produce only one kind of boot. It must have been impossible to avoid giving in to that temptation.

And so I became the convenient kind of boot. "Black" was allowed to stand in for Richard Swartz; reality was sacrificed to fiction.

And why not? What would hinder General Lieutenant Kratsch's subordinates from producing—making up—a file all on their own? Or at least from inventing a lot of information about someone? What would have stopped them from contacting strangers or people they disliked privately in order to put together an empty conversation for a report that would attest to their praiseworthy watchfulness in the service of the state?

The secret police worked under a minimum of supervision. This was the very nature of their work, and so there was probably no other sector of society in which it was easier to produce material just for the *plan,* just with the goal of satisfying a superior's formal expectations; in no other sector could it have been easier to produce piles of pure garbage, things that were completely useless or at least trivial, without being detected—while the lines of people out on the street made it easy to detect the stores where there was hardly anything to buy. They couldn't conceal lines. Lines were all too striking. But the Stasi didn't have to concern itself with such open situations where their attempts to fulfill the quota would have been right in front of peoples' noses; they could add pears or subtract apples without anyone noticing. I was one of the objects that could be used in their arithmetic. For the Stasi's own purposes, it was necessary to busy themselves with a spy instead of a journalist, and so with every new "plan of action" my person was ever more stylized as the Stalinist cliché of a class enemy.

Everything they thought they knew about me was pointed toward that goal.

Black begins to live a life of his own. Suppositions about Swartz become facts about Black, supported by the appropriate fantasies, even if these came into conflict with what had been established as fact in earlier reports.

Toward the end of the eighties my "homosexual tendencies" of the seventies had become confirmed homosexuality; my travels back and forth through Eastern Europe for the newspaper had been transformed into courier duties under direct orders from hostile powers, and in order to complete the image of the typical spy from the West, I was equipped with money problems and an illegitimate child in the Soviet Union (!), as well as "intimate contacts with journalists from Israel or of Jewish background."

What I wouldn't have given for the KGB to have furnished me with that child!

A great deal of this fascinated me. On the second, or perhaps it was the third, day in Building 7 I no longer read the information about myself as a report or a document, but as a novel. The creators of the reports began to interest me, and it irritated me that they almost always were anonymous or, like Kafka's heroes, forced to appear only as initials. They interested me because I saw that they struggled with the same problems I do: how to best depict a scene, what the hero ought to do or ought not to do, what could be stricken from the text and what must absolutely be left in, and finally, what impression their text would make on a reader about whom, like me, they couldn't know much more than that they wanted to captivate precisely him and no other.

Without meaning to, they had become authors. They had put on a uniform, a light green and soft dove-gray uniform, sworn an oath, and now to their own astonishment they sat behind desks in front of a blank sheet of paper and on that paper they had to write something with which to entertain their audience, in this case a rather critical reader, one who wouldn't set the report down in the middle of a sentence and turn off the reading light on the night table.

I began to feel a mild sympathy for them; for Kl., HgH. or S., and especially for JJ., who didn't use many adjectives. It was sad to have to note that they remained quite miserable writers. Time after time they used rather dubious means to solve problems in their stories. They furnished them with details that were no longer grounded in their own observations, but which they probably believed could make their fables more beautiful and believable. I, who in any case knew something about what they were narrating, had my doubts about this strategy. It reminded me of a fading prostitute who tries to hold on to her customers by applying a thick layer of powder over her age.

Here and there a glimmer of talent appeared, or a justified pride in a successful bit of phrasing, but I am afraid that they cheated their reader too much—all of their cleverness was directed toward the plan. They wrote for the plan. As soon as they took pen in hand it was as if they could not trust their own experiences, as if something held them back from putting them into print.

Maybe there was a longing for discretion here. Was it out of respect for their victims that they falsified reality? Did they want to fashion such a fantastic biography for me that no one could take it seriously? Were they like Istvan Gáll? Did they want to protect me? They were the ones, after all, who best knew how innocent I was. Or was I just a victim of their total lack of talent? I saw all the trouble they went to for Black, but also how awkwardly they took up the task of breathing life into their *homunculus*. Dully he trudged on through the pages without giving a single person joy. I read on, growing more and more distressed. Distressed about what the pages actually contained, but distressed at the same time that what they had created was for the eyes of a bureaucrat and not those of a real reader, and that the writers had been true neither to themselves nor to reality. It struck me that I certainly could have helped them here and there if they had plucked up their courage, revealed themselves, and shown me a little more faith.

But in the end they chose to hide behind their initials. They never introduced themselves, they never called, they never wrote; they contented themselves with spying on me and bugging my conversations. It was a shame. I believe I could have helped them. Together we could have written a rather decent novel, something readable instead of this uneven epos.

On the first of August in 1988, the Stasi determines that their goal in the case of Black is to prove that the subject is liable to conviction under the Articles 97, 98, 99, and 100 of the Criminal Code.

I have to admit that I never even bothered to look up those paragraphs.

THE STASI'S STYLIZATION OF INFORMATION AND OF REALITY ITSELF went hand in hand with an incompetence that is often comical. This incompetence was that much more dangerous, because it began in the fieldwork itself. The result was that the reports that eventually ended up on Lieutenant General Kratsch's desk bore from the very beginning a closer resemblance to tall tales than an attempt to describe reality. In Black's case this is not so important, but it must have made it next to impossible for East Germany to unmask real spies.

On the sixth of April in 1987, the Stasi notes that I turn up at East Berlin's Schönefeld airport with an "unknown female person." The excited tone of the report implies that they believe they've hit upon a real find: this must be a really intimate contact, probably a lover (what happened to my homosexuality all of a sudden?).

The report describes how the subject checks in for Budapest with one piece of luggage (Samsonite; color: black) and how the two of them, the subject and the unknown woman, then "take leave of one another with several embraces and kisses on the mouth." The report gives a careful account of this intimate scene:

"Be well, my darling," says the "unknown female person" to the subject. "I'll be waiting for you, we'll see each other soon."

According to the report the subject then goes directly to passport control and customs, while the female person returns to her car, which she has parked outside the entrance—a white Lada with the license plate number INY 9–81. For safety's sake the whole departure scene has been documented in a series of five photographs, all attached to the report, which is signed in an illegible scrawl.

Well, Inge—what do we say to that?

The pictures are rather blurry, but it certainly is you and me, that is undeniable. But on the other hand, I have a hard time believing that you expressed yourself in quite the lovesick terms recorded by the spy. I imagine that you probably said something like "Come back again soon, dear, we'll be expecting you."

But I admit I don't really remember—it was a long time ago, and so my recollection will have to compete with their record. But still, Lieutenant General Kratsch, sitting at his desk, must have wondered a bit about those kisses on the mouth. When he reads "several kisses on the mouth" and then takes a look at the photographs, he must see that the mouth has become a cheek—actually, two cheeks—and even Goethe already knew that the devil is in such details.

A mouth is not a cheek. I know of course that this is the position of a boring positivist, but worlds can lie between a mouth and a cheek. He who makes a mouth of a cheek risks mistaking his ass for his elbow. I am pretty sure that Lieutenant General Kratsch knows his Goethe, or at least his Faust, and he would have been quite aroused if we had accused him of working with the Devil. The Lieutenant General's task was to protect the workers' power on German soil; thus he was on the side of Good, and therefore we cannot exclude the possibility that it was he who underlined the word "mouth" with a pencil, and then put a question mark in the margin.

I can imagine how the poor Lieutenant General sighs as he scribbles down that question mark. Lieutenant General Kratsch is in a bad mood. He is sighing over his employees. Nothing is the way it ought to be anymore. Whom can a person trust in this world, he asks himself, and sighs again. But of course, Inge dear, this is nothing more than pure guesswork, a supposition without a proper foundation, and I am a little ashamed that I commit to paper such fantasies about a completely unknown person, so that the fantasies are printed and others can partake of them.

But still I think the Stasi ought to have been able to identify you. Your file is many times thicker than mine, after all; if nothing else, your license plate should have put them on your track. In my file nothing indicates that they discovered that my lover is the wife of Stefan Heym, the writer who all on his own must have kept a whole series of Stasi departments occupied for several decades.

I don't recall what Stefan was doing that day, and you most probably don't either, dear Inge. Maybe he wanted to stay up in his attic and write. Or perhaps he stayed behind in the garden? It might have been a beautiful, sunny day, although it's hard to tell from the photographs, since they were taken indoors. Maybe Stefan wasn't even at home in East Berlin that day. I don't recall. But it was nice of you to take me to the airport, Inge.

SCHÖNEFELD WAS EUROPE'S MOST APPALLING AIRPORT. IT REMINDED me of a prison camp, the last place where you felt you could come and go as you pleased. It was worst in Arrivals. At Schönefeld the police took their sweet time looking over passports; small gates had to be opened to allow passengers to continue to the next station, and from somewhere behind the thin walls came the barking of dogs. Big dogs, you could tell from the barking. The dogs barked, but they never showed themselves. I never saw them except at night, and it still happens occasionally that they turn up in my dreams. They have survived the state they used to serve; in my nightmares they keep on barking while I try to sleep, they pull and struggle in their choke chains and threaten to be my last living memory of East Germany.

The fact that I was an accredited journalist did not speed up the process; on the contrary, it was extended to the furthest possible limit every time I appeared at Schönefeld with my passport and the little green booklet with stamps and signatures from the foreign ministry.

The passport control officer sat in a gray cage behind thick glass, open only a thin crack that did not allow me to see the table in front of him. Once he had surveyed my passport for a while, the telephone in his cage would happen to ring, as if by chance. The same thing happened every time my passport was inspected, so that eventually I realized that it must be the man in the cage who called himself; when he inspected my passport he found that my name was on his list, and by pushing a button somewhere in the cage he could make his own telephone ring. He could pretend to answer, actually just mumbling something into the receiver in order to warn his colleagues. All of this inspection, telephoning, and mumbling took a lot of time, and it used to irritate whomever happened to be stuck behind me in line.

I was forced to wait even longer for my baggage; the meters of microfilm in my Stasi file are explanation enough for that. Still I was only halfway through. I still had to go through customs. How could the men with the dogs in the basement inform customs that there was something in my bag that required it to be opened? The customs officials stood behind low tables. There were no telephones there. After passing through passport control you had a good view of customs, and while I waited for my bag I tried to keep an eye on the officials: but no one showed up to whisper something in their ears, and the time it took to inspect my passport, when I couldn't yet see customs, was too short for the men in the cellar to have photographed my papers and warned their colleagues.

I was never asked to open my bag for customs. It was one way to demonstrate that this state adhered to the formalities, that all of the state's officials respected those special documents that proved my accreditation, in which the foreign ministry asked on behalf of the document's holder for special cooperation with the handling of his baggage in customs.

So elegant! The German Democratic Republic loved to adhere to such formalities. But soon I realized that it was all an illusion. I knew that they had already turned my bag inside out, and every time the customs official politely asked me if I had anything to declare, and I just as politely said no, I wondered how he had received his information from the cellar—that there was nothing designed to overthrow the GDR in the bag, that the bag shouldn't be opened, not this time, that the moment had not yet come to strike at Black.

How did it happen?

Through pure chance I managed to catch the Stasi out, when a customs official "happened"—as if by accident—to turn over my bag's address label after one of his obligatory questions.

It was that simple! One single cross, a dash, a little mark on the label—that's all he would have needed in order to ask me to open the bag. Once I had figured it out, I felt stupid that it had taken me so long, and maybe that's why instead of answering his question I myself began—as if quite by accident—to turn over the address label when they asked me if I had anything to declare.

I did it right in front of their noses. It was my private revenge, and many customs officials had a hard time containing their rage. Their faces turned beet-red. They realized that I had seen through them. But it didn't seem to shame them; they weren't ashamed, they were just angry.

Instead, I was the one who was ashamed. I was ashamed that I had let myself be drawn into their brand of police logic, using my time and imagination to attempt to break their codes and discover their tricks, imagination that would have been better used for other purposes.

THE FEELING OF SHAME WAS SOMETHING THAT I PROBABLY SHARED with most of the others who sat with me in Building 7's reading room that week in March. I looked around. In the reading room sat other people, complete strangers to me, and the only thing that united us were the stacks of files on the tables in front of each and every one of us. Now and then someone sighed so loudly that none of us could have avoided hearing it; it could have been a sigh on behalf of all of us, the sigh of collective shame. When I looked up occasionally from my own pile of papers, it seemed to me that my eyes fell every time on someone who was shaking his head, slowly, as if exhausted or aggrieved.

Shame? Yes, shame. Shame over our own helpessness that was recorded up and down the pages in our files; shame over having been "subjects" that were now really just objects, shame that our real names had been transformed into aliases; shame over this insolent intrusion into our private lives, and shame that we had allowed it to happen without resistance.

Yet my shame was different from theirs. I was not a citizen of the GDR. I was just an outsider, someone who was able to come and go as he wanted; to call me a victim of the system would have been to rob the word "victim" of all its meaning. The damage done to me was infinitely less serious that the damage done to them, my right to indignation was less, but perhaps also my shame. With me it was more a case of embarrassment—that the Stasi had forced me into routines and a cautiousness that I, today even more than then, perceive as unworthy.

What was there in all of this for me to take pride in?

I had let myself be poisoned by the atmosphere that the Stasi had gone to such lengths to create. I had behaved as if every telephone were tapped, every stranger a provocateur; I had never written down anything important, I had acted as if a microphone were hidden in almost every room I entered, and all of this accommodation had almost become second nature.

There was a particular gesture of accommodation that pursued me throughout all my decades in Eastern Europe: someone looks hard at me, falls silent, and points to the ceiling. The gesture means that it is in our best interest to keep quiet about what we really wanted to talk about, that we shouldn't ask each other quetions about what truly interests us. The dumb-play toward the ceiling indicated that we should devote ourselves to filling our time with empty talk, and it was the police with their microphones who were stealing from us, stealing all of our precious time that belonged to our lives and not to theirs, so that it sometimes seemed to me that this everyday, metaphysical petty theft would be a worse punishment than being locked up in a cell.

This submission was doubly dishonorable because it was usually unnecessary; my own file was evidence enough of that. The Stasi were not only incompetent; Erich Mielke's resources were simply insufficient to keep track of the collective madness that infects every normal European at the end of this century. It was an impossible task to watch everybody who needed watching. There was neither sufficent personnel nor enough funding for that, so Mielke was forced to place his last hope in the notion that all of his subjects would more or less voluntarily behave as if the Stasi were always at hand. Mielke's ideal citizen would act as if the threat that was actually only seldom there really existed.

A part of our shame emerges from the fact that we often did act that way. In the case of East German citizens, this could have come from an instinct of self-preservation, and for outsiders like me, it was the concern not to get a friend or acquaintance into trouble. These kinds of concerns suited the Stasi perfectly; they knew far better than we about their own helplessness. Of course it is true that we were careful to protect ourselves and our friends; but it is also true that caution contributed to the spread of a sickness with which I had already come into contact during my student years in Prague, a sickness we called "espionagia." The person afflicted with espionagia soon convinced himself that he was being watched when he was not, felt guilty without having done anything, and perceived every form of protest as meaningless, even when it wasn't. At any time the snare could close around him, and we caught this sickness from each other; all of us had caught a bit of the espionagia that the police, with our cooperation, made such an effort to spread, because in the end they could poison the environment much more easily than they could control it, and found it easier to incite depression and mania than to really create a fear of something real in us.

Without trying to defend ourselves, we sickened with espionagia, since this seemed, paradoxically enough, the only way to stay healthy. Involuntarily we did what we could to infect one another, at the same time dimly aware that we were working on behalf of the police;

instead a certain amount of everyday credulity, of naïveté, would have been better for our personal hygiene. Only a few of us understood that. Most people did not have sufficient courage for such insight.

We conformed. Obviously, this did not make us accomplices to the police. But it was simply dishonorable, a conformity that could look like quiet submission; that was the source of our shame.

ON THE TWELFTH OF MARCH I CLOSE MY FILE FOR GOOD. AFTER A week of reading I have had enough of police documents and the reading room. The twelfth of March is a Friday with spring in the air. Outside a dull Berlin sun is shining, and pigeons patrol back and forth on the window ledge. I return the three folders and the binder to Mr. Schwalm. It is actually painful that I cannot tell him what he had hoped to hear.

But how would it be possible?

Unfortunately my file can not even be used as an addendum to my journal; for fifteen years the Stasi took the trouble to know all about me, and the only thing I could learn in five hundred and twelve pages of reading is how infinitely little they knew that really was important, how easy it is to be mistaken, with what energy they decided, time and time again, to misinform themselves.

Not even the things that they might have considered useful found their way into my file. It is strange. Over so many years there must have been a thing or two that I would not have wanted to stick under their noses; not necessarily anything political, but the things that a person might be ashamed of, a moment's weakness, a trifle that, in the hands of an ill-meaning person could be made into more than a trifle.

For almost twenty years I was accredited as a journalist in the GDR, but in my papers there is not a single instance of that sort registered. I must admit that my vanity was a little injured.

Outside the sun is shining, and I have no desire to sit here any longer—I have had enough of you: Lieutenant General Kratsch at his desk, your colleague W. Damm, a Major General responsible for relations with the socialist brother nations, Master Sergeant Weber and his mediocre German, Colonel Roth, who tried for so long to figure out if my name was Carl Axel Richard or just Richard (couldn't he look in my passport?), the "unofficial collaborators" (*informelle Mitarbeiter, IM*) Lutz, Ricki, and Frieda, acquaintances who spied on me and whom I neither can nor wish to identify.

I have had enough of all of you; I am making you a present of Black, for I have no use for him. You may keep him for your own purposes, whatever those might be; perhaps he will even enjoy your company.

Friendly Mr. Schwalm allows me to copy some pages from my file. I only want a few. Three of them I'm thinking of sending to Péter in Budapest; the rest I'll keep for myself. If, sometime in the future, I want to remind myself of your years'-long labor, I need only take out a page or two from my desk drawer—for example, the following notes on a tapped telephone call of April 12, 1983:

"Mr. Heym informs Mr. Swartz, once greetings have been exchanged, that he is on the way to West Berlin, but that his wife would like to speak to Mr. Swartz. The remainder of the conversation is carried out between Mrs. Heym and Mr. Swartz. Mrs. Heym informs Mr. Swartz that she and her husband will return from West Berlin no earlier than around eight o'clock. For this reason Mrs. Heym suggests that Mr. Swartz go to Mr. Hussel's house before that time. Mrs. Heym gives Mr. Swartz to understand that she and her husband will also be visiting Mr. Hussel, and she suggests that all of them can then go to the Heym family apartment. Mrs. Heym points out that Mr. Hussel already knows of this plan. Mr. Swartz acknowledges this and states his agreement."

I take leave of Mr. Schwalm, and on the steps to Building 7 I count over my copies. The notes to the telephone call lie on the top, the sun is shining, and I feel something rise within me, not a sigh any longer, but something that has been suppressed all too long: laughter.

YOU WANT TO KNOW, CAN I SPEAK GERMAN? WHY SHOULDN'T I? SUCH a strange question! And still you want to see the synagogue so late in the day? Yes, sure, German and a lot of other languages, if I tried to count them on the fingers of my right hand there wouldn't be enough, so many fingers as I have needed languages in my life no one has, and they were all necessary, you understand, all of them came to use sooner or later. Not even you have so many fingers. What is your name, by the way? And on your mother's side? Schwarz? So, Schwarz, my fault it wasn't. It wasn't me, it was life that loaded me down with all of those languages. It was life itself that demanded that I be able to say something in every one of them, and what was more important, I had to understand what was said to me, and most important of all what was yelled or whispered. People yell at you until your ears give out, there is a terrible lot of screaming in this world, but what is only whispered in your ear is even more dangerous. That's how it was with the languages, and if someone had bothered to ask me, I would have been happy with just one, the one I sucked from my mother's breast, but me nobody asked.

You probably know how it is with languages, how it is written? It all has to do with the Tower of Babel. You can't have forgotten that already, how it was when we humans were still living in the dark and there were no telephones or printed books and the people angered the Lord by building a tower that was supposed to reach up into heaven? From this tower they thought they might take a peek at His dwelling place, they even carried ladders up there, they wanted to climb up on them, such idiocy the world had never seen, but nobody seemed to have thought how they were going to get back down to earth climbing backwards.

What do you think, Schwarz? Had they really thought the thing through? Have you ever seen a crab on a ladder? So, Schwarz, if you ask me, I am just about certain that they would have started blacking out and falling down, one by one, in a great big pile, and I would not be surprised if there were some heart attacks, the heart is the most precious thing we have, but also the most fragile, not much more than a trembling baby bird in its nest, and to punish the people the Lord stole the ladders from them before He tore down their tower in His wrath, and instead of a single language He gave us Hungarian, Romanian, the gypsies' language, Russian, Armenian, and all of the other languages, and to us Jews both Yiddish and Hebrew, one for getting through this world and the other for speaking directly to Him when we needed it, and certainly we needed it, but He did not listen, did He, may the Lord forgive me.

At home in Fogarasch we spoke Yiddish and prayed in Hebrew. I was born in Fogarasch and when my mother died, may the Lord have mercy on her, my father took a new wife and my father was pious, he kept the languages separate, he did everything as it was written, he spoke only Romanian with the gendarmes, but yelling at me he did in Hungarian. In Hungarian you can argue and swear better than in any other language. That's because the true Hungarians were actually wild men from Asia who came riding here on dirty little horses, and when they got down from their horses they kept their language that no one else understood, they kept it for themselves, people need something to hold onto, and their Hungarian language was like the wind from a horse when it lifts its tail. My father really appreciated Hungarian when he was in a bad mood, but with the curses that blaspheme the Lord and all of our mothers, yes, Schwarz, unfortunately there are many Hungarian words of just that kind, with them he wanted nothing to do, no, such Hungarian words were not acceptable, and I never heard such curses from my father's mouth, may the Lord have mercy on his soul.

Yiddish was the language we used on the street. Our laughing we did in Yiddish and our crying, too, of course, but when I dreamt at night my dreams were so full of sin that all of the languages seemed to get mixed up, and the languages were not languages anymore but had become a single color, that's just how it was, but as soon as the dream dipped its brush in color and began to paint the inside of my empty head the color suddenly changed to many colors, I dreamt red, green, pink, and sometimes black; white was the only color I did not dream. You must dream, Schwarz, it's good for the digestion. So do you maybe have stomach problems? Only daydreams are harmful dreams, the Lord doesn't like to see those, a person who has his head stuffed up with that kind of dream gets lost here in this world. It's easy enough to recognize when someone is a daydreamer. The dream sort of lights up his face from inside, his face burns like a lantern in the darkness, but he himself is not there, he sees neither money nor his own days, and if he smiles, it's at something in his dream that the rest of us have nothing to do with because it's there, inside his own head, do you understand? In my family there were many who dreamt by day and none of them accomplished anything worth remembering. Early in life they gave up. One drowned himself in a river in broad daylight. Others left and never came back, they did not even send a telegram home, and at least for the women a postcard or some kind of sign would have been a comfort, you know how women are, but I stayed home and just dreamed at night, the Lord had thought out another fate for me, one that had nothing to do with my head, but with my voice.

My voice is the finest thing I have. How should I say it? It was the most beautiful voice in Fogarasch. Yes, Schwarz, the most beautiful. Today I am old and my legs don't carry me as well as they used to; if I were to fall down in the winter out here and break my leg, the Lord forbid, I have no idea who would take pity on me. But my voice! There is nothing wrong with it, it still carries, I still have my voice, and if you come with me to the synagogue I will sing for you so that you can hear for yourself that everything I say is true. At home in Fogarasch I sang more beautifully than all the others. I could also sing loudly, though I wasn't any bigger than you see me now, and in Fogarasch they admired my voice and said, look at that little Ernster, such a voice, a cantor he should be, and it was too bad that I was so little in size, but my voice got people to forget how awfully little I really was. *Ja.* I was very little already back then, and much bigger than that I haven't gotten. As a young man I suffered terribly because of it, and only later in life did I discover that for a woman the voice is more important than the size of a man, not even about what's missing on top does she trouble herself, not at all, Schwarz, in Fogarasch I had a neighbor who was completely bald on top, I had only my voice and he had not one strand of hair, but still women came to us both, both to him and to me, what do you say to that? Do you understand women, Schwarz? So little we understand of women, you see, and when we begin to understand a thing or two it's no longer of any use. How many times have the women whispered to me, you're little, Ernster, but no one has such a voice as yours, such a sweet and big and irresistible one, now hop into my lap and kiss me again!

My Jossele, my wife used to say, sing for me! What do you want to hear? I asked. It doesn't matter, she said, sing whatever, when you sing it's like on the gramophone, and I sang for her, right into her ear, if it was a song that should be sung with feeling, or far away or loudly, as strongly as only I could, if it were a song made to be heard everywhere around, and what I sang was not just what I had learned from the cantor in Fogarasch or picked up from my uncle, who had been in Vienna when he was young and learned to play the clarinet so that when he went totally blind he still found all the keys, no Schwarz, I sang what was popular, too, back then, I sang Joseph Schmidt, he was from Czernowitz, "Ein Lied geht durch die Welt" ("A Song Walks Through the World,") or "Tiritomba" I sang, but not so that my father could hear it, and he was even smaller than I was, Joseph Schmidt I mean, but what a voice, even with the rasping of the needle, such an unbelievably strong voice and out of such a little body that you might have thought such art would have rescued him, but no, Schwarz, Joseph Schmidt starved to death in the middle of the war, in Switzerland, can you imagine, not even in Switzerland did they have enough food for such a great artist, who most certainly did not take up much room, and with a golden voice that had gone several times around the world on the radio, already at that time, Schwarz, before the war.

I sang in the synagogue also, of course, but completely different melodies. It was there I saw my wife, may the Lord be merciful to her soul, I mean for real, for the very first time, except what I actually saw of her was just her red hair, a lock of it was sticking out from under her shawl, I think she let it stick out on purpose. And why should she hide such hair? What do you think, Schwarz? Do you understand women? It was that lock of hair that got me to notice her up among the other women in their section, and at that time we were not in Fogarasch any longer but here in the city, right in the synagogue next door. My wife was from here in the city, which is of course much bigger than Fogarasch. Her red hair was the reddest I had ever seen and once I had gotten a look at it, it gave me no peace, I wanted nothing more than to be allowed to lay my hands on it.

It was desire, Schwarz. It was the same sin as in my dreams, but so long ago that I don't remember much more than that red color, though the synagogue is still standing out there, even if the window-panes are broken on the second floor and the spiders are crawling over the women's benches, yes, like a miracle the synagogue is still standing, though I cannot grasp what the Lord needed such a miracle for, because nothing is left inside it but the books. Well, the benches, of course, they're still there. But what is a bench? In every bench there is a little drawer and if you pull it out, the book is still there, and on the cover of every bench there is also still the name, each one engraved on its own brass plate, no bigger than the iron the shoemaker uses to put heels on boots, and every plate is screwed fast into the bench cover for eternity, so that even today you can see who sat where, Berman next to Kussmaul, Berger beside Kohn, Kohn next to Neumann and then Feivel, just like that they sat, the plates show precisely how they sat then and always had sat, and it would never have occurred to a Neumann to sit in a place intended for a Klinker, for in the drawer in front of his seat each one had his own book, in the drawer in front of Klinker was Klinker's book and not Neumann's, and everyone knew that, so the problem wasn't finding your place, you understand, Schwarz, no, the problem was that the Lord decided in the end that none of them should have any place to sit any longer, that was the problem, Schwarz, no place at all, but He did not find the books. Or maybe He didn't care about them? They stayed in the benches. The books He forgot, so that what I'm looking after now is no longer a temple but a library. That's how it is with books. They remain. Pull out a drawer! Sit down on a chair, light a candle in the attic, you will always find a book! And so it is written: in the beginning was the Word, and when everything has been fulfilled you can be sure that what will be left will be only words, precisely like in the benches in the synagogue, and if the words happen to have been destroyed and burned up in one language, you can be sure that some of them will have managed to creep into another one and set up house there, that much at least you can be sure of, so it is with words, Schwarz, the Lord has just simply too many languages to keep track of, so many that the words amuse themselves by dancing around in front of His nose, also words that are not at all appropriate, even though the Lord Himself has more than a little responsibility for those Himself, I mean because of that notion of giving us more than one name for one and the same thing. That tower, again, Schwarz! It was that tower that angered Him so that He decided to punish us, but without thinking first, and wouldn't it have been better if a stone were always called a stone and we didn't first have to think about where we are and to whom we are talking before we can be certain that a stone is not called something completely different?

Tell me, Schwarz, what is it that holds the world together? What do you think? You don't know? The Lord Himself, Schwarz, of course, just as He created it. But only as it happens to suit Him! With His right hand He holds the world together, but with the left hand He covers His ear to keep from hearing our screams, there is a great deal of screaming here, the person who does injury screams as loudly as the one he injures, and even though they are completely different screams they irritate the Lord the same amount, who is He to distinguish among us, He has to listen to everything, and it makes Him so enraged that He loses His grasp on His own creation, the Lord's grip on the world is no longer as tight as we would like, and when the screaming is at its worst, He lays His right hand over the other ear, too, so that we have to take care of ourselves completely on our own, Schwarz, without the help of His hands.

All these misunderstandings! But if you will excuse that I say it, it is the Lord Himself who is the cause of all this chaos, so that the books are left when the ones who read them are gone, and that has to do with the languages again, all of those languages that spread around many more books than necessary. The Lord should have been satisfied with a single language. That would have been more than enough for both Him and us to keep track of. But seven? Or seventy thousand? That's an impossible task. Not even the Lord can remember them all, but what He does indeed remember is that we humans have made noise and caused trouble and angered Him with that tower, so terribly that He decided to punish us all, so that I can find the Manger family prayer book in the synagogue, but no more Mangers. No Mangers. No Neumanns or Feiwels, either. Just their books, and I have thought a great deal about that, there is nothing here in life that I have thought so much about, but without growing any wiser. The head is a greatly overrated part of the body. Do you agree, Schwarz? If we had been provided with two of them, like those calves in alcohol that they show for money, we would surely have understood how many other parts of the body are more important, and the feet are among the most underrated. My own head is too feeble to grasp why the books should be left. A whole life has not been sufficient to understand that, or maybe there is nothing to understand, perhaps it doesn't please the Lord that we think about things that He Himself doesn't comprehend.

What do you think, Schwarz? Who gets the last word? Is it so certain that the Lord Himself always knows what He's doing? Do we have to give up the hope that even He can sometimes make a mistake?

It could be that He hasn't yet decided, that what seems for us to be eternal and so awful that we can do nothing but scream, is just an experiment for Him that takes not much more than a second, and of time He has enough. *Ja.* Who can really know how finished His creation is? Who, Schwarz, we humans, maybe? Our greatest sin is that we are constantly tempted to get to the bottom of things. The human being wants to dive into the depths, even when it draws him down, he wants to burrow behind things, even though there is nothing but emptiness and darkness there for him. False paths, nothing but false paths! Hasn't the Lord commanded us to stick to the surface of things where He has been good enough to spread out all of life before us? Shouldn't that be good enough for us? And it is of course the dangerous head that leads us away from the surface and down into the depths, while the heart keeps trying to hold us up on top for as long as possible, keeps on ticking so faithfully day and night that any one of us should take much more comfort in a body part like that than in our heads, except it's true of course that we have all got both a head and a heart, but the heart is the part of our bodies we should listen to.

The heart, Schwarz, don't forget. You can fill a head with anything, but the heart has room only for love or sorrow, and often enough for both at the same time. For it is not true that the heart forgets its sorrows with time, and it never forgets a love, but you know yourself that our sorrows often are our loves, so it is, Schwarz, and my own heart wants to break every time it remembers my dead wife, may the Lord have mercy on her soul, it almost breaks every time I am in the synagogue and pull out her drawer and see her prayer book there. The head? But a head forgets everything! Nothing sticks in it, everything except the names of the days of the week and two plus two falls right out, and certainly humans get more use out of their feet, even for art the heart and the feet are more important than the head. Didn't Joseph Schmidt sing about how a song walks through the world? But of course that's not to be taken literally, it's just for the gramophone, but it is true that feet and song belong together, the pious used to both sing and dance to the glory of the Lord, and even though mine are small and not so pious, I should be much more grateful to my feet than to my head.

During the war, for instance! In wartime everything that has to do with the feet is important. Most wars are decided by feet, remember that, Schwarz, if you can keep your feet warm and dry, that's good, but if they should swell, *oy vey,* your nails fall off and you can be certain that the end is near, or you use them to storm the enemy or cut and run, it's all the same, it's always the feet that decide what will happen to you, in wartime, I mean. One pair too many of sore feet? All at once the whole war is lost, and for those who wear no uniform it is truly a catastrophe, though even we Jews had our generals, King David was a great general, did you know that, Schwarz? In the camp it was important to keep your feet clean and wrap them in any rags you could find. Those who didn't keep up the nerve to do it died, they died like flies. When the Russians finally came they needed reinforcements, the war was still in full swing in the west, at night we could hear the explosions, boom boom, cannons are happiest at night, and many of us were sent to the Polish legion in Galicia, but we were all afraid of the Poles. It was said that the legion was full of anti-Semites, so when those of us who still had some health were lined up outside the barracks and a fat Russian major walked along our file and screamed at us that he needed a shoemaker, I called out "Here!" and took a step out of line, though it was a lie, I was no shoemaker, may the Lord forgive me.

A lie, Schwarz, I lied! Why did I do that? "Shoemaker Ernster at your service!" Don't ask me. It was completely counter to my philosophy. Do you have a philosophy, Schwarz? Get yourself one, you have to have a philosophy to get through this life. Look at me! What do you see? A little person, my hands are small and my feet are, too, my whole self is small, and everything you can see on the outside is small too, Schwarz, but what you can't see is that I am just as small inside. *Ja.* Inside of me it is crowded, my entire self has to fit inside that space, and with us little people it is just like it is with whole nations, the little ones are the very worst, just think of all the horrors that have to squeeze into little countries, and then look at a big one and you see how much more space there is for all the terror, it sort of thins out and doesn't seem so awful any longer, but in someone like me there is no room, and everything would have ended badly if it hadn't been for my voice that turned all the terror in me into song, just like Joseph Schmidt, who was even smaller, so that they didn't want to put him on the opera stage, he was only good enough for the gramophone, Joseph Schmidt would have made the prima donnas look ridiculous with his being so small, that's what people said, except it was actually his voice that was too big, Schwarz, his voice was the real reason, but they didn't say that, of course, and absolutely not to him personally, though of course he knew the score, he was from Czernowitz, you see, but everybody was certain that in such a little person as Joseph Schmidt there must be a constant boiling and bubbling, without interruption, like in Napoleon, so that it was impossible to put such a little person on the opera stage, and we won't even mention dwarves, the kinds of unpleasant surprises a dwarf has in store, and it is not completely untrue that in a big, tall person there is enough room, anyway, even if that is the only positive thing about him, while all the thoughts and fluids and horrors that have to squeeze into a smaller body can easily boil over, they push us small people up and out without our being able to do much about it, sometimes higher than everyone else, like Napoleon, toward the top, or at least out of line, and that was my case, precisely.

If only you knew how many dangers lie in wait for a person like me!

The little person lives a dangerous life, and my plan of defense was to try to hold back everything that was boiling and bubbling inside me. Don't get nervous, Ernster! Breathe deeply, I said to myself. Count to seven! Sit down for a second! Just like that! As a short person I was forced to choose, choose between being visible, despite my size, or to use it for what it was good for, for keeping my head down. But it was necessary to choose, once and for all, and I chose to keep my head down and so I can't explain the shoemaking thing, I don't know why I called out "Here!" that time and stepped out of line, it wasn't my philosophy. *Ja.* Besides that, it was a lie. Believe me, Schwarz, I have lied often in my life, but never of my own free will. Instead it was as if life itself were lying through me, and when you have to save yourself, any profession will do, it's like with languages, the first one that comes along will do, and if you don't know the grammar or how to cobble a shoe, the only important thing is that you don't let anyone else find it out. But believe me, Schwarz, it's hard to pretend to be a shoemaker.

The Russian major needed new boots for himself, and at home in Fogarasch I had seen how the shoemakers first used to have the customer place his bare foot on a piece of paper, so I asked the major for a newspaper. The next day he brought one. Under his arm he had a roll of black leather. I tore a page out of the major's newspaper and asked him to stand on it. With a piece of coal I traced his feet on the paper. What's the meaning of this, he yelled, are you trying to make a fool of the Red Army, and I answered, Comrade Major, we are just taking your measurements, no foot is like any other, and not just any boots will do, what we need are two boots, one to fit each of Comrade Major's feet, and he just grunted in answer but kept standing on the newspaper, the *Red Star,* a soldier's newspaper, and this made me even more nervous. He hadn't taken off his socks and they stunk terribly, I thought that they must stink worse than his feet would have if he had taken off the socks and stood barefoot on the newspaper. But he had given me good leather, a whole roll. He was still angry. "The devil take you, Jew, if you destroy my leather!" And then he left.

That evening I sat on my cot and didn't know which way to turn. A tailor from Iaşi came and sat down beside me, and I explained everything. Ernster, he said, you unfortunate! Then he went back to his cot, but he soon returned. Look here, he said, I've never worked in leather, but it can't be that different from cloth, and I've seen the major, we have his feet on the paper. So, Ernster, we'll give it a try!

And with the knife the major had lent me the tailor began cutting the leather, though his specialty was pants, and while he cut he stuck his tongue out of the right corner of his mouth. I sat beside him. My only thought was focused on the leather, it was if he were cutting in my own skin, and Schwarz, you know already that the whole thing was *Betrug*, a big lie, and when he was done cutting and two boots lay cut out and waiting on my cot, as flat as the dough for a strudel, he said to me, Ernster, the war is almost over and God knows if we'll survive the butt end of it, but if I don't I want you to go to Iaşi and tell my folks that before the war was over, the two of us made a pair of boots together, and without me, you should also say, you wouldn't be alive. Rosenstrasse 18, he said, and I have remembered that address until today because it is in my heart. In my heart, Schwarz, not in my head. Rosenstrasse 18. But the tailor's name I have forgotten.

So it is, Schwarz. To measure and cut out are the hardest things, and to stick to that pattern later is almost an impossibility. The rest does itself. The major provided the thread and the tacks, though they were too long and rusty. A locksmith from Humenne remembered that before the war he had seen a film about the Baťa shoe factories, and he showed me how I should fasten the upper to the sole; the major gave me the glue, something sticky that the artillery greased their cannons with, but still, Schwarz, the boots didn't look so bad, as long as you didn't get too close. But when the door flew open and the major stepped into the barracks, I was afraid. The Polish legion! Just think if the boots should split when he pulled them on, maybe he would step through the soles, *oy vey,* and then the major began to scream, where are my boots, "Here!" I yelled, just like when I took that step out of line, and if I could have taken it back at that moment, I would have.

The major looked at the boots. Comrade Major, I said, they are maybe not so beautiful, but they don't leak. We dunked them in the barrel of rainwater and they didn't take in a drop, I swear by everything that's holy, in my boots you can march all the way to Vienna if you want, and when you celebrate your victory you will of course have a pair of real German army boots to dance in. The major took a step backwards, looked at the boots again, and then he screamed, villains, he screamed, I should have the whole lot of you shot, his face was deep red and he looked as if he were about to die on the spot and I got even more afraid, this time about what might happen to the major's heart, and then he screamed again that he was going to shoot us all, he screamed until he choked, and we ran back and forth and finally ran up to the major and took him under both his arms. Carefully we sat him on my cot and I loosened his collar, a stiff uniform collar, so that the major could breathe properly, except he was already wheezing more than breathing. The Red Army, Schwarz! None of us dared to say anything, and we saw how his body began to shake, it shook as if he were crying, and it was true, the boots really deserved a good cry, and so the fear took hold of me again, but then the major exploded in a laugh, he fell backwards on the cot and laughed so that he had to hold his stomach with both hands, and we looked at each other and then we began to laugh, too, one by one, all of us laughed together, until the major sat up and gasped for breath, he dried his face with both hands and said, though it was more like panting than speaking, is that what you call boots? Yes, we said. Those are supposed to be boots, said the major and loosened his uniform belt, he was fat, you see. Yes, we said. You damned villains, said the major, did you want to trick me? Yes, we said, that's what we were thinking, anyway. And so the major began to laugh again, he hooted with laughter and we laughed with him, I'm going to have all of you shot, he screamed, and I thought, mercy, if only I were home again in Fogarasch, I guess someone has to die even on the last day of a war, and the major kept holding his belly with laughter, we all laughed together.

Say what you like, Schwarz, but that's the way it is! I'm right, right? Not only your feet, but everything about them is underrated, and if you discover a tear in my eye now it's not because I still fill up with laughter from what I've been telling you, even though the Major was a good person, but because it got me thinking of my wife, may the

Lord have mercy on her soul, the Major's feet and boots got me thinking of her feet and her feet or the corset, you know, one of those girdles with elastic, with garters for the stockings and all. A corset. Of the finest quality, and I had bought it in Bucharest, my wife asked me to do it. Jossele, she nagged, my whole life I have wished for a real French corset and there are none to buy around here, only on the boulevards in Bucharest, and don't you dare come home without one, but it has to be pink, so then I was forced out on a hunt to Bucharest after her corset, though I had other things to do, my business, Schwarz, but in the end I found one, not a real French one, maybe, but the most expensive, packed in a paper carton with plastic and so ingenious that you could see the whole glorious business without opening the carton. It was pink, too, and imported. So I came home with the corset and my wife took me in her arms. Jossele, she said. This is just how I had imagined it, such a husband I have! One who can take care of the most difficult business all on his own, and she kissed me on the mouth and put the carton with the corset from Bucharet in the bedroom wardrobe.

Aren't you going to put it on, I asked. Not yet, she answered. Ja, Schwarz, that's what she said. There was no trying it on that day or the next, either, the carton just sat there in the wardrobe, and so I asked again, when are you thinking of putting it on, and she just smiled, later, she said. Not now, she said. And at first I was disappointed, but I got over it and time passed, too. Soon I had forgotten the whole thing.

But Schwarz, so it is written: for everything there is a time, and that's how it was with the corset, too. Only many years later, when I had forgotten about the corset and the carton a long time earlier, the night came when she woke me up, it was dark outside and dark in our room, and my wife whispered to me, Jossele, I am so terribly cold. It is so cold in the bed.

Schwarz, tell me, what can a person do in such darkness? It was in the middle of the night. What would you have done?

I tucked the covers around her more tightly, but it didn't help. In the middle of the night, it was, and my eyelids were heavy with sleep, and in the darkness I heard her say something, Jossele, she said, I'm freezing. Warm up my feet, please. And under the covers I took both of her feet in my hands, I rubbed them between my hands, but it didn't help. Her feet were as cold as ice. What could I do? What would you have done, Schwarz, and my wife whispered to me, Jossele, she whispered, do you remember the corset? I think I want to put it on now.

And only then, when she said that it was time for the corset, did I really wake up, though it was in the middle of the night. I got up and felt my way to the wardrobe, it was as black as coal in the room, my legs were trembling and I said to myself, *oh Lord*, don't let it happen, not like this, and I took the corset out of the carton, my hands were shaking, too, and my wife said, please, help me put it on. And I did as she said. I helped her put on the corset though I knew that it was going to take her from me, and I cursed it. I cursed the day I had bought it, and I cursed Bucharest too, may the Lord forgive me for it.

Ja. Then I lay on my back beside her in the bed and didn't dare move. My limbs felt frozen, as if my legs and arms had taken all the cold from my beloved's body to make her less cold and to keep her with me for a little while, the tears began running down my cheeks, but in the darkness, praise the Lord, so she didn't have to see it.

My life has been a waste, I said in the darkness. I've made nothing of it. I struggled to hold the tears back. My life has been in vain, I said.

Don't say that, said my wife, and her voice was so feeble and weak that I almost couldn't hear it. No one may say that, she said. I loved you.

It's not true, I sobbed.

Yes, it is, said my wife, it is true, and I could feel her squeezing my hand under the covers, and she didn't even have enough strength to do that.

Don't leave me alone, I whispered, and in the darkness we lay, both of us motionless on our backs beside each other, she unable to move anymore and I too frightened to, one movement would have hastened what already had been written, and I held her hand, I tried to give her all the strength I had.

You mustn't say that your life has been wasted, she whispered. Promise me that. No one may say that.

And I felt how the tears ran over my cheeks again and she couldn't see any of that in the darkness.

Don't talk like that, she whispered, and it was as if she were speaking to a child, do you understand, Schwarz? For me it was suddenly as if she was no longer my wife but my dead mother, only the corset and that body were still my wife, but the voice was already my mother's though it didn't sound like hers, it was much weaker, as if nothing interested it much anymore, and I had loved her so much that I could no longer decide if it were my mother or my wife speaking to me in the darkness, and both of them I had loved so much that I would have given my own life for them if I had been able, but how could I have done that, Schwarz, is there a person who can decide the moment of his own death?

Warm me up, she whispered. My feet are so cold. And I cupped my hands around them again, like this, her feet were completely cold, she was about to leave me, just as it had been written.

That other peoples' lives are more difficult than ours, that they suffer more than we do is perhaps true, but it doesn't help us, Schwarz, it doesn't comfort you when your own wife is dying, and on Thursday next week it will have been twelve years ago to the day, and so I heard her say, Jossele, you need three eggs.

That is what she said, I believe. Three eggs.

For what? Where am I going to get any eggs?

Three eggs for scrambled eggs, she said. Beat them in the pan with a little milk. Milk, I sobbed, you know that there's no milk around here, where am I going to get milk? Or a little water, she said, and her voice was so low that I had to press tightly against her in the bed to hear.

A little water. My Jossele, can you remember what I'm saying, and I said yes, yes, I'll remember all of it, I promise, every word. And a dab of lard, she whispered. Melt it in the pan first.

Lard, I whispered.

Yes, Jossele my own, she said. Sometimes I used lard. Forgive me for that.

And that was the last thing she said.

Forgive me, she said, Schwarz. But was that directed to me? How should I know if she might not have been talking to someone else?

I lay beside her for a long time in the bed, and now I could no longer hold back my despair, I wept loudly in the darkness, and I wasn't able to collect myself until she didn't seem to want to let go of my hand, it was toward dawn, her fingers were still holding onto mine, and in the midst of my despair I was so frightened that I got out of bed, and though it was still night and dark and there was nothing to see, I carefully pulled the cover over her so that it even covered her face.

Ja. I wanted to see her face but at the same time I didn't, and the Lord came to my aid with His darkness, as He always comes to our aid when we don't know if we're coming or going and no longer can help ourselves.

And it was a lie, Schwarz, do you understand me? A lie! I had lied again. I didn't remember anything, not a single word of what she had said. Sure, I had heard what she said, but her words no longer meant anything. No word is like a person, words and books are left with us but they can never replace the person who goes away, and so everything we promise is worthless. Scrambled eggs? Not even today can I make scrambled eggs.

Do you understand me, Schwarz, do you grasp what I'm talking about? Are you married? Not married? But let me take care of that, we'll take a walk together and visit all the unmarried ladies, good day, Miss Rosen, but first we have to greet her mother, good day, Mrs. Rosen, good day to all the blondes and to the redheads, too, but watch out for that color, and as soon as you know it you're married, but that was of course before the war, why have you come so late, Schwarz, why didn't you hurry, I have to sit here alone in my room, you can see for yourself, not much more than a hole in the wall, and listen carefully to what I'm saying now, because this is what I have come up with in my solitude to comfort myself: a person has to be allowed to lie when another person has to be spared from the truth he cannot bear.

Ja. Forgive me Schwarz, but what is the time? You wanted to see the synagogue, and now it's already getting dark. Where can the key be? Let's go. What time is it, anyway? Can you take my arm, that's it, forgive me, come on, let's go."

A DOCTOR MUST CONDUCT HIMSELF LIKE A DOCTOR, ONLY THEN DOES a doctor become a doctor, at least in Vienna, and since this doctor's diploma happened to be both genuine and from Prague, it would have been possible in Vienna to be a double doctor (Dr. Dr.); *Herr Doktor Doktor* Schwarz would have been the form of address used by the Viennese, but in Vienna he who does not conduct himself like a *Doktor Doktor*, or even like a regular *Doktor*, remains, despite the doctorate, a *Herr*.

His friend Doctor Weiss, on the other hand, who had no doctorate but had earned his title in Vienna by conducting himself like one, was addressed as *Herr Doktor*, and when he declined that title, the Viennese said: "Certainly, as you wish, *Herr Doktor*."

"Help me," said Doctor Schwarz to his friend Doctor Weiss. "You know that I am a doctor, a doctor of economics, even a doctor *honoris causa*, but no one here addresses me as *Herr Doktor*, while you, who are no doctor, are called *Herr Doktor* wherever you go. I, on the other hand, am only a *Herr*. But you are a *Doktor* even when absent," said Doctor Schwarz to his friend Doctor Weiss, who was not a doctor, but in Vienna treated like one.

Doctor Weiss, who had no right to his doctor title, regarded his friend Doctor Schwarz, who was not from Vienna, thoughtfully and at length, and even in Doctor Weiss's penetrating gaze there was something genuinely doctoral, of course not definable in academic terms, but obvious to any butcher, at least in the city of Vienna.

The two doctors, both the false and the genuine, looked at one another, and Doctor Schwarz sighed. "My dear Schwarz," said Doctor Weiss at last. "You lack an umbrella. You do not even own a bow tie. You are filled with your doctorate, but it is invisible."

"What do you mean, invisible?" asked Doctor Schwarz.

"Try an umbrella," said Doctor Weiss.

"An umbrella?" asked Doctor Schwarz.

"An umbrella," repeated Doctor Weiss.

"At the butcher's?" asked Doctor Schwarz.

"Just don't let on who you are," said Doctor Weiss.

"But I have a diploma," said Doctor Schwarz.

"A diploma?" said the astonished Doctor Weiss, who had no right, strictly speaking, to his doctor's title.

For Doctor Weiss, who had no doctorate but conducted himself like a doctor, had received his title as part of a package deal, so to speak, while buying cold cuts at the butcher's. But it sometimes happened that the Viennese took away his "Weiss," so that he became *"Herr Doktor* Schwarz," and when he corrected them, pointing out that his name was Weiss, the Viennese said, "Naturally, as you wish, *Herr Doktor* Schwarz."

This disturbed Doctor Weiss. But since Doctor Weiss was from Vienna himself, he knew that there was nothing to be done about this *"Herr Doktor* Schwarz." He would however have been glad to help Doctor Schwarz, but since he, that is the Doctor Schwarz who really was Doctor Schwarz but in Vienna Herr Schwarz, was not from Vienna, Doctor Weiss knew that there was no way to help him.

"Try an umbrella," said Doctor Weiss, but he did not sound very convinced. "Just do not start up with the diploma. For God's sake!"

"An umbrella," said Doctor Schwarz.

Doctor Weiss looked at him, perhaps for the first time with true interest.

"My dear Schwarz, with an umbrella you will become a doctor like me," said Doctor Weiss. "You will become me."

"But I am Schwarz and you are Weiss," said Schwarz.

"That depends," said Doctor Weiss. "You are Schwarz, but sometimes I am Doctor Schwarz, and though you are the one who has earned the degree, you will not be the doctor you would have been if you had been me. And you do want to be Doctor Schwarz," said Doctor Weiss. "Right? After all, you are the one who is do-doctored."

"So I am the one who is Weiss," said Schwarz.

"No," said Weiss. "If you were Weiss I would not be Weiss, but

Schwarz. I am the one who is Weiss. Not you. But now and then I am Doctor Schwarz, and that is because I am not do-doctored."

"Do-doctored in what?" asked Doctor Schwarz.

"That is not important," said Doctor Weiss, irritated. "Where is my umbrella, by the way?"

"Your umbrella?" asked Doctor Schwarz.

"My umbrella," said Doctor Weiss, and bent down to look under the table.

"My dear Doctor Weiss," said Doctor Schwarz. "Since when do you have an umbrella?"

"I have always had an um-umbrella," said Doctor Weiss and looked around. "I had it with me. I came her with an um-umbrella."

"I have never seen you with an um-umbrella," said Doctor Schwarz.

"That can't be true," said Doctor Weiss.

"I swear it. Never," Doctor Schwarz assured him.

"You can't mean it," said Doctor Weiss.

"Yes, I certainly do, my dear Doctor Weiss," said Doctor Schwarz. "If there is an um-umbrella here it is mine. It must quite simply be mine."

"Yours?" said Doctor Weiss suspiciously.

"Mine and no other's," said Doctor Schwarz, who had never owned an umbrella, but who was now beginning to feel like a real *Herr Doktor,* even in Vienna.

"And which of us is actually Weiss," asked Doctor Weiss. "You, perhaps?"

"No," said Doctor Schwarz. "Not Weiss, but *Doktor Weiss,* please."

"Certainly," mumbled Doctor Weiss, who had just found his umbrella. It had happened to fall under his chair. "As you wish, *Herr Doktor.*"

IT IS THE ROOSTERS THAT AWAKEN ME, RIGHT IN THE MIDDLE OF the city; they crow from every corner and all directions, and though it is Sunday morning and I manage to get back to sleep, they creep into my shattered morning dreams and keep on crowing there as if nothing were holy or private anymore.

I soon give up my struggle with the roosters and get dressed to go down and eat breakfast. For breakfast there are omelettes and ham and eggs; eggs are the last thing I want. A cup of coffee? There is no coffee. Outside a clear and still-cold sun is shining. I am alone in the dining room. While I am waiting for my breakfast, I see that the terrace facing onto the square is covered with shattered glass. I chew my way through the ham, long for a cup of coffee, and cannot stop thinking that the crushed glass splinters outside on the terrace are the remains of my morning dream.

What could I have dreamed that had so much glass in it? And I curse the invisible roosters who keep crowing out there, despite the fact that it is Sunday.

The square outside the window is like all the squares of this region: big and oblong, its cobblestones mantled with a pale layer of asphalt. There is nothing special about such a square. On a Sunday like this it resembles an empty sack. On weekdays it is a square for geese in baskets and squatting old ladies in black, but even then the sheer size of it is still unpleasant. The square is quite simply too big; you can see that especially when it is empty and desolate, as it is now. There is more space in it than the geese require, and on an early Sunday morning like this it is obvious that such a square, even though now empty, is more appropriate for parades or pogroms than for farmers' markets.

On my way out for a morning walk I stumble on the stairs leading into the hall and just about fall down them. When I turn around I see that pieces of the last step are missing. Large pieces of it must have been broken loose with an object harder than stone.

In the hall a woman sits alone and regards me over the top of her glasses.

"One day we all work and drink coffee together, and the next we kill each other," says the woman, who is knitting something blue and watching television.

I look angrily at the step. In my thoughts it is connected to the broken glass and the roosters, all the things that have conspired in concert against me this morning, and so early that they bid fair to destroy my first free Sunday in a long time. I see that several of the steps are marked with dark stains; stains that I did not see when I arrived late last night.

"This ought to be cleaned up," I say.

The lady at the reception desk does not look up from her knitting.

"Do you really think that we want them back here after all that has already happened," she asks.

"I was only saying that this ought to be cleaned."

"And who ought to clean up after them, do you think?"

She has a dark blue jacket across her shoulders. On television they are showing a Catholic mass. A very old priest bends over a piece of paper, the paper is trembling in his hands, and with a voice that also trembles, the priest reads a greeting from the Pope in Rome.

"Leave your passport here," she says when I ask for it. "What do you need your passport for on a Sunday?"

I look at the stairway in the hall. Blood that is soaked up by stone or marble loses its fresh color and soon looks dusty. Within the stone the blood stands still, perhaps because it no longer has the task of pulsing and giving life to the body of a human or an animal. Strictly speaking it has no task at all, and it is not until the cold light of this Sunday morning that I discover that several of the steps leading up from the hall to the second floor are full of dusty, soaked-in stains of dried blood.

"Mr. Tănase called," says the lady in the reception when I come back from my walk.

"Mr. Tanăse?"

On the television the mass is nearing its end; the old priest holds a cross lifted on straight arms above his head.

"I don't know a Mr. Tănase."

"He will receive you at his home at one," says the lady, laying a piece of paper in front of me on the counter. "Here is the address. It's not far at all," she adds, and on the television the priest is still holding the cross aloft and singing a Catholic hymn whose melody I think I recognize. The priest's mouth moves on the television screen.

"But I don't know any Mr. Tšnase," I say.

What time is it, anyway?

On the wall behind me in the hall there are four big digital clocks showing local time in Moscow, London, Paris, and Bucharest. All of European time has been arranged into a synchronicity up there on the wall, though it is a synchronicity in different time zones. Still, the fact that London or Paris vouch for the time here must make life easier to bear for both the staff and the guests, even if there is no coffee.

But in Moscow on this Sunday, time has been eliminated. Only two blinking red dots are left to mark Russian time, and without numerals the dots seem to belong to a different calculation of time from ours. What at first looks intentional proves to have a quite natural explanation, even if it happens to be Russian time that has suffered the most—none of the four clocks on the wall is correct.

Their works must be out of order. The Russian clock is broken and even the Romanian one works badly; certainly the situation in Bucharest is chaotic, but not so chaotic that time moves from 10:00 to 23:44 from one moment to the next, or that from midnight we are suddenly propelled into the dawn at 4:22. The digital clocks on the wall work any which way, just as most things in this hotel work, and no repair is going to help that, but it is too bad about the lack of correct time. At least I could have stayed on real European time.

On this early morning I discover that the hall, too, is slovenly. In the corners, which dust rags and brooms reach only when well paid, lies the same broken glass as outside the dining room on the second floor.

Perhaps it is the roosters who keep track of whatever time is needed here. The roosters are enough and clocks are not needed, just as no map is needed to find Mr. Tănase. A map would be of no help here, either to show the way to Mr. Tănase's or anywhere else; to have a map or ask for directions would only unmask me as a stranger, and I prefer to follow my nose. The sun is already high in the sky and the road lies open; this Sunday I am sharing it with white, waddling geese.

A stranger was the last thing I wanted to be. It was not enough for me to visit this world—a better word than "world" does not occur to me—as a mere stranger or guest; I wanted to make it *mine,* and this arrogance was overshadowed only by the attraction this other world had for me. My curiosity knew no bounds, since I was convinced that I could always save myself by stepping back over the border between my world and theirs. But in this way I had created more confusion and awakened more hopes than I myself could understand, hopes for those who were out to save themselves, and who saw me as a part of their rescue. Even so, their self-respect did not allow them to grab me as a drowning man grabs a lifesaver. They wanted no sacrifices to their cause, they did not want to beg for anything, instead they wanted to soften hearts. They wanted to be seduced, and so we met in an erotic embrace, but they were unable to figure out whether it was I or my passport that had seduced them. My pride rejected the idea of the passport. I wanted nothing more than to seduce and in the bargain make their world mine, and it was only when I discovered that it was the passport they were after, that they put more hope in it than in me to rescue them and make my world *theirs,* it was only then that I withdrew; I prepared to go back over the border to my own world, but when I turned around my baggage was gone.

My bag had been stolen.

The bag with my clothes was gone. Six pairs of socks and my suit was stolen. I was forced to buy a new one, one of the two models available here, and so what was more, I even looked like them. Did they think it was a question of solidarity? Maybe they wanted to believe that, though they knew about the theft and were secretly happy about it. But they also knew that at home in Vienna I had other suits hanging in the closet—that the suit I was now forced to wear would immediately land in the trash once I found myself on my side of the border. Still they were flattered. They would be glad to forget that I did not have a choice, just as they long ago had been forced to forget that they themselves had none, and this masquerade could have amused all of us a while longer if in the end they had not begun to consider it a bit too intimate and ingratiating of me to struggle into a synthetic suit, even if there was no other suit available.

What could I do?

I had to put something on my body. But they were no longer open to such reasonable arguments; in the end they would have rather seen me walk around naked. The suit I had pulled on could not be mine because it was *theirs,* and that I had slunk into it anyway was an impertinence. Out of pure meanness they pinched at the back and waist to convince me how fantastic the fit was, better than any suit from Savile Row, and just because I felt sorry for them I agreed; we lied to each other out of honest affection and malice. Savile Row, indeed; I stuck my hand in the pocket of my suit jacket and drove it right through the lining, and no matter how badly it fit, it still did not make me one of them, while they tried to convince me that I ought to buy even more of them while I had the chance—several synthetic suits, cut for the absolutely ideal figure, just not my own, with a fit that was unmistakable.

So my suit remained a cover for what it could not change, just as they convinced themselves in time that my curiosity and my interest in them was only pity, that everything was a cover, and even in such a suit, exactly like their own, they would have no difficulty whatsoever recognizing me. They would all be able to jump on me as if I were their whipping boy, just as the geese on this muddy road suddenly attack me, hissing and waddling, with fluttering wings, as if even the animals are able to tell that I do not belong here, have no business being here, and that such an impertinence must be punished.

They do not even want to share this oozing country road with me, and when I stop, quite frightened, in the middle of the road in my muddy suit, someone calls out to me not to be afraid.

I should not be afraid of the geese. They are not dangerous.

"Mr. Tănase?"

The man who stands outside the house on the right side of the road and washes his car, a Trabant, nods while he dries his hands on a rag.

"Dumitru Tănase," he says, and takes my hand. "Wonderful that you could come."

Mr. Tănase is dressed in a blue sweatsuit with white stripes. He has a little gray head with tufts of hair in the same color, his head looks like a dirty gray pear covered with burrs. Once more he dries his hands and asks me to come into the house with him. Together we walk through the little garden and on the steps to the house a woman welcomes us; it is his wife, in a robe and with a grainy layer of purple on her lips. She smiles at me with even teeth.

Her eyes glisten. Madame Tănase is both excited and upset. Some strands have escaped in disorder from her upswept black hair, they have fallen over her face. When she stretches her hand toward me the nails are painted the same purple color as her mouth.

I have brought a present with me, balls of marzipan dipped in chocolate, with the great composer's name and picture on the carton.

"All the way from Vienna," sighs Mrs. Tănase.

The Tănase family has acquired a satellite dish, a white shining disc on the roof, and for the first time in her life Madame Tănase has seen American wrestling this Sunday morning on her television.

"Have you ever seen big guys like that fight? No? *O, là là!*"

Everything in the house is prepared for the guest. The television is standing in the little hall where she has set the table for us already;

on the table stands a bottle without a label. We drink to one another with *țuica*, plum brandy, and on the sofa sits a plump younger lady with coal black hair, Lidia, together with a melancholy man who says nothing, he only mumbles something that could be hello or welcome, but could just as easily be his name.

On the wall above the sofa hangs a print that depicts King Ferdinand and is a tribute to the Romanian army during the first World War. Around the king a group of men has gathered with drawn sabers and standards. They crowd around the center of the print, and around them and the king there is nothing else pictured; the royal group's lances and gun barrels stick into the sky like the hair on the back of a mean dog. Without the war depicted on Mr. Tănase's print, Transylvania would not belong to Romania today, and after the revolution, which was now four months ago, he went and got the king down from his hiding place in the attic.

"How do you like our hotel?" asks Mr. Tănase.

"I just got here late last night."

"It is the best in the city."

Lidia laughs from the sofa and Mr. Tănase says that the Hotel Grand was stormed on the twentieth of March, that was a month ago; the fixtures on the second floor were destroyed and the staff and the Romanian hotel guests were beaten with canes and wooden clubs. Later that same day at least six people were killed outside on the square.

"Five or six."

"I know," I say.

Mr. Tănase sits quietly for a moment as if he is thinking about the significance of my answer. His face is tense, a tension that seems to have to do with his inner world, not the outer one. Even Lidia and the melancholy man beside her on the sofa are silent. Madame Tănase has left the room. She is not visible.

"Well, let's have a drink, then," says Mr. Tănase and lifts his glass of plum brandy. "To our guest."

"What you might not know is that a Romanian journalist was also killed in the hotel," says Mr. Tănase when he has emptied his glass and licked his lips.

"In the room next to mine," I say. "I know."

"Koko," calls Madame Tănase and suddenly her face with the red lips appears from behind the door.

"That's from a film," says Mr. Tănase irritably.

Madame Tănase brings in a homemade nutcake from the kitchen. When she cuts the cake, liquid runs out of it, and her husband says that this kind of nutcake cannot be made from a cookbook, it is an old family recipe, and that his wife learned to bake the cake from his own mother. "As a child I ate the same nutcake. Not the one in front of us on the table of course, but no one would be able to tell the difference between this one and the one I ate as a child."

"Except that cake was eaten long ago, of course," he says, and at this Lidia laughs with her mouth full of nutcake and the melancholy man on the sofa beside her says nothing. He is occupied with shoveling nutcake from his plate into his mouth with his knife.

We eat our cake. Mr. Tănase has the floor. In what he is saying I sense something left unsaid, so that the thing that lies closest to his heart and yet remains unsaid makes the features of his face unnecessarily tense; like those of an animal, I think. Indeed, an animal: the little head, the jaw, the skin stretched over it, even the teeth when they are bared in a grin, not at all disagreeable, but just natural, like an animal that has to trust its instincts a little more than its heart.

"Where is our cassette?" asks Mr. Tănase, turned toward the mute on the sofa who, in his sudden terror, forgets to shut his mouth, a completely black hole in a perpetually tortured face, and he pushes his plate away and leaves the room.

"Excuse me," he mumbles as he pushes past me with his back turned. It is the first thing I clearly hear him say; at least it sounds as if he is excusing himself.

The nutcake has made Mr. Tănase talkative. Carefully he brings a white paper napkin to his lips, he does no more than brush it against them, and when he has laid the napkin away on the table he continues to explain about the cake and the family recipe, and of this nutcake he makes an entire cuisine.

"Ah, no one makes such wonderful food as we Romanians," says Mr. Tănase, and Lidia nods from the sofa, "Of course," she says.

"And without our Romanian recipes we never would have accomplished anything," says he and I nod, their food does always taste pretty good, "if we had not stuck together we would not even be able to fry an onion today," says Mr. Tănase.

"Bravo!" cries Lidia, clapping her hands.

Mr. Tănase explains that all Romanians from their birth on are taken into a single great community that is much older than Christianity. Not all of his sentences get finished, his jaws are working. Mr. Tănase talks and eats at the same time.

"*Vatra Românească*" he says, "Our Romanian hearth! That is how a cuisine is made."

Madame Tănase trips into the room again; now I see for the first time that along with her robe, she is wearing high heels without stockings. She is serving white wine in glasses, and when she leans over the table I get a glimpse of the upper edge of a pink nightgown under the robe.

"What is he up to, anyway," grumbles Mr. Tănase, turning around.

The mute has disappeared as if swallowed by the earth, and behind her husband's back Madame Tănase takes the opportunity to wink at me with her left eye. She has formed her purple mouth into a round pouting "o"; maybe this is from the same film.

"What have you been up to," says Mr. Tănase angrily to the mute, who has come back into the room with a package under his arm. Without answering he sits down in front of the television.

"Sit on the sofa so you can see better," says Mr. Tănase to me while his wife tosses her head nervously a few times; it is probably the loose strands of hair that keep falling in her face. She gets up from the table and disappears into the kitchen again.

"It is not that we have anything against the Hungarians," says Mr. Tănase. "There is nothing wrong with them. You know. Hungarians!

People have just excited them. It's always the same. Manipulation! The intellectuals, of course. You know. Right? Bah! Four or five of them at the most. Just lock them up! The Hungarians, I mean."

"We were here first, you know," says Lidia, and without turning toward us the mute suddenly lifts his right arm into the air and snaps his fingers. There is a crackling in the television, an image flutters across the screen, "Aha," says Mr. Tănase and takes a case out of his right-hand overall pocket, opens it, and sets a pair of glasses on his nose.

"Make yourselves comfortable!"

On the screen a crowd of people appears. The crowd is in color. In the background, over the crowd's head, glimpses of the Hotel Grand sometimes flicker, but the camera moves uncertainly back and forth as if the person who was making the film did not know what his film should include, nor did he have any idea where he could find what he needed for it. You can see that the crowd on the screen is excited. It is shouting something in chorus, but the rasping sound from the television drowns out all the words, and the crowd consists only of heads that billow back and forth over the screen, from left to right and back again, heads like the topmost scum on the crest of a wave, and the wave itself is the common body, all of the individual bodies there on the square that have flowed into one common body, a collective body with thousands of heads.

"Listen to what they are saying about us," says Mr. Tănase.

"What are they shouting?"

"Shhhhhh!"

"Most vagy soha," says Lidia beside me on the sofa.

"Now or never."

"You can hear for yourself," says Mr. Tănase, straightening his glasses on his nose.

"They send books from Hungary that say that we are not descended from the Romans," says Lidia.

Mr. Tănase searches for an even better scene, and the mute, squatting next to the television, winds the tape back and forth so that the sound rises to a falsetto and the crowd disappears. The mute hacks the crowd into a single mass of heads that flow out over the square in all directions, so that it is impossible to see which heads are Hungarian and which Romanian, though Mr. Tănase has pulled his chair close to the television, and like a field-marshal he points to the right or left part of the screen with his whole hand and cries out "there, did you see?" or "here!" but then the mute has already managed to wind the tape farther so that Mr. Tănase cries "Stop, this isn't working at all!" and his wife trips in from the kitchen again, this time with a large platter with sour cream, white bread, and Transylvanian cabbage rolls.

"Go get my briefcase," Mr. Tănase calls to her, but instead she sits down at the table. The mute turns off the television. The cabbage rolls must have come directly from the oven; they are steaming. The scent of cabbage fills the little room.

With the cabbage rolls we drink both white and red wine, as well as the remains of the plum brandy. We pour the sour cream over the cabbage rolls and it is so thick and solid that it does not even melt at the edges, it just sweats a little.

"Don't you ever think that it is sad to visit us here in the East?" asks Madame Tănase.

She smiles and looks at me, her mouth is a glistening red in the middle of her face. She looks at me as one looks at an ignorant child who demands a great deal of patience, a child of whom it would be unfair to expect anything.

"Tell us something about Vienna," she says.

"How about that briefcase?" asks Mr. Tănase irritably.

"Who wants coffee," twitters Madame Tănase and I dry my mouth and give my honest opinion, that I have not eaten so well during my entire week in Transylvania, not the week before in the Banat either, and she smiles with delight. For the first time that Sunday afternoon her purple smile contains an almost girlish shyness that makes me like her even more.

"Don't forget the briefcase," Mr. Tănase calls after her, and when she comes back from the kitchen she really does have a thick briefcase with her, but also another platter of cabbage rolls, and her husband immediately begins to dig through the briefcase, and quite soon he finds what he is looking for, a newspaper. While we eat another round of homemade cabbage rolls, he reads to us from the April 25 edition of *Cuvîntul Liber*, the article begins on the front page and is so long that it continues in the back of the paper. It tells of the murder of five Romanians in December of last year. Mr. Tănase reads to us about how the murderers cut off the head of Dumitru Coman in the presence of his family and then set fire to his corpse.

"Dumitru Coman, Liviu Ceuchisan, Gabi Dănica, Ferenz Imre and Aurel Agache," he reads from the newspaper, and Lidia nods with her mouth full of cabbage roll.

Mr. Tănase lets the paper from the twenty-fifth of April fall down on the uneaten food left on his plate. He shakes his head.

"We are probably the only people in the world who let a minority form its own party," he sighs.

"That is true," says Lidia.

"In Louisiana there are eight million Frenchmen," continues Mr. Tănase. "Eight million! Not six or seven but eight! What do you say to that? But do you think they have their own party?"

"This is just the kind of thing people want to read about," says Lidia, meaning the newspaper. "People want to read about the kind of thing that could happen to any one of us."

"Well, I don't know about that," mutters Mr. Tănase, fiddling with his briefcase. "It's not going to happen to me. But it is shocking, that is what it is. Every day one has to expect the worst."

But there is something else he wants to show me, and yet again he plunges into the briefcase with both hands, "I just had it right here," he mutters angrily, and while he is looking in his briefcase, his wife looks at me over the table, and Mr. Tănase cannot find the paper he's looking for.

"I have a surprise for you," says Madame Tănase suddenly, clapping her small hands together.

She leaps from the table so that the dishes clatter and leaves the room. When she comes back, she is carrying a pair of gloves. She pushes my plate aside. The two gloves she lays before me on the table.

"A present for you."

"I just had it right here," mutters Mr. Tănase.

"Try them on," she says. "They are too small for my husband. His hands are too big."

"I don't know."

"Try them!"

I take one of the gloves from the table, the right one, and pull it on. Actually it is too warm for gloves now at the end of April. But the glove feels comfortable, it closes tightly around my fingers.

"Does it feel good on?" asks Madame Tănase.

"Yes, not bad at all."

"Those are really nice gloves," says Lidia, as if she had seen them before. She has gotten up from the sofa and sat beside Madame Tănase.

"Pigskin," mumbles Mr. Tănase without looking up from the bundle of papers in his briefcase.

"Why don't you put on the other one, too," asks Madame Tănase, leaning forward across from me over the table.

"If you really think I should."

She nods.

With my already gloved right hand I take the other glove from the table and pull it on, bit by bit, the whole way over my left hand, but the left glove feels tighter than the right; my middle finger almost does not have enough room. I have to squeeze the glove on, it is not easy. Madame Tănase watches attentively as I try to push my middle finger all the way to the end.

Mr. Tănase rustles his papers. He has pushed his glasses up onto his forehead.

"There," I say with relief as I finally manage to put on both gloves. I move my fingers inside them. "I have to make sure that they're all still there," I say, and then I let them hang, as if they need to relax after a great effort.

Lidia laughs.

"Would you like to have them?" asks Madame Tănase.

I don't know what to say to her, I just sit there wearing the yellow gloves, and in front of me on the table there is still a half-full platter, cabbage rolls with sour cream, bread, and sticky wine glasses, and I would like to have taken some more of everything if it hadn't seemed inappropriate to eat with gloves on—Mr. Tănase's gloves, to boot.

"You can have them if you like," says Madame Tănase; Lidia has laid her arm around her shoulders. Together the two women regard me with curiosity.

The toilet is suddenly flushed, it must be the mute. He has to pull the cord several times before you can hear the water rush into the stool. I had not even noticed that he left the room.

"How do they feel on?"

"Not bad at all," I say cautiously.

"Not bad, you say?"

"They feel good on."

Lidia laughs again.

A door to the room is opened, then closed. The mute is back from the toilet.

"Ah, here it is," cries Mr. Tănase, waving a piece of paper in the air, while his wife, with a bored expression, looks at her red polished nails instead of me.

"I knew I had it here someplace!"

Madame Tănase gets up from the table and leaves the room. Her heels crack and I can see that she really is not wearing any stockings; her white calves gleam.

"Let's see," says her husband, setting his glasses on his nose. "Here we have it! A paragraph written Saturday, the twelfth of April, 1940. More than fifty years ago. Ha! Here is what Goebbels writes in his diary, just listen!"

"The Hungarians," he reads loudly from the paper, "persecute the

Romanians in the annexed territories bloodthirstily. A band of dirty swine! *O bandă de porci murdari!*"

Mr. Tănase whacks the paper with his index finger to show where the place about swine is. He gives me the paper, I hold it in my hands with the gloves on, and indeed: there is the sentence about the Hungarian pigs, and someone, probably Mr. Tănase himself, has translated just that part of the paragraph from the diary that interested him most, so that between the lines one reads *O bandă de porci murdari* in black ink.

"What do you say to that?" asks Mr. Tănase.

"Would you like more cabbage roll?" asks Lidia, who seems to have taken over the role of hostess since Madame Tănase left the room, but at the moment I say no, thank you, she turns up. She has combed the strands of hair back from her forehead, they have been reunited with the rest of her hair.

"Yes, yes," says her husband, taking the paper from my hands. "Goebbels! I know, I know. Bah! Of course he was a criminal. But this is from his private diary."

"A diary is a completely different story," says Lidia.

Madame Tănase has sat down with us again, but you can see that she is bored. It seems as if she has lost interest in the gloves. While she begins piling up the dishes, I take the opportunity to take them off; I do it stealthily, as if embarrassed, I hope that no one sees. Carefully I push them away. Without my hands nearby, the gloves seem quite harmless.

Madame Tănase has forgotten the coffee. With her left hand she holds her robe together over her breasts, and when she comes back from the kitchen she does not sit down. She remains standing while her husband sits, and Mr. Tănase has stopped digging through his briefcase. What time could it be? This afternoon time seems to have stood still or shrunk to two red dots, the eyes of a beast in the night.

"Where are my glasses," asks Mr. Tănase, and everyone can see that they no longer sit on his nose or forehead.

His wife says nothing. With her left hand she is still holding the robe closed over her breasts. Her nails shine against its fabric.

"And what are my gloves doing here on the table?" Mr. Tănase asks, and I can tell by his voice that he is irritated again; it is April, after all, and who needs gloves in April, in Tirgu Mureş no one even goes to church at this time of year in gloves.

It is almost five in the afternoon and Lidia whispers to me that it is time to go, but loudly enough for everyone to hear it, and so Mr. Tănase takes the opportunity to say, "It's too bad that you already have to go."

"Stay a little while," says his wife to Lidia, and Lidia stays, and with her the mute. Madame Tănase gives me her hand: a chalk-white and lifeless hand, as if it were my fault that it did not have any of the freshness of her magenta nails and lips.

In the hall Mr. Tănase takes a cane in hand, a rattan walking cane, and he walks ahead of me through the little garden. With his cane in hand he walks in silence through his garden, which now on the way from the house to the gate looks badly tended, a garden with dried, dusty bushes, with pale plants or plants with no color at all, and as he walks ahead of me towards the gate he begins to beat the bushes with his cane, one blow, and then another. Together we walk through the garden and the whole time Mr. Tănase beats the bushes with his cane, to the right and the left, ever harder, and only when he gets to the gate does he stop beating, and he turns to me.

"I didn't quite catch your name," says Mr. Tănase.

"No?"

"I mean your whole name," he says, and pokes in one of the bushes with the cane. I say my name while he continues to poke.

"Why are you hiding something from me?" he suddenly asks.

We avoid looking at each other.

"Yes," he repeats. "You are hiding something from me."

"Have I disappointed you?"

"You can hear for yourself," says Mr. Tănase, and looks straight into my eyes. "All you do is ask questions. Questions, questions! Don't you have anything to say for yourself?"

"Most everything here is strange to me," I say. "I wonder if you can understand that."

Mr. Tănase lets his gaze glide over the garden and begins to beat the nearest bush with his cane again, but loosely and without direction, as if his thoughts were elsewhere.

"No," he says. "I do not understand that."

"Really?"

"No. We have only spoken of things that anyone could understand. People are the same everywhere. That is the way it is here with us, anyway."

"I am not from here," I say.

"What am I supposed to think of you," says Mr. Tănase in a low voice. "We are not used to people hiding things from us here. What harm have we done you?"

"Why did you even invite me?" I ask, now with the same low voice as his. "What did you want from me? Didn't I eat your wife's cabbage rolls? They were very good."

Someone calls to him from inside the house.

Mr. Tănase looks at me. Close up his face reminds me of one of the papers he was looking for in his briefcase.

"You look tired," he says.

Someone calls him from the house.

"It's the roosters' fault," I say. "I had hoped to be able to sleep in today."

"So, the roosters," he says, disappointed.

Then he begins to beat the bushes again, but as if he has already forgotten why he is holding a cane in his hand and is attacking his own bushes.

From inside the house I hear laughter; I can make out Madame Tănase's, shriller than the others'.

"Aha, the roosters."

Mr. Tănase looks at the ground.

"Well, good-bye, then," I say.

I have reached out to him, but he does not take my hand.

"They crow all the time," he says. "They never give us any peace."

Mr. Tănase has lifted his cane and lets it rest on his right shoulder. He no longer beats the bushes with it.

"Those goddamned fucking roosters," he says.

Down by the gate to the street are some empty rabbit cages, two piles of cages with no rabbits.

"You ought to behead the whole bunch," I say.

Mr. Tănase nods absently.

"Yes," he says. "That would probably be the best solution."

I END UP IN PRŻEMYSL BECAUSE OF THE POPE AND AN OLD POSTCARD. The postcard is from the very first years of the First World War and depicts the city's fortress. It is hand painted, and the gray of the fortress has spread over the card and discolored the light blue sky over the city.

Prżemysl is still in our hands," is printed at the bottom of it.

For years I have wanted to see the fortress and the city that is almost the geographic center of Europe. But when I get there it turns out that Prżemysl is no longer located in the center of Europe but at its border; the city lies where Europe ends or where Europe begins, depending on one's perspective, and it takes less than three days to convince myself of this.

For the traveler who is coming from the east and gets off at the railway station here, Europe begins in Prżemysl, while the traveler who gets on a train to travel eastward leaves Europe behind. The city itself seems to be unconscious of this fact, and perhaps that is because the two travelers, the one from the east and the one from the west, never meet at Prżemysl's train station. They do not meet, because they happen to be one and the same person: a traveler who arrives from the east and then leaves several days later, from the same station, heading back east again.

In the quarter of the city near the station I look for a hotel. The train station in Prżemysl was built in 1895. It is a solid building from a distant and better time, and it looks like all the other railway stations, theaters, hospitals, and barracks that were built by the Habsburg monarchy on the periphery of the empire. Along with the buildings came lieutenants, doctors, tax collectors and ballet girls to show that European civilization had come to stay. But even then it was most often more wishful thinking than reality. At the end of the last century the Galician author Karl Emil Franzos wrote of the world that begins just beyond Prżemysl, calling it *Halbasien,* Half-Asia, a designation that made it clear that European civilization here was not much more than a thin layer of veneer, something like the paint I see flaking from the walls of the railway station.

Inside the station I find a man behind a window in the wall, a man employed by the railway, and when he opens his window he says that there is no hotel here in the city. "Why would there be a hotel in Prźemysl?" he asks with a grimace. Then he begins to count a bundle of banknotes, no longer concerned with me. "The one we have is closed for renovation," he says, when he discovers that I am still there and do not appear to be about to leave him in peace with his money that, strictly speaking, is neither his nor mine.

The station is under construction as well; it is being restored. The structural framework of the great hall and the frescoes of the ceiling have been brought back to their original condition. Old dust and dirt have been taken away, and the frescoes shine now in clear and light colors, but once they had finished the frescoes it looks as if their enthusiasm for renovation, or at least the money for it, disappeared. The scaffolding rises inside of the hall; boards and planks form a great labyrinth of wood that seems to keep the building from caving in and burying the waiting passengers inside. I open the door to the waiting room, but close it quickly again—the smell of sleeping people who have been wearing the same clothes for several days rushes out at me. In the same clothes they put on hundreds of miles from here, the people go on sleeping. On the wall above the sleepers hangs a clock with black hands that have stopped; it is twenty-four or twenty-five minutes to three, though you cannot tell whether it is daytime or nighttime, and there is nobody awake enough to ask.

Not many trains arrive at the three platforms, but even so there are people waiting day and night for them. The waiting people stand, squat, or lie on the platforms, surrounded by their plastic bags and worn cardboard suitcases held together with string. They are Ukrainians, Russians, Huculs, Bulgarians, a Boyk or two, Romanians, or Gypsies; when asked where they come from, they utter no answer, but simply point with their hands, always toward the east. All of them have come here for the same reason: to visit Europe.

From Halbasien they have traveled to Europe, a Europe which for them does not mean Paris or London, but Prźemysl.

They do not get any farther than this. Once in Prźemysl, they walk up and down the city's streets and admire the overabundance in the shop windows. They admire all of the products that they cannot admire in Halbasien. In Prźemysl's shop windows there are deodorant, beer in cans, an astrological calendar that shows the way to Happiness, a keychain with a Mercedes symbol, soap from East Germany (which no longer exists), dresses that bristle when one runs a hand over them, and small, portable televisions, made in Korea.

At the Russian Market, as it is called in Prźemysl, they sell what they have dragged with them from home. They try to sell a doorknob with no lock but made of brass, a bicycle chain, small wooden souvenirs, or a jar of dirty gray, dried-up caviar, so that they can buy a mini-calculator, string, a baby carriage, or some cans of beer from the Polish merchants. When the cans of beer have been drunk, they are placed like trophies or decoration on top of the television. But that is when they are home again. Here at the Russian Market they exchange Russian rubles or Romanian lei for the Polish złoty that has already become a sort of half-Asian hard currency in the places the Russian or Romanian travelers come from, places to which they will soon return.

Sweat runs down the brows of the black marketeers; a fat gypsy with a face like a pulpy melon fans the heat away with a bundle of dollar bills. A little old lady sells half a goose, another sells some teeth, fastened to a piece of pink plastic that is supposed to look like gums. What is taking place at Prźemysl's Russian Market is called market economy by those who have never been here, but not one of the merchants who devotes himself full time to this haggling and bargaining in Prźemysl, neither a Pole nor anyone from the other side of the border, has ever become affluent or a large-scale businessman.

I decide anyway to try to find the closed hotel, since the renovation might have been finished three months ago, or perhaps it was never more than a grand notion, a dream that has preoccupied Prźemysl the last twenty—or at least the last fifteen—years. I cross Plac Legionów, and there, across from the station, is a newspaper stand where someone has glued a picture of the Pope behind the glass window. I look for something to read, a local newspaper, and among the newspapers lies a pale carton with a plastic model. The carton reads "Grumman F-14 A Tomcat Plus," an American fighter plane that makes Marshall Piłsudski's legionnaires look like they belong to the age of knights and tournaments. A group of Romanians are admiring the carton with its flying monster; a little Romanian boy presses his nose flat against the glass, and the Polish lady in the stand says something that cannot be heard through the glass, but her twisted, mean mouth makes words superfluous.

Everyone here on the square is carrying or dragging something. On the square children are carried half asleep, as well as suitcases, sacks or plastic bags; here a drunk is being dragged or a box that not even two full-grown men can lift, and all this carrying and dragging is sufficient unto itself, everything else has been shoved aside, so that on the Plac Legionów there is only carrying and dragging, there is not enough room for even a smile or a hand lifted in farewell, a hand that waves instead of gripping a handle. It is only out on the three platforms that the carrying and dragging stops; the carriers and draggers sit down exhausted among their baggage, they light a cigarette and look out with dull eyes over the railroad tracks, which burn in the sun and disappear at a bend on the horizon.

THE HOTEL IS INDEED CLOSED FOR RENOVATION. THE WINDOWS LACK curtains and the door is nailed shut with boards. Not even the sign is left, and I stand there in front of the closed hotel's door, unsure of what to do. Then I walk back to the station to ask the man in the window for more information, but the window is closed, so instead I walk straight through the station and out onto the first platform to ask advice of one of the Polish policemen who patrol the platforms with their batons. The policemen's faces are just as dull and expressionless as the travelers'; they do not see any of them anymore, no individual people, just the mass, and then all of the suitcases and packages that someone must have dragged out onto the platform. But they are not interested in who among the crowd might be responsible for this, and the passport and customs inspection here is little more than a formality, a sleepy routine check of the sleepers. The main thing is that the platform is eventually swept clean of this rubbish heap of baggage and people, and when the police herd the crowd toward the sign that says customs in Polish, this also happens as if in sleep, almost in exhaustion.

For safety's sake, *contrôle des passeports* appears under the Polish word for customs, since Prźemysl does not want to be *Halbasien*, and the French text is supposed to bring Europe a bit closer. But there are no Frenchmen getting on or off trains here.

In the absence of Frenchmen, the people on the platform have to make do with one another. They fight over their seats on the train that does not come, elbow each other and throw curses in various languages after one another, words that are made no milder by the fact that the same poverty is inscribed on their neighbor's face as on theirs. Wherever they look they see poverty and so are reminded of their own, of their own pain and all of their personal injuries, of the fate that caused them to be born on the wrong side of the border that divides Europe from *Halbasien*.

I stand with them on the platform and feel as if I have done something shameful. I neither carry nor drag, I do not even smoke. I am not dressed as they are, and it is all too obvious that I am not getting on an eastbound train, that I do not even come from Prźemysl, but from a world beyond their Europe, a distant world, a place far to the west, closed to these people. Cautiously I move forward among the people and their baggage, careful not to step on anyone, but just the fact that I am not on my way anywhere betrays me. My presence is a mockery, a provocation, and I cannot imagine a single word or gesture that would bridge the abyss here on the platform between our two worlds.

A hotel, I think. Mustn't there be a hotel here?

But the half-Asiatic world's instincts of subservience are so deep that the people around me leave me in peace. For several centuries they have been practicing this mute equanimity, until the face no longer betrays the heart. A shy glance, a cigarette butt cast at my feet; nothing more happens. I am not worthy of their hate—their hate is reserved for their own world. It is reserved for their neighbor, and in the underground tunnel that connects the platforms, in the coolness under the burning tracks, I read on the wall "Poland for the Poles." It is sprayed in red, and paint does not flake underground as easily as above ground, but just so that there is no misunderstanding, someone has written a little farther on, "To the gas chamber with the Ukrainians," and after that the murderousness comes on in wave after wave: "Death to the Gypsies," "Castrate the Poles,"—in Ukrainian—and when everyone has been painstakingly maimed or murdered, someone writing in Polish ascends to a Solomonic *gówno rośnie*, "the shit is rising."

In the center of Prźemysl, above ground, all of the slogans were painted over with white paint before the Pope's visit to the city. Now the Pope is back home in Rome, and the walls of the buildings are full of neatly painted white spots, houses like piebald dogs, Dalmatians, the Pope has left a dog-city behind. The hate has been hidden under a thin layer of paint, doomed to peel as all paint does when left without protection in the wind and weather. But down here in the train station no one has bothered to paint over the slogans, perhaps because it is impossible to imagine a Pope underground, or because no one who counts comes down here anyway.

I ask one of the policemen on the platform about a hotel.

"In the fortress," he answers. "People who want to stay overnight stay there."

First I think that he's joking, but then he writes an address on the first page of my Polish newspaper: Ostrów Polonia, a youth hostel just outside the city. "The Holy Father's Unforgettable Visit to Our City," says the newspaper's front page.

IT IS THE WRONG FORTRESS, NOT THE ONE FROM MY POSTCARD AT home in Vienna, and the hostel is a wooden barracks with only cold water in the room. While the bleached blonde who manages the barracks signs me into her ledger, I take a walk around the remains of the fortifications. The fortress lies in a grove, and its ramparts are overgrown with high grass and bushes. The walls are built of square blocks of stone and red brick. Thoroughly rusted, heavy doors still hang here and there on their iron hinges. Tunnels open behind them and then disappear into the ground and a moist, musty darkness. A solitary bird suddenly flies up out of the grass in front of my feet; frightened, I stop under the sheltering crowns of the trees and listen to my pounding heart.

The bird has disappeared. It seems that it has flown into one of the underground passages, and right where it flushed I find an empty cartridge in the grass. It is eaten with rust and dented in the middle, like the cigarettes the Russians make from any available paper, hardly rolled, just pinched tightly at the center.

I put it in my pocket.

During the night I sleep restlessly, and some time after midnight, it must have been closer to two, I am awakened by a rustling and groaning outside on the gravel. In the crack between the curtains I see that a bus with Ukrainian plates is causing the ruckus. The bus is full of what must be Ukrainians from the other side of the border. Since it is too warm to fall asleep again, I get dressed and go out into the corridor, where the blonde is haggling with the Ukrainians. In every room there are two cots, and the Ukrainians want to pay 30,000 złoty, about three dollars, per cot. The Polish woman thinks that is too little, and when she realizes that the Ukrainians had planned to sleep two to a cot, she drives them out into the night.

They go back to the bus to sleep there, and I myself only get back to sleep at dawn.

In the morning there is no breakfast to be had, and the bleached blonde just shakes her head. "You can buy a beer," she says. In the shower out on the corridor there is no water. Inside the men's toilet there are three sturdy Ukrainian women filling a kettle with tea water; one of them smiles kindly at me with a mouth full of metal teeth. The bleached blonde lets them boil water on a primus stove in the corridor, and I wonder how much she charges them for it, but I don't ask. The electricity has gone out throughout the barracks.

"Vandals," says the blond Pole, nodding after the three Ukrainian women who carry the kettle filled with water out to their bus.

The Ukrainians have all slept in the bus. Now the men are standing out on the gravel lot and smoking their morning cigarettes. It is the first cigarette of the new day. The men's suits are black or gray, and all of them are busy smoking. In the distance, between the trees, Prźemysl is visible; a collection of church towers and cupolas in the summer sky, and all of this churchliness seems to rest uneasily, as if in a bowl of quivering heat.

It looks as if it is going to be another hot day.

Today I will be going on to Warsaw, and while I pack the car the Ukrainians, one by one, venture up to me. Silently they watch while I clean the dust from my windshield. It is my car that interests them, and their bus driver, a nimble little man who is the only one who doesn't smoke, breaks the silence.

Are those tires completely new? How often do I have to change them?

The others form a ring around us, and all at once their faces are solemn, almost worshipful.

The driver wants to know what I do when the motor gives out. If it gives out? I answer that I take the car to a mechanic, and this response seems to astonish the Ukrainians. Silently they look at one another, as if they were only able to absorb the word "mechanic" communally.

There are silences that are more painful than peaceful, and to protect myself from this Ukrainian silence, I ask the bus driver if he wouldn't like to test drive my car. First he throws up both palms in a gesture of refusal, but I insist, and finally he sits down anyway behind the wheel. Together we drive two laps around the gravel lot, two very slow laps, and in the middle of the gravel lot the other Ukrainians stand and follow us with their eyes as if this were a rare animal on display in a circus menagerie. The tires crunch in the gravel; a completely different sound from that of horses' hooves in sawdust.

Afterwards the bus driver's eyes shine with pride, and he asks if I want to buy a refrigerator from him, a used one, but it works. He has it in the bus. The refrigerator is really all right, says the bus driver. When I says thanks, but no thanks, he is not disappointed; poverty cannot afford that kind of disappointment, and where he comes from the poverty has never really ended.

Like war it just goes on and never stops, until, precisely like war, it starts up again, and when I begin my trip to Warsaw the Ukrainians stand in the gravel lot and wave after me, they wave a long time, and all of us know that this is not until we meet again, but farewell forever.

(ABOUT WATER) THE FIRST TIME WE MET, I TREATED HIM TO SHRIMP. This was more than twenty years ago in a kitchen in the Söder district of Stockholm, and he looked at the shrimp for a long time without touching them. Finally he asked how you were supposed to eat them.

"Haven't you ever eaten shrimp before?"

Dragan shook his head. Where he comes from there is no water. Was it embarrassment that caused him to avoid my eyes? I looked at his hands. They looked superfluous, more used to earth or fire than water, and as if in the presence of an unfamiliar element, he didn't quite know what to do with them. Where he comes from there are no shrimp. Not any mussels or oysters, either; all of the fish that happen to be served there have to make do with the same name, though some of them deserve better.

The shrimp on the plate could have taught us a thing or two about the meaning of water, but we were not attentive enough, and soon I was busy showing him how to peel them. Instead of letting him stuff them immediately into his mouth, one shrimp after another, I taught Dragan to gather them into a little pile in order to put them on a toasted and buttered slice of bread, and then snip fresh dill over the whole thing.

The shrimp could have helped us. The sea is both a generous and a harsh master, and it happens sometimes that those who go down to the sea come back as better people; in any case they have a few seashells in their pockets and stories—stories which no one really wants to believe, since they do not conform to what everyone knows and always has known. No one has ever seen or heard of yellow people with slanted eyes, and to eat with wooden sticks seems stupid, almost indecent, as long as a person has his fingers and a knife. But still the seductive power of these stories should not be underestimated, and we have the sea to thank for this and more, for I have not even mentioned the scent of drifting seaweed, or the calming influence of swells on the soul, or little seahorses; but where Dragan comes from there is no sea.

There it was a rarity if someone returned home with shells in his pocket to tell of another kind of horizon, a thin strip of watery blackness that keeps the sky from floating out to sea, or maybe it is the other way around. And while we peeled our shrimp in Stockholm, we unfortunately missed our chance to push off together into the open sea, where even a person who avoids the depths and just keeps to the surface can learn a great deal more than on land.

Dragan lived in Belgrade, the white city. I had come to know it before the two of us knew each other. On foot I had tried to become acquainted with it from all sides, without ever understanding where the city began or ended. The last telegraph poles staked out the city's claim, but the grass was already growing around them and threatened to take back its territory. On the abandoned construction sites the iron reinforcements were rusting; animals and garbage descend upon the land as soon as the city turns its back.

At the edge of the city I always came, sooner or later, to some inn, half buried in a hillside. Any one of them was like any other. This kind of inn had long ago sunk into the mire and mud; only the roof and the upper part of the windows stuck up out of the ground, and before the whole thing was swallowed by the earth, one had to quickly bend down (always this bent back) to slink in and take shelter in the warmth and dust. The dust here filled lungs and clothing.

The white city was not white, but gray and dirty.

In such inns meat was served on skewers, *ražnjići,* or *čevapčići,* ground pork and beef, and both were grilled on an open fire. Over the table lay cloths spotted with the blood that people in the white city still only whispered about or filled newspaper columns with, and the blood was bad wine. In such inns I rested and ordered something to eat, a grilled kebab or grilled meatballs, and at the tables around me the other guests spilled wine from their glasses and on the tablecloth more spilt wine turned into bloodstains, and only when the blood had dried was it wine again.

In such inns the tablecloths were of coarse linen, pale yellow like the wax candles in the churches in the city, but the city was far from here. At the tables sat guests who drank and stared down at the tablecloth without seeing anything other than the stains from spilt wine, and when they looked up the wine had turned to blood. Such inns were like churches, and the guests got just as drunk on the miracle of the tablecloth as they did on the wine that rose in their glasses until it ran over the rim as blood. Here there were bloodstains everywhere, and when all the wine had been drunk the waiter showed up and turned the tablecloth, and on the other side there were the same spots of dried blood, but those that had been face down before were now face up, so that everything could begin from the beginning again.

The waiter turned the cloth. In the wine glasses the blood rose until it once again ran over the rim, and if there had been napkins in such an inn the napkins, too, would have been soiled and stained with all of that spilled wine.

Where was the water here? Who in this place could have served Dragan even a single shrimp?

More kebabs and meatballs were brought in from the kitchen. At the next table *ražnjići* was being served with the wine, a kebab made of a medieval king; the skewer went right through the royal guts, and the ground meat was made of the remains of some especially pious saint, of the saint's fingers and toes, and when the guests sank their teeth into the flesh, tears ran down their cheeks; they cried as they ate, and even their tears were of blood, and with the wine in their glasses they washed down all the kings and saints, so that when their misfortunes proved to have neither an end nor a beginning, they laid their arms around each others' shoulders and cried together, grown men mourning the sweetness of death, and their tears fell into the wine in their glasses, which was blood, and presto, the waiter was there and turned the cloth so that everything could begin from the beginning again.

How could a person escape from such a house in one piece? And at the next table the guests stood up and sang a song about the king they had just gobbled up, a song with many verses, and in every verse there was a new king who was waiting to be eaten, but despite the monotony of their diet, seldom had I seen such healthy and splendid people, like contented crocodiles in their proper element, except theirs was a river of blood instead of water, and when I thought that it was all over and everyone had eaten his fill of kings and saints, the waiter arrived and turned the cloth over, so that everything could begin from the beginning again.

So many hopes chewed down to the bone! So much poured out and wasted on one and the same plate!

Why are you sitting there smiling to yourself, they ask me. *Marš, marš, marš, Carigrad je naš!* Carigrad is ours! Why do you keep your hands under the table? You are so quiet, they bellowed. What are we supposed to make of you?

So many princes and saints on such a small plate! All that flesh that turned to spirit, or at least filled the city's newspapers, and on the tablecloth all of the wine that had changed to the blood that the papers wrote about! And when all the blood had been drunk it was time for the dead to rise again.

This service never ended, and it was here that it was celebrated, here in the inn, in their true and half-buried church, and instead of a priest they made do with a waiter, who was always standing ready to turn the bloodstained cloth so that everything could begin from the beginning again.

On my way back to the city from such inns it sometimes happened that I walked a part of the way along one of the two rivers that approach the city from out on the plains. It was restful. For a while, I had company. From the plains the rivers approached, but just where they could have broken through the city walls, they joined and formed one great river, curving gently around the city.

They avoided it.

Or was it the white city that withdrew from the water? Was it the city that kept to the land, so enamored of itself that it protected or destroyed what was strange or different, as it had already leveled all of its mosques and the houses of the different and unhappy people who no longer lived there? Though it was an old city, a visiting stranger would not be able to read its age. The white city lived outside time. All of its buildings had been poured from the same sack, sewn and patched by the city itself, until there was nothing more to pour from the sack, and so great was this city's love for itself that all of its quarters looked alike, none of them older or newer than the others, all of them unpainted, like a virgin confined to a convent, and the city as it now stands fills its inhabitants with pride.

So great was this city's love for itself, it seemed, that it no longer wanted to hear any opinions other than its own. The white city did not listen to any sounds other than its own. Stealthily it followed every stranger, so that behind his back it could sweep up the tracks he had left behind. I saw how it was with my own eyes; how the stranger's footsteps were rolled up and used to light stoves in winter, or to seal leaky shoes. The whole winter the city's inhabitants sat in their apartments in front of their crackling fires and roasted chestnuts. As far back as anyone could remember, the fire had spoken the same language as the people of the city, and outside the windows, the jackdaws slept in the trees. From the city's old fortress, the inhabitants could see out over the plain and its two rivers, though it was in another world. There, in the other world, the houses and church steeples were different; on clear days you could see them clearly from the fortress, but if, during a moonless night, these foreign houses and church steeples had managed to cross the water and enter the city, they would have been immediately torn down.

In the winter it could sometimes happen that the police, or at least people in uniform or wearing a mask, broke down the apartment doors of the city's inhabitants. They stole the money that had been sewn into a red pillow, and on the pillow was the embroidered Savior, surrounded by white lambs. The next day they returned to take a detailed report of the theft; they took a stamp from their pockets, drank a glass with the man of the house and pinched the littlest girl's cheek. They disappeared down the stairs and promised not to come back, but then toward the end of winter they were back again, along with some superior with a black mustache. Now they just wanted to ask some questions of the man of the house, and they stayed for a long time in the room behind the kitchen. Voices could be heard from in there, and one of them belonged to the man of the house. And then they all suddenly left the apartment together, and not until the beginning of spring did the man of the house return.

But still people said that this was progress, anyway it was better than back when nothing but the head of the man of the house returned (in a sack). One day not long afterward the others also returned, at least the subordinates without mustaches, to ask how everyone was doing and whether there was anything they could do for the family. Before they said their goodbyes and disappeared down the stairs, they pinched the littlest one on the cheek, and then one spring day when the family returned home and least of all suspected it, they surprised a man in a mask or uniform who stood in the middle of the room, shaking out all of the pillows in the house, even the empty one with the embroidered Savior and lambs, and this time the masked man held a knife in his hand, a knife he had stuck into the pillow with the Savior.

That's the kind of thing that happened in the winter in Dragan's city. If you were unlucky, it could happen in the summer, too. The broken-down doors! The knives! The white city needed an enemy to keep from laying hands on itself, and when its fear became over-whelming and the violence finally broke out, the world outside was blamed for their pain. Now and then one of the city's people tried to save himself. But leaving the city meant putting one's whole existence at risk. If a person nevertheless dared to try, he risked falling directly into an abyss, actually over the edge of a map, since the world was considered flat in the white city. Anyone who had taken off and yet survived must have joined the enemy.

And of such a person there was nothing written in the newspapers that the people of the city discussed in the cafés.

(MORE ABOUT WATER) I USUALLY STAYED AT A HOTEL IN THE MIDDLE of the city. In front of it was an old well that was no longer used. From the fifth or sixth floor at the back of the hotel I could just barely get a sense through the haze of the two rivers out on the plain. On the first floor of the hotel there was a café where Turkish coffee was served on a tin tray along with a glass of water. Earlier, between the two world wars, this hotel had been considered of the highest class. That was before my time. At that time the hotel and a newspaper published here had been considered the two institutions that made the white city a real city. I liked the hotel's name, Moskva, which is of course not only the name of a city but also a river. On the third floor there was a spring-water well of mosaic tiles, decorated with doves. From their beaks bubbled a quiet water, a water that kept running even at night, while the guests slept.

The hotel's café was an oasis. In the evening they offered live music. It was played by very old musicians who held their instruments together with rubber bands, musicians with one foot already in the grave. Even the music they played was very old. The musicians refused to die, they refused to change their repertoire, and the city let them have their way. The white city was not particularly musical. The inhabitants preferred to read and discuss their newspapers, drink their coffee and smoke their cigarettes; the music was only there as white noise. In the café they listened absently to what was played. No one had discovered that it was not the musicians who played the music in this café, but the music that played the musicians: it was Waldteufel that played the musicians, it was the potpourri from Giselle that played the musicians, and the musicians cut capers on the stage. But most of all they launched out onto the great blue river; the Danube played the musicians so that they waved their arms wildly like drowning men, though they were safe on dry land.

With the blue Danube another world flowed into the Hotel Moskva, but no one in the café noticed it. Nor did they care about the river Danube out there on the plain. No water interested the white city.

Only the musicians kept the great river out there on the plain alive.

In this city my friend Dragan lived and wrote his poems. He had already written several books. The summer before the war I visited him in the middle of the worst heat. We had not seen each other for a long time. I knocked on his door, the door was open. Dragan lay on his back on the bed, unshaven. "Come in," he said, though I already stood in the middle of his only room. He got up from the bed and began to talk about the book he was reading. There was a map of Croatia in it. Dragan was sleepy and in a bad mood. It was late in the afternoon and he put water on the stove for coffee. Then he opened the book and showed me the map.

"Croatia looks like a croissant."

I could not agree; it looked more like a jellyfish or an octopus.

"Unnatural, anyway," Dragan thought.

It was summer, toward the end of July, the very warmest month in the white city.

(STILL MORE ABOUT WATER) WHEN THE WAR BETWEEN SERBIA AND Croatia broke out, I went to Dragan's city, and the same afternoon we were already sitting in the café at the Hotel Moskva. Everything was as usual. The war was elsewhere. In the café people continued to drink coffee and read newspapers and in the newspapers there was no war. The old musicians played as before, and if it was out of tune it was not due to the dissonance of war, a shift in accords that had crept into the city's music, but because the band played badly and out of tune even without a war; it was a band that would not have played any differently had it been right in the middle of the action.

When it was time for the "Blue Danube" it was just as beautiful and blue as it always had been, except not very far from here, upstream, maimed corpses were already being thrown into the river and floating to shore just at the edges of the white city.

Dragan is happy to see me. At first we talk about poetry, which after all does seem more appropriate to a café than what brought me here, but then he says that there is something he wants to show me.

The waiter has just put the tin tray with coffee and water on our table. Dragan digs through the books and manuscripts in his bag under the table and finds what he is looking for: something heavy and big, an empty shell casing, as big as a vase.

He puts the shell right between us on the café table's marble top. The brass must have been polished recently. It shines dully.

Dragan turns the empty casing upside down to show me the factory mark engraved on the detonator. It says M. Weiss, Budapest 1914. I happen to know of him. Manfred Weiss was an immensely rich Jewish industrialist in the old Austro-Hungarian empire. Apparently he also earned money in the war that ended the dual monarchy.

"Where did you get that?"

I feel uncomfortable and look around the café. This kind of projectile, armed or disarmed, really had no business here.

The shell was a gift to Dragan. He got it from an Orthodox priest in Bosanski Petrovac, a small Serbian town in Bosnia, near the Croatian border in Krajina. Dragan says that Bosanski Petrovac is a town of perhaps twenty thousand inhabitants, and I admit that I am not even sure I could find it on a map.

"Petrovac is just thirty kilometers from Grahovo," explains Dragan.

On the road from Knin, just after Strmica.

"Gavrilo Princip was born in Grahovo."

Gavrilo Princip? I once literally stood in his footsteps. There was a cast of them in the asphalt of a sidewalk in Sarajevo, right at the spot where Princip stood when he shot and killed the heir to the Austrian throne, Franz Ferdinand, and his wife, Sophie. I had not been able to withstand the temptation, and my shoes fit into the cast as if it had been molded especially for me. A momentary lack of caution, a step in the wrong direction; that is how easily one becomes a murderer. There I stood, relieved not to have a revolver in my pocket. If at that moment I could have stepped out of the murderer's footsteps, bent down, rolled them up, and stuck them in my pocket, I know I would have done it.

"Here on this spot on St. Vitus Day, the twenty-eighth of June 1914, Gavrilo Princip proclaimed freedom for his people," I read on a memorial.

A month later the great war had broken out. Within the course of a month the bullets in Princip's revolver had been replaced by Manfred Weiss's shells, and from the very beginning the Europeans decided that there was something special about this war, and they gave it the title "world" war.

But I can not understand what a Serbian priest in Bosanski Petrovac has to do with Manfred Weiss's shells. A priest is after all not much different from the peaceful waiter who is now approaching our table again to brush the cigarette ashes from the marble tabletop with his hand, and I would like to believe of him that he thinks of his guests as more than Serbs or Croats, that he does not wonder whether his guests are from the right or wrong nation.

Though in the newspapers that the people discuss in the café, a completely different position has already being taken. The newspapers have put on an ill-fitting language, too large for them: I read "honor" and it sounds like a provincial lawyer beating his breast. Or I see "heroic," and behind that word a farmer could be hiding, someone who thinks he has made something of himself and has moved to the city. And it is the same way with words like "fate," "victory," "territory," or "border" and even bigger words served up with our coffee, words that must have something to do with the white city's own fear, a fear that nowadays seems to be able to both read and write.

Or a word like "cleansing"! What clothes were they thinking of laundering? What car were they going to wash? Or did this "cleansing" I read about in the newspaper no longer apply to either clothes or cars—had it already launched into more bold adventures?

No shells have fallen on the waiter's city yet, but just the thought that the war could suddenly knock at the door and gain admission to even his café seems to irritate him. A café is always a café. One has to be able to demand even of a war that it conducts itself according to the same rules as a guest, and the waiter steals a suspicious glance at the empty shell that, together with the coffee cups and the untouched water glasses, stands on the table between Dragan and me.

The Orthodox priest in Bosanski Petrovac had brought the shell down from the steeple of his church to give to my friend. The priest had to climb up to the last bit of the steeple on a ladder and take hold of his robe like a girl gathering her skirts, Dragan tells me.

One of the priest's predecessors might have hidden the shell up there among the bells during the First World War. There it stayed until September of 1991, and before the priest gave it to Dragan, he had it dusted and polished.

The empty shell casing is the priest's gift to a poet who took the trouble to visit the priest's parish in distant Bosanski Petrovac. Along with several other authors, my friend was invited to read from Serbian literature, the classics, and his own work. The priest himself invited them. Then he presented Dragan with a shell, a very unusual present, at least as a gift from a priest to a poet.

Even Bishop Hrizostom was invited, Dragan says, while I struggle to make sense of this mixture of priests, poets, and shells. Another Serbian bishop had been invited from Šibenik, an older, venerable man, but on the way to Bosanski Petrovac his car was stopped at a Croatian roadblock. Šibenik lies on the Dalmatian coast. From Šibenik to Bosanski Petrovac the road goes over Knin and Strmica. The Bishop of Šibenik was interrogated. The Croatians first took his episcopal necklace. Then he was forced to remove all his vestments. Only after an hour was he allowed to go on. The bishop asked them for a glass of water. He was thirsty, or perhaps shaken, but they gave him nothing to drink.

"When he got out of the car in Petrovac, I saw that his hands were still shaking. I did not want to ask him if he was allowed to keep on his underwear while the Croatians searched him. I did not ask. A bishop is not just any priest," says Dragan. "I could not ask him something like that."

"What poems did you read?" I ask.

But Dragan has already begun to tell about how he was sitting in the first row along with all of the priests and bishops, on the podium that was cobbled together of unpainted wooden planks in front of the church in Petrovac. It is a hot day and there was no cool breeze from the mountains. The folk dancers whistle and stomp on the wooden floor, the planks sway under their feet, the church bells ring. Many people have gathered. There is clapping and all of the priests and poets are shaken in their chairs as if in a boat on the high sea, and in his lap my friend has the shell casing that he has received as thanks for his journey all the way to Bosanski Petrovac to read his poems.

After the folk dancers' performance Dragan feels he ought to say something. The audience expects it of him. It does not happen that often that they have visitors from the capital, and a real poet to boot. And the times are such that the people expect something of their poets. As long as there is peace the demand for poets is not so great, but now it is war, and the hour of the authors has struck.

My friend rises from his chair, and with the shell in his arms— though it is empty, it is heavy—he holds a short speech for the audience. Where he stands on the podium in front of the church he speaks just as the words occur to him. Dragan says that the Serbs have a long history, and that just a few miles away it is repeating itself, and that it now looks as if today's enemies are the same as yesterday's.

Haven't the Hungarians delivered weapons to the Croats, he asks with the empty shell in his arms. And isn't that the same thing that happened during the First World War? Yes, indeed, that is just how it was! Just as they did then, the shells are coming from Vienna and Budapest this time, even if Manfred Weiss no longer has anything to do with it, and below the podium people laugh as he holds the empty case in the air; they are probably laughing at Manfred Weiss.

Just as they were then, Germany and Austria are on the Croats' side. The Swabians are marching again, Dragan cries to the audience. But who cares to listen to us? Who can claim that he has opened his heart to our cries? Whose eyes see our spilled blood? Where are our true friends, he asks from the podium, and the audience becomes restless. Someone shouts something, but he cannot hear what it is.

Just as in 1914 and 1941 we are now at war, Dragan cries to the audience, and it is the gift from the priest in Petrovac that inspires my friend the poet in his speech.

"You said all of that?" I ask.

"Yes. More or less."

But still I cannot understand why a priest, and then several priests after him, would have kept a shell in their church for more than seven decades, as if it were a relic. Not in the nave, not behind the iconostasis, but still, up in the steeple with the sanctified bells. It does not seem especially Christian. And if people occupy themselves for such a long time with the things of war, isn't the risk great that one day war will break out again?

Why hadn't the priests been more careful with that shell?

"But it was empty," says Dragan.

It is possible that they first thought of the shell not in connection with war, but with the idea of using it for something completely different. Perhaps they wanted to make some kind of useful object from the metal? Perhaps mold a little bell for the church? The people of this province are poor. They have always been poor and obliged to make use of all kinds of useless items.

"A brass shell case could be used for so many other things," Dragan says.

"Yes, certainly," I say.

But it is not a useful item or a bell but in fact a shell that we have in front of us on the table. Furtively I watch my friend while he continues to tell his story. I try to imagine him as a poet in the service of the god of war, Mars, but I cannot quite succeed; Dragan looks all too peaceful, a civilian who stirs his coffee and sadly shakes his head every time the war between the Serbs and Croats is mentioned. As usual, he is unshaven. To imagine Dragan in uniform is an impossibility.

For a poet, it seems to me, even an empty shell case should be more than sufficient to get him to imagine all of the horrors of war.

BUT IT TURNS OUT THAT EVEN MILE PRINCIP WRITES POETRY, THOUGH Dragan says that his poems are bad and not worth remembering. Mile Princip is about thirty, almost six and a half feet tall, and the son of Gavrilo Princip's nephew, the same Gavrilo Princip who not so long ago shot Franz Ferdinand in Sarajevo; here in the Krajina it happened yesterday or early this morning. Mile Princip comes from Grahovo, too, and he is just visiting Bosanski Petrovac with all of the other poets and folk dancers.

There, in Petrovac, he also meets my friend, the fellow poet.

What do they talk to each other about? About poetry? It's more likely that they talk first and foremost about the war. Mile Princip has come directly from the front, if one can say that there is anything worth calling a front in a war that seems to have set itself up here and there, in church steeples and soon in the cafés as well, not to speak of the hearts and minds of people and all of the other places people tell themselves that they can use to hide from the war. In Krajina the Serbs are fighting the Croatian fascists and the Croats are fighting the Serbian terrorists; the poet Mile Princip is one of them. In Bosanska Krajina he is popular, almost a hero, and his popularity does not only have to do with his famous relative.

I forget to ask Dragan whether Mile Princip was also standing up there on the podium in front of the church, reading his poems, or if he was sitting down with the audience. It seems most likely that he was sitting with the audience. Not because his poems are supposed to be too bad to be read aloud from a stage—the demand for even bad poetry is great in times that await a redemptive word—but because Dragan tells me that Mile Princip was one of the people who came up to him afterward especially to thank him for his speech, and that Princip, perhaps in his capacity as poet and creative colleague, wanted to show his appreciation with a special gift.

He has the gift in his pants pocket; a gift from one poet to another.

But it is not a seashell but a cartridge, a live one. Mile Princip has several cartridges on him, in both of his pants pockets, but Dragan gets just one of them as thanks, and when he tells me about this in the Hotel Moskva I look at the empty shell in front of us on the table, I look at my empty water glass, and I try to imagine Manfred Weiss's shell as a live shell.

This means one fewer of them, Mile Princip is supposed to have said to Dragan with a smile as he gave him the cartridge.

But my friend brought the empty shell from the First World War to the café, not Mile Princip's live cartridge. A true poet's inspiration: the live cartridge is just one of uncountable live cartridges and thoroughly mundane. Anywhere in this country anybody at all can fill his pockets with ammunition, while Manfred Weiss's shell is empty and, precisely for that reason, different. An unexpected find that sets the imagination in motion.

"And with that 'one fewer of them' he meant . . ."

I do not finish my sentence. Instead I make a rather awkward gesture with both hands that is reminiscent of how the old first violinist in the Hotel Moskva's café moves when he changes his music on the stand in the evenings.

Dragan looks at me. He does not understand my question, it was not completed, anyway, maybe it was not even comprehensible.

He just moves his hands in the same awkward way as he did in my kitchen twenty years ago, though here in the café we are in the world of human beings, no longer in the realm of the shrimp and other sea creatures. His gesture is as helpless as mine, and it requires no imagination to understand it.

STILL LIFE

VASSILIJ TELLS ME THAT THERE IS A CHURCH IN ROME WITH THREE paintings by Caravaggio, which for centuries have been illuminated only by the sun, and that he has always dreamed of seeing them.

The sunlight that falls through the windows of the church is supposed to give the paintings all the light they need. The artist painted them where they hang; every color was first mixed and attuned to the sunlight from outside before it touched the canvas, and when Vassilij finally gets to Rome from Kiev, poorer than all of the cats of Rome put together, he finds that church.

But then it turns out that the sun has been replaced by a machine. If you put five hundred or maybe five thousand lira in it, the three paintings by Caravaggio will be illuminated for two minutes by a spotlight, and in four languages the machine tells the visitor what he is looking at. With the help of a tape player and artificial light one can do without the sun that even in Rome is not always dependable, and in fact the day that Vassilij visits the church, the sun is showing no consideration for art; it has hidden behind some Roman clouds.

The sky is ashen gray; not the faintest glimmer of sunlight falls through the church windows.

Since Vassilij is convinced that this spotlight is not the light in which the artist once painted his pictures, and that these two minutes of electric instead of natural light actually destroy rather than illuminate Caravaggio's canvases, he despairs.

It is his only day in Rome. Every second is precious here, but not precisely in the way he had imagined; he can hardly afford the lira for the machine. Will he ever return to Rome? While tourists in shorts linger inside the church to escape from the heat outside, he flees. But before he flees, he catches a glimpse of the sweat running over the tourists' half-naked bodies, sweat that will later cool and then penetrate bone and marrow as a new and uncomfortable cold that soon drives them, too, from the church. It is more comfortable out there despite everything, especially since clouds cover the sun whose light has fallen in through the windows for centuries to illuminate Caravaggio's paintings, all three of them, and the machine keeps grinding on in there in its four languages until dusk falls and Caravaggio is swallowed entirely by darkness.

Maybe the tourists in shorts will remember Caravaggio as a place where they were cold, and Vassilij tells me that one cannot view Caravaggio like that, least of all three paintings at once, not in a spotlight when the sun was intended to be the only permitted illumination. Only nature's own path from darkness through light and then back to darkness makes the viewing possible that was conceived by the artist himself for that space in the church, says Vassilij, and I forget to ask him if he had five hundred (or was it five thousand) lira for the machine, or if he had to wait for a Japanese or German to stick money into it.

I don't tell him about the Loreto church in my old neighborhood in Paris, either. Time has become so precious in that church that a special altar has been erected where the visitor can light a candle and ask God for forgiveness that he cannot stay in the church long enough to pray properly; a candle like that costs two, or maybe five, francs.

Caravaggio's paintings can at least count on cost-free sunlight now and then, but that is no comfort to us, since it is not likely that Vassilij will ever see Rome again.

I feel sorry about both the art and Vassilij. Tourists in shorts have money instead of time; Vassilij on the other hand has no money, but as much time as it takes to stand in line for milk or toilet paper or to wait for the right stamp in a ministry back home in Kiev. In Rome, time is his only resource. Instead of money in his pocket, he has plenty of time, but Rome plays him a nasty trick, and I wish that the Eternal City had not felt it necessary to steal from him his one and only asset, giving it back in the form of ransomed and expensive segments of time just two minutes long; I wish it for Vassilij's sake and for the sake of art.

Of course I cannot compete with Caravaggio. I can only help my friend with art, in an image of my own making. On my next empty sheet of paper I am planning to set down Vassilij alone in front of Caravaggio's three paintings; at the most I will place an apple and a penknife next to him on the pew. When the last tourist in shorts has left the church, I will shut the door and lock Vassilij in. He can then sit alone in there through the night, in the dark, instead of having to stand in line at home in Kiev.

I will have him sit there the whole night. And just at dawn a hint of light will seep through the church windows, the very first morning light.

As I have imagined it, this light will dissolve his waiting as if it were a morning mist, and then it will reach Caravaggio's paintings, too, so that gradually at first, one by one, they become visible. The sunlight itself will paint them out of the darkness as it once, with the help of the artist, painted them onto the canvases.

A first brush stroke comes clear in the light, then another one and more and more, so that all three of Caravaggio's paintings return to the church in the same way they once entered it. That is how I have planned to cleanse them of that artificial, two-minute light, and my thought is not only to make a gift to Vassilij of this picture on the sheet of paper; my plan is also a selfish and calculating one.

I have given Vassilij an assignment. I have imagined him as performing a representative act. Invisible to the world, he will have to sit in there in the church to see what we in the West no longer see, and for this assignment I cannot use a Japanese or a German, that would be impossible, only someone from the East without a penny to his name.

He will sit there on behalf of us. And only the next evening do I plan to unlock the door and let him out, just in time for the train home to Kiev: a hungry and wonder-struck Vassilij.

IN A ROMANIAN NEWSPAPER I SEE THAT LÁSZLÓ TÖKÉS IS ACCUSED OF having worked for Securitate, Nicolae Ceauşescu's old secret police. The newspaper wants to make a real agent out of him, while Tökés himself says that he was forced to report one or two conversations, pretty much like everyone else in Romania.

I believe him on that point. But still, László Tökés is not exactly just like everyone else. In December of 1989 he was one of the revolution's heroes; today he has the bishopric in the Reformed Church in Oradea, a city which, despite all the catastrophes of our century, has not quite managed to hide the fact that it has a proud past. A little more than five years ago, in Timişoara, László Tökés was still quite an ordinary priest, like most others, though later he could well have become the greatest hero of the Romanian revolution if one thing had not stood in his way: he was a Hungarian, not a Romanian.

The wrong blood was flowing through his veins.

In the end, every revolution is about just that, blood, and it is important that the blood flowing through the revolutionaries' veins is of the right type, just as it is important that the blood of the revolution's victims is of the right color. When it comes to victims' blood, blue is always the favored color. The demiurgic and plebeian nature of revolutions determines that blue blood is the best for spilling, and only when that blue has proven to be just as red as the blood of the revolutionaries does the revolution reveal one of its many paradoxes: the color blindness which, far more than the revolution's original intent, contributes to the actual transformation of our world.

In addition, a revolution has the characteristic of almost always granting power to people other than those who created it. Sometimes this happens right away—as in Romania—but sometimes it takes longer, as in Russia, where the Bolsheviks had to put up with Aleksander Kerensky for a while, or in unreliable France, where a

Corsican officer was able to make use of the early revolutionaries' groundwork, but only after several years.

Often the revolutionaries of the first phase end aggrieved and disappointed. Without their quite understanding it, the reins of power have slid from their hands. But when exactly does this occur? The telephones on their desks no longer ring, and soon the desk has become a coffee table, the telephone an ashtray, filled to the brim. Important meetings take place, and no one calls them; they only get to hear about them afterward, from a cleaning lady or a drunken security guard. There are no more decrees to sign. They miss the decrees. And the people have forgotten them.

There is not much to be done about that, although for more than one revolutionary this fall from power can be the stroke of fortune that saves his neck. But this is no comfort for the true revolutionary, who is more interested in History than heads, whether his own or other peoples'; at least this is what History teaches us.

Instead the revolutionaries of the first phase usually maintain that those who now happen to be in power were not part of the revolution from the beginning, and that no one from that time has even heard of them. Most often this is true, too; that is what accounts for the pathetic aura around the forgotten revolutionary.

I remember an irritated Václav Havel on the evening some economists showed up at the Laterna Magica in Prague for the first time, on the empty theater stage where the Velvet Revolution held its press conferences every evening. The two economists were Valtr Komárek and Václav Klaus. Havel hardly knew them; neither of them could be called a dissident. Both had been hibernating at the Academy of Science's Institute of Economic Research, forgotten by almost everyone, with their noses planted in papers devoted to an economy that did not exist. On that evening they had more or less invited themselves in, because even a revolution needs to talk about money, and today it is Klaus, not Havel, who minds the Czech shop.

The revolutionaries of the first phase usually experience a total desertion, and this desertion is harder to face than being forgotten. In the beginning, betrayal is a harder blow than the people's indifference, and in the revolutionary it gives rise at first to astonishment, then a deeply injured resentment. In especially hard cases this resentment can mutate into a maudlin air, since literally none of the old comrades ever get in touch; they tend to avoid those who are no longer equipped with office telephones.

The period of involuntary inactivity that now begins gives rise to a talkativeness in rejected and abandoned revolutionaries (perhaps as compensation for the lost telephone). And this self-prescribed therapy, paradoxically, only emphasizes the fact that these people no longer have anything to do with the revolution. Nothing at all! Their own revolutionary program is in fact already on its way to becoming a footnote in an as-yet-unwritten history book for stupid schoolchildren. They have been left sitting alone, at the café or the *editorial department*— or less frequently, in other places—where one can look them up to hear them pontificate about which direction the revolution actually should have taken, and this they do in such a halting way that we are forced to stay and chat with them wherever we happen to sit down. That is, in a café or a newspaper's *editorial room*.

Their revolution was betrayed; or at least, it lost its way. It is only *when* and *how* this is supposed to have happened that they can not account for. They can talk about everything else. But once they get to the part where they have to explain why we are sitting where we are sitting, a black hole opens in their litany.

When? How? That they do not know. My disappointment is just as great every time, though perhaps I should not be surprised. Birth, death, the missed chance, the betrayal of others; everything important here in this life is left in darkness.

In the East I have met a number of talkative revolutionaries, and László Tőkés was no exception to the rule, though the café in his case was a church. The church was on Strada Timotei Cipariu in Timișoara, and I met him there less than half a year after the revolutionaries rounded up Nicolae and Elena Ceaușescu like Bonnie and Clyde and shot them dead.

It was a Sunday. Tökés was dressed completely in black. Only what I could see of his shirt shone white, the cuffs and the collar, and all that black brought out the dark rings under his eyes. The black was appropriate to his office. But Tökés himself looked like the classic revolutionary from posters or documentaries, with broad shoulders and vigorous features, more like a worker than a pastor. His gaze was steady and serious. His face was perhaps not quite attractive, but it was honest, his handshake firm . . . and still there was a melancholy in his whole being that might have been resolution or—how devastating for a priest—a poverty of spirit. The burning was lacking in him; the inner revolutionary fire seemed to have been replaced with a dull, heavy solemnity, which I found as much Calvinistic as Hungarian.

There could be no doubt that László Tökés really had ended up in the right denomination. I do not think that he would have brought out the urge in anyone to confess.

After the service he received me in a room off the sanctuary. Tökés shook hands with each and every member of the congregation; in his left hand he hid a lit cigarette. Later he took me aside. We sat down at a large table. The walls were covered with portraits of priests in black robes with white lace collars. These were his predecessors. And Tökés's world, too, was black and white. His "yes" meant yes and his "no" really meant no; but it was difficult to ascertain what he was actually saying yes to.

It also surprised me that he was so soft-spoken. His tone was confiding, as if our conversation concerned a close relative or a conspiracy. He seemed not to want to convince me as much as to point out the obvious—the already revealed—just as for him, a priest, it would have seemed incompatible with the dignity of his calling to lay out proof of God's existence. Romania was an unhappy, unjust country. The country's injustices had become his own path to insight. But God had held him in His hand; it was God who had given him the strength to confront them all, and the very number of injustices convinced him early on that he was walking his Via Dolorosa with an entire people, and that for that reason a revolution was unavoidable. He had imagined this revolution as a purification, a catharsis, and in this case, too, a Calvinist priest was the right man at the right time.

This is how he had conceived his mission: to proclaim the unavoidable revolution.

After my visit with Tökés I walked down to an eatery by the river, the place was called Flora. It was only a stone's throw from the church. There I ordered something they called pizza, and before it was brought to my table the waitress explained why it would be served wrapped in paper. "Otherwise the others will be envious." An excursion boat went past out on the river. The boat was called *Pelican*. A man with a white beard, perhaps a poet, stood up and gave a speech that sounded like a sermon, until the waitress pulled on his suit jacket. "He is a little sick," said the waitress. At the table next to mine an alcoholic sat and seemed to chew up, rather than swallow, a water glass full of vodka; it was Sunday, after all, and when I went to pay the bills in my pocket were a wrinkled wad of paper. It seemed to me that I had been through all of this before, a long time ago, when my childhood hamster disappeared one time for a whole week in order to chew up my father's white vest.

I took out a paper and pen and tried to remember in detail what Tökés had said, but I could only remember smells. His room had smelled of melted wax and mothballs. But aside from all those injustices the only thing I could remember from our conversation was that he had spoken a long time of the necessity for a new revolution. A *second* revolution was unavoidable.

The first one had been stolen from the people.

IT IS MY EXPERIENCE THAT THE PEOPLE WHO MAKE REVOLUTIONS ARE seldom politically astute. They lack the cool distance necessary for analysis, a distance which, at the decisive moment, most certainly would have kept them from climbing up on the barricades and setting the revolution in motion. Instead they are hotheads, and they are so close themselves to what is happening that they do not have a proper perspective; they see nothing but what is right in front of their noses. And since they do not have time to concern themselves with too many details at the same time, they have to decide that just this, the thing that happens to be in front of their noses, is the revolution itself, neither more nor less, and so where their noses have led them, and not so much what they have written in their pamphlets, forms the basis of their decisions. They take command and give orders, much more guided by their noses than any plan worked out in advance.

When Tőkés spoke so warmly for a second revolution, it was out of disappointment over the fact that the first had changed so little in Romania. I could agree with him on that. But at the same time this was about something else; more precisely, it was about his inability to grasp and submit to the fact that what he had set in motion himself had now been taken over by others, and that it was his own nose more than the others that had betrayed him, and that this is what happens in well-nigh every revolution.

Tőkés did not understand this. Instead he was indignant, truly indignant; a maudlin air would not have been worthy of a successor of Calvin. And his feelings were genuine, put forth with the energetic stubbornness that even in the most pure-hearted revolutionary can seem a bit frightening to us ordinary folk. In Communist Europe I met many both courageous and likeable dissidents, but in retrospect I am relieved that a few of them never came to power. I think that they could have ended quite badly. Their uprightness, hardened by all the carefully chronicled injustices, would have created an even greater misery for people than what less upright but—thank God—tired *apparatchiks* had already brought about.

Still, Tőkés's second revolution did not seem as dubious to me as Lev Trotsky's permanent one. A continuous revolution? Day in and day out, without rest? A state that was more interested in whether a revolutionary lost his job than whether a worker did? In which people like Trotsky therefore would be equipped with a kind of universal insurance against unemployment? Tökés seemed more moderate than Trotsky, in any case; or maybe he was just not so bad a loser. A worldly eschatology has been smuggled into this idea of a permanent revolution, an eternal perspective that the priest did not need, since he already had his heaven. As far as Tökés was concerned, a second revolution could follow on the heels of the first, but this would not necessarily lead to a third; that would lie in God's hands, and it was certain that He did not let anything on earth continue into eternity, while Trotsky did not have any such inhibitions, so he was happy to imagine heads rolling throughout eternity without end, and no amen. Tökés, on the other hand, could count to two without feeling obliged to go on like a parrot, and it was God and no other who had helped him with his method of counting.

But I did not understand how he was thinking of carrying out his second revolution. Who was going to climb up on the barricades with him? While we were sitting at the table discussing the future, there were plump, friendly ladies busily putting out pastry on the tables behind us for coffee after the service (as it turned out, there was not enough coffee for everyone). Now and then they looked in our direction with motherly concern and a touch of worry in their eyes.

The people of this country want another revolution, said Tökés to me, banging his fist on the table and startling the coffee ladies.

One of them turned and smiled at us. She nodded kindly at the priest and me.

"No need to worry," she said. "Of course we have tea for those who don't want coffee."

Here I want to add that it also seems that the revolutionaries of the first phase are mistaken on a still more essential point: no revolution can create a tabula rasa from the old order. Not only would that be a physical impossibility, it is also a serious tactical error that revolutionary theorists, at least, usually understand; the only modern exception I can think of is Trotsky again, with his vision of the permanent revolution, and of course Pol Pot with his Rousseauian madness.

Every revolution is actually a rather stillborn enterprise. It may overthrow those in power—often they are killed—but this is mostly cosmetic, entertainment. Because once something has been released into the world, we cannot get rid of it so easily; the old order will turn up again soon enough, but first it will open up a new front, although "front" sounds much too martial when one considers that the really effective counter-revolution is utterly civil.

The old order usually does not take up the struggle with a weapon in its hand, but armed with its sense of etiquette: with its refusal to call the square of its childhood "Square of the Soviet Armored-Car Driver," with the help of a slip-knotted tie or with the habit of saying "good day," while lifting one's hat. Under especially difficult circumstances, as in Romania's case, the old order's return has to come in an even craftier form, namely in the form of the first problems the successful revolution has to deal with. A revolution might lead to a new so-called system, but even if it does, it only rarely can overcome the same problems the now-murdered former leaders failed to escape. This, sooner than the spilled blood, is the undercurrent the revolutionaries have to try to swim against, an undercurrent headed against the revolution, and so strong that the revolutionaries are soon more occupied with treading water than trying to move forward in it, and the more water they tread, the more certainly the water will turn to blood.

Perhaps Tökés did not understand how strong this undertow is, but he clearly saw that Ion Iliescu had something to do with it. Iliescu held the power in Romania. Tökés was accusing him. It was Ion Iliescu who had stolen his revolution. We were in agreement on that. Tökés asserted that Iliescu was a "wolf in sheep's clothing," and I could agree with him about that, too; I had just met him in the presidential palace in Bucharest.

Iliescu had sat across from me in a gilded armchair with a smile like barbed wire. On his feet he wore the best shoes I had ever seen in the Balkans, a pair of welted black brogues, impeccably polished. This was the nation's president. His time was precious; his watch was, too. Iliescu listened carefully to my questions, but only to find out what lay behind them. I realized this and tried to conceal my actual views by being sincere, but without success. Sincerity was an all too easy trick for Iliescu; he is one of those people who, when they say "good day," tempt us to look up at the sky first to make sure that it is not dark and full of stars. With his head slightly tilted to one side he listened to one question after another. He managed to make that barbed-wire smile ingratiating. With cunning calculation, it seemed to me, he broke eye contact only now and then to cast a quick glance at his watch.

Perhaps Iliescu really wanted to smile like any one of us, but he must have suspected that his smile was more of a sneer, which made him exert himself with it that much more. He smiled, but so forcefully that the sneer froze on his face; anyone who saw it there realized that this man was really lying, and it would have been better if he had not tried to smile at all.

A liar? But he did not want to have anything to do with lies; he did not need more than one or two, no more, and not very big ones. But on the heels of the first lie and the second more had followed, although it was not so easy to figure out where they had come from, and when there were so many of them that he no longer could keep track of them all, he must have felt obliged to accommodate them, and now it was done. The lies had taken over. They had forced him into their harness so that he had found it best simply to own up to them, and in that respect he was a perfectly honest and sincere person. If anyone had tried to deny it, it would have made Iliescu very angry; such a person was quite simply lying.

I was fascinated by his shoes. A uniform makes a person in the Balkans someone to be reckoned with, but all too often they forget about the shoes. Iliescu's were shining and bright.

I must admit that I appreciated the shoes and the fact that the nation's president was wearing a pin-striped suit instead of a uniform, as well as the fact that he, smiling the whole time, was able to divine with such certainty what lay behind each and every one of my questions, and for that reason he said no when I wanted to know if he went to church. He hesitated for just a second with his answer; a hesitation that had nothing to do with whether God exists or not.

Ion Iliescu was a genuine political animal. To steal (there was that word again) the revolution from the people or László Tökés was one thing, but to lay claim to God would have been going too far for the former Communist. He had understood this. Still, for a moment he was tempted; he had not quite managed to conceal his first impulse, he was much too surprised for that, and I celebrated this as a secret, though modest, victory. But he had pulled back at the last moment, and for that I felt a grudging respect for him.

Not everything can be stolen in this world, and I had listened with growing suspicion in Timişoara to Tökés's interpretation of the stolen revolution. Wasn't it a misunderstanding, or at least a simplification? Even an Iliescu was forced to come to grips with almost the same problems as the murdered Ceauşescu, and this—and not only what happened to be under Iliescu's sheep's clothing—gave rise to a kind of melancholy Romanian continuity that I think Tökés took too lightly.

Too lightly: perhaps because it would have been all too painful and heavy for him to admit it.

Nevertheless, there was that connection to the past there. No revolution allows us to keep swimming against its dark undercurrent in the long run, though it is a part of the revolution's eroticism that it seduces us into believing that precisely this is possible. Anyone who has experienced several intoxicating, sleepless days and nights when the world seems to have been turned on its head knows that this is just how it is—and that there is nothing you can do to protect yourself against that emotion. Because not only blood makes up a revolution, also the rush, the rush that leads to still more blood, but at the same time to the exhilaration that turns a revolution, at least for some time, into a true folk festival.

IF LÁSZLÓ TÖKÉS WAS THE FIRST TO CLIMB THE BARRICADES, MIRCEA Dinescu was the Romanian revolution's death-defying jester. Wasn't he the one who had drawn a picture of Communism with a human face on a piece of paper for me? A few quick strokes of the pen and it was finished: a skull in a grinning clown's mask.

I think it happened in another palace, the one where the writers' union held its meeting. How Dinescu had become the chair of the union no one could explain to me.

Dinescu was a poet. His courage was as great as his madness, and the only thing that surprised me was that his face was not painted like Pierrot's. I was very fond of him, if one can be fond of a person who is more electricity than human. It was not possible to take him entirely seriously. Dinescu never sat still. The moment he managed to sit down in a chair, he flew right out of it. He had the habit of getting very close to a visitor without listening to him; instead of answering a question he might stroke the embarrassed visitor's cheek. He usually began a new sentence without having finished the last one, and this feverish restlessness was also a part of the revolution; at least of its very first stage.

I got to know him after he already had the peak of his revolutionary career behind him. He himself was the only one who had not realized that. If he had, I think he would have considered it irrelevant.

Mircea Dinescu seemed as if he wanted to thrust himself into the future while there was still as much as possible left of it. The electricity in him was not just energy—it was neurasthenia. Everything has its end in this world; most of what lies before us is already on the decline—light, bananas, bread and other pleasures, not least the future itself—and if we were to turn back to inspect what we have left behind, we would find that has already turned into something quite different from what it was when we still had it ahead of us, so that the past can not be used at all, other than perhaps by a poet or two.

Dinescu was not one of their number. It did not seem to be his style to play the flaneur in the garden of his childhood, meditating on what he happened to find there on the gravel paths. This was not his temperament. Here was a poet who did not gather up the past; it was dead and gone, it only frightened him, while the time that lay before him insisted on being used. But even it kept running out, and he did not know how he was going to be able to keep it ahead of him for a little while longer.

Mircea Dinescu seemed bewitched by the future, and the revolution was his instrument to help him claim as much as possible of it. But it also made it difficult for him. In the end it would make his situation untenable, since the revolutionaries with the longest lives, those who have managed to survive the first phase of the revolution, are bound more to the past than to the future, paradoxically enough, an outlook they share with poets, the ones who write about gardens, that is, and whom they therefore distrust. Dinescu? They could make use of him without fearing him.

And the future? It is of interest only to utopians or a poet like Dinescu; he paints it in bright, clear colors, almost as if it were a house he was thinking about moving into, and he never tires of saying how much better it will be when it is completely painted and we can live there. The genuine revolutionary, on the other hand, turns to the past long before the actual revolution, scouting out the injustices that are even more important to him than his program for overcoming them. It is this kind of injustice that becomes the yeast for his revolutionary dough. In Timişoara László Tökés had spoken at length with me about the people's "wounds" and the "outrages" that had been perpetrated against them, and in order to find as many wounds and outrages as possible he had gone back rather farther into the past than we really had time for on that Sunday.

With this kind of yeast the priest had baked a rather bitter bread, and I had let a piece or two fall under the table when he was not watching me. On the wall behind Tökés I had been especially captivated by two large paintings in heavy frames. Under the eyes of

Kalvin János (1509–1564) and Zwingli Ulrich (1484–1531) he had broken his bread, and without noticing had eaten more of it than I had, so that when we parted his handshake seemed to me even stronger than when I had taken his hand the first time, right after the church service.

Every revolution has its rhythm, its own breath. If László Tökés seemed to breathe in and out more through his mouth than through his nose, Mircea Dinescu lived in the very inhalation of the revolution: he had kept himself ready and let the revolution fill him, as if it had been his destiny. In this there was something both fatalistic and religious/mystical that I do not believe he himself was aware of, though the very thought of such a connection, with Fate or the heavenly angels, would have enchanted him. It was Mircea Dinescu's pale, unshaven baby face that announced the revolution on television, that *declaimed* the revolution as if it had been a poetry reading, while other people stood there silently and solemnly with him, people who were not as courageous and who had only limited interest in poetry, but who breathed both in and out and were in less of a hurry.

They were a different kind of revolutionary. Many of them were not only more interested in the past than the future—they were also stuck in the past. These people were neither poets nor utopians, and if they had any conception of the future, it was not as a vision, but as a future in a pruned, strictly cut form, just right for fitting into a party brochure. They would have no problem with such a future; it would be manageable with the help of a simple manual or a single command.

But still they were silent, and while Dinescu spoke about "the people" the others already knew that he, the poet, had nothing to do with the people. It was still just a poetic delusion that would not propel the revolution forward. For the people, Dinescu was just a gaudy bird, a fool; not one of them, anyway. Like a mute funeral cortege, the other revolutionaries stood there behind Dinescu in the television studio while he chopped up his own revolutionary sentences into ever-smaller futuristic pieces, into bits of sentences, to a few pattering words in a megaphone that they soon would take from him.

When does Mircea Dinescu lose his role in the revolution? When do the others get rid of him?

The poet himself must have been unaware of what was happening behind his back. It was the same as it was with the past; it would not have occurred to him to turn around. He truly believed that he was one of the people, and in his childlike, moving way he was true to the people, though they did not care about him. But Dinescu had decided not to abandon them. To the astonishment of many, he remained remarkably serene even in the hour of defeat, with clean hands, while the other revolutionaries had already begun to dirty theirs.

After that, Mircea Dinescu became his own revolution. Perhaps that was best for all concerned. In the end even the others had realized that he lived in the kingdom of his own poetry; in truth he had never left it, not even during those days in December. They left him in peace. In his own kingdom he continued to intoxicate himself with the revolution, and this was probably not entirely harmless. But something solidly reasonable, hidden so deeply in his being that no one had discovered it, seemed to protect him; he was not cut out to play the bitter loser.

One of the flighty and fantastic aspects of his nature was that he never really understood that carnivals and folk festivals have to give way to the everyday, and that nothing here in this world continues without interruption, that is to say *for all eternity*; that in the end, the audience all goes home. People get tired, even in revolutions, in any case the majority of us who do not consist solely of electricity.

And that is what happened in Bucharest. For quite a while the crowds there took part in a sort of street theater with real blood. But the ones shooting did not really shoot with the thought of hitting anyone, especially since it was unclear who that ought to be, but rather the shooting was an end in itself; it was the noise the revolution needed, it was the din that was indispensable, and people shot without aiming and there was no one to aim at, and just for that reason it was necessary to shoot all the more so that someone really would get hit, and all of this shooting and the blood that finally did flow was there to show that something had happened.

In refined, European Timişoara, some of the revolutionaries spoke of the mob, the *lumpenproletariat* in Bucharest. I thought that this was unfair. It is true that it was not the same middle-class, disciplined crowd as in Prague the month before, but this Rabelaisian multitude had still made its contribution to the Romanian revolution, if only for the sake of fun and noise, and Silviu Brucan had driven around in this crowd for several days in an armored car; in contrast to Mircea Dinescu, without the slightest contact with the people.

FOR HIS ENTIRE LIFE SILVIU BRUCAN HAS SERVED THE REVOLUTION, AND he ought to be grateful that he has not already, like Trotsky, ended his days with an ice pick in his head. Inside that armored car there were a few people who really thought they had a plan for the revolution, or at least they tried to keep a cool head. Brucan was their *eminence grise*. He had his training in the Communist power apparatus, had survived more than one political purge, had seen the world and spoke several languages. During the fifties he was already demanding the death penalty for enemies of another revolution in the party organ *Scîntea*, and with his good contacts in both Moscow and Washington, he was now at last, at over seventy years of age, going to get to make a revolution with his own mind. And, indeed, no bad mind! While Mircea Dinescu probably does not know whether you open a tap by turning it clockwise or counterclockwise, or how you get the lead into a lead pencil, Brucan was a person who had given similar problems and their solutions a great deal of thought, especially with reference to politics.

Impatiently he had awaited his turn; he now knew better than anyone else. His experiences as a revolutionary under Antonescu and then Hitler, Stalin and finally in opposition to Ceauşescu, were going to stand him in good stead.

But even Silviu Bracan was mistaken. Even this guru was outmaneuvered by others, though his revolutionary career was longer-lived than either László Tőkés's or Mircea Dinescu's. Even so, one day he disappeared from his large office in the government building, where I had visited him a few times. In the corridor, dirty soldiers slept with their submachine guns between their knees; some of them were guarding Brucan's door. Behind the door it was warm. The air was shivering over the radiator, and in the air floated the scent of a not too expensive, but good, shaving lotion.

Brucan himself usually received visitors standing behind his desk. He was wearing a dove-blue cardigan of a quality that had nothing to do with either Bucharest or the revolution, and he knew it. A small, contemptuous, and self-satisfied smile confirmed that he had seen that the visitor, too, had understood this; that such a cardigan has nothing to do with Bucharest.

But here we were at the heart of power. A person who received visitors here could allow himself whatever colors and quality he wanted, and the dove-blue color of Silviu Bracan's cardigan taught me more about revolutions in the Balkans than all the other colors and clothes together.

"How did you find your way here?" he asked, with the small smile hanging on his lips.

Brucan opened his eyes wide; they were strikingly watery. He looked as if he did not expect an answer from a person with so little political experience as myself. How many revolutions had I experienced? Brucan wanted to convince me that the revolution in Romania had not yet won, that its enemies were still hiding in the woods or in the sewers, and his fantastic interpretation was more appropriate than the blue cardigan in a land populated by vampires, the impaled, and kidnapped children (the gypsies, always these gypsies), where in any case the unimaginable of the underworld was always more important than the imaginable in the world above ground.

"Do you really believe what you are saying?"

"No," answered Brucan. "But I had hoped that you would."

This was part of the revolution, too: the chess player who tries to use squares outside the board, and who, when his opponent points out that there are not more than sixty-four, immediately returns to the board again.

But one day Silviu Brucan, too, was gone. How had it happened? He, who had outwitted so many opponents, was in the end outwitted himself, and since the irony of History seldom allows us to be reconciled to our own sad fate, I assumed that Brucan was disappointed.

I was disappointed, too. No one stood behind the desk anymore to receive guests with that sarcastic smile, ready to comment on what was happening in Romania as if it were a chess game rather than politics.

Brucan fascinated me. Despite the fact that he had always had more time for me than Iliescu, my impression was that he was a much more inaccessible personality, probably more because of his experience than by nature. But I had fallen for his little smile. With Iliescu I had been captivated by his shoes, but Brucan's smile had the advantage of being a part of the man himself; probably it had already been in place when little Iliescu was still running around barefoot at home in the village. An arrogant, but at the same time enchanted, smile, a little crooked, as if to show that he already knew most everything and had heard it all before; and that was most likely true, too.

Sometimes it troubled me that his smile looked precisely like Iliescu's, the smile I had seen when the president was sitting in his gilded armchair in the palace, though in one case it was a loser's smile, and in the other, a winner's. But despite the similarity there was an important difference—Iliescu's smile was dissimulation, an attempt to veil the fact that he was on his guard, while in Brucan's mocking superiority there was also something challenging, or rather, a wish to be challenged.

Silviu Brucan was an intellectually curious person, and this made him vulnerable. He liked to talk about other people behind their backs, could be led into speaking of things about which he had not the foggiest idea, and always wanted to hear the latest joke so that he immediately could tell one of his own, a better one, of course, and even newer. If you told him that you had already heard his joke, his eyes shone with delight. In addition, he was fascinated by the word "if"; by its inherent ambivalence, although it was one of the words which, in the middle of a revolution, could be deadly poison. From the word "if" it was not far to pure speculation and relativism. Brucan would have known that better than anyone. But still he could not help playing with it.

If Mircea Dinescu had refused to leave the kingdom of his poetry, Brucan was never far from the café. In Bucharest, where there was not even any real coffee—only lukewarm Turkish grounds—this was a real accomplishment. But it was nevertheless fatal to Brucan's relationship with the revolution. A person who takes up residence in a café soon descends into the hypnotic questions posed by chess games and newspapers. The person who has wandered into that maze is lost. It was the only explanation I could find for his disappearance from the government.

The café! Brucan must have spent much too much of his time there, and so perhaps he was not the true revolutionary he claimed to be; the café life had kept him from it. Instead of occupying myself with his cardigan, I began to take an interest in his breathing. His nose did not seem to play a special role in the process. Silviu Brucan breathed quite normally, sometimes through the nose, sometimes the mouth, like most people. His chest rose and sank in a rhythm like that of a person who is reading a newspaper without much interest. While Tőkés and Dinescu spoke incessantly of the people, Brucan did not utter the word. What he lacked, quite simply, was the excitement of the other two revolutionaries; I suspect that such exhilaration would only manifest itself as a migraine in Brucan. If one set aside his youthful political sins (or were they in fact the deeper cause of his calm?), Silviu Brucan was not an adherent of extreme feelings or standpoints. He pulled away from them—perhaps not so much out of intellectual or moral conviction as the fact that he did not find it worthwhile to waste his strength on such exertions.

He had no desire to squander too much of his energy on anything other than himself.

I had met him once already before the revolution, and then I had seen him in the midst of it, but most of all he fascinated me when he had lost all—or almost all—of his power. A little more than five years after the revolution I decided to look him up. Considering his long experience and Macchiavellian intellect, I imagined that Brucan would be the only one who could do what Tökés or Dinescu could not: analyze what actually had happened to the Romanian revolution.

At what point do the revolutionaries of the first phase lose their power? When does the revolution become a counter-revolution? Who got rid of Tökés, Dinescu, and Brucan?

And how?

I WANTED TO FIND THIS OUT, AND SO I INVITED HIM TO LUNCH; AT Capşa. Capşa, in the center of Bucharest, has remained through all the revolutions the city's most elegant restaurant, even if nowadays it can no longer live up to its reputation except through the staff's arrogant and impertinent attempts to pass off cod roe as Russian caviar. I invited Silviu Brucan to lunch by telephone.

In a hoarse and rather weak voice, he promised to come.

The man who came was an old man on frail, slow legs. It was a very cold winter day in January. The staff greeted him with a respect that carefully ignored that any revolution had taken place, and as if this particular man were their most esteemed guest. In the coat-check they took his black Russian cap with outstretched hands; a king's crown would not have been treated with greater care. This is how better restaurants and service people survive upheavals—by paying them no mind—and this denial allowed Capşa to uphold more of Romania's best traditions than all of the country's equestrian statues put together. Capşa did not concern itself with politics. The restaurant's only problem remained getting hold of vegetables and a sufficient number of eggs for the kitchen, a difficult enough task, but one that was not noticeably influenced by whether there was revolution in Bucharest or not.

Capşa's rooms are arranged in a line, and in the first one a waiter, his hands behind his back, officiated over diverse antipasti. Brucan and I inspected them together. Various hors d'oeuvres were arranged on plates and platters. Black olives, endive, mayonnaise, pickle or sardines. On other platters there were small salads and something billed as caviar. Brucan rubbed his hands and bent over the table while a waiter pointed and whispered in his ear. In just this way he probably once leaned over the newspaper pages in the composition room in Casa Scînteii to make a last-minute check that no printing errors had found their way into his articles, the articles in which he demanded the ultimate punishment for the enemies of the people. But the years had made a smorgasbord of the newspaper, and a banishment to Bărăgan had become *ouefs à la russe*. Silviu Brucan asked the waiter for goulash and a vodka.

Goulash was his favorite dish, and the food interested him more than my questions. I asked him about László Tökés.

"A Hungarian," answered Brucan, without looking up from his plate.

Dinescu?

"A poet."

And Iliescu?

Brucan looked carefully over his shoulder, as if he were not quite sure whether ice picks were out of fashion.

"What do you think?" he said. "We couldn't just hand over the revolution to the people in the streets."

The waiters stood idle against the wall. Brucan declined another vodka. We continued to eat our goulash in silence.

"Do you know what Elena said?" asked Brucan suddenly, putting down his knife and fork.

I did not know. But it surprised me that I understood so clearly what he was talking about and immediately grasped what he was getting at, as if every revolution can be reduced to a handful of lines and events without betraying its contents. As if everything but these lines and events would only confuse, or prove to be superfluous, so that I had understood immediately that Brucan must be talking about that moment on the twenty-first of December more than five years ago, when the first shots were fired on the square between the royal palace and the Party Central Committee building.

Nicolae and Elena Ceauşescu are already up on the roof of the building, waiting to fly away in a helicopter, and before Elena Ceauşescu gets in, she is supposed to have turned to General Victor Stănculescu.

"She asked him to take care of the children," said Brucan. "Those were her last words. Victor, take care of my children."

Brucan looked at me searchingly.

In the middle of the day, the heavy drapes were drawn in front of the windows on to the street. In the cracks between them the winter light sifted into the restaurant; dust shimmered in the air.

"The most important ministries are always the ones in charge of the army and the police," said Brucan. "The army, the police, and the courts."

Surprised, I put down my knife and fork.

"It is not the same with us as it is with you," he continued. "In a democracy there might be completely different ministries that are the most important. But not with us."

I, however, was still up on the roof. My impression was that it was not so much the Ceauşescu children that interested him. The General was more important. Stănculescu, who had promised Elena to take care of them, but who later that same day would break his promise and go over to the revolutionaries' side. It was that betrayal that seemed to interest Brucan, and even if he and the General had ended up on the same side because of it, I think it bothered him.

What is all of our experience and all of our preparation worth if we can not even depend on an officer's word of honor? This kind of betrayal, within the course of just a few hours, and in a General's uniform, to top it off! This is how the human factor makes all planning meaningless in practice. People, even very high officers, simply can not be depended upon; at any time they can betray us.

Everything that Silviu Brucan had learned about revolutions must have seemed useless at such a moment, and this seemed to be what he was thinking while he poked at his goulash with his fork; that is, the role of chance in a revolution, while I kept thinking about blood; in this case, a mother's care.

Blood is in any case thicker than water. At the moment of danger Elena Ceauşescu is not thinking about the people or about power. She is thinking of her children.

"What should we say to that?" Brucan interrupted my thoughts, and his question was not about the children.

After a thoughtful silence he repeated his question, as if he were holding a seminar with a sole student, and it was precisely this question that was appropriate for discussion here in a restaurant, right between the lunch and dinner hours.

"What should we say to that?"

During the fruit compote, Brucan said that the great mistake of the revolution had been to let the secret police, Securitate, come under the command of the army, so that all the people who should have been thrown out remained at their posts. The army protected the secret police, and that was not my decision, said Brucan. Once he had said that, he said nothing more through the rest of lunch. Nothing of how he himself was deposed, nothing about that moment when the revolution changes actors and direction; that decisive moment that I was so curious about.

Instead he told me about his life as a retiree—how these days he was sitting at home at the desk, putting together a political encyclopedia. It was going to be a reference work with all the political concepts and terms, the very first of its kind in Romania.

"You are still a young man," said Brucan, drying his forehead with his white napkin. "You are still young, but you will get older, and you still know nothing of politics. Politics is weather. Remember that! All of politics is about weather."

Weather?

I must have looked skeptical.

"Nothing happens in the winter," said Brucan. "In the winter there are no politics. In the winter one can go abroad and take a vacation from politics. Everything political happens in the summer, when it is warm outside."

What could I say? But these conclusions drawn from a long political life bewildered me, just as much as his work on the encyclopedia with the most important political concepts, as if an author, occupied his entire life with writing novels and plays, would suddenly, in the autumn of his life, devote himself to constructing an alphabet.

But probably most bewildering of all was his conclusion that everything is only weather.

Meteorology as the key to the world's affairs.

At the coat-check a uniformed doorman helped him into his galoshes. His uniform was threadbare, but still a kind of uniform, and the doorman's little smile had a quiet melancholy that was much older than he was.

Then the old revolutionary shuffled homeward in the slush, fearful, though it was not clear to me whether he was afraid, like all old people, of falling down and breaking his hip, or whether he feared that a truck would suddenly appear out of nowhere and intentionally run him down.

Only when he had disappeared around the corner onto Calea Victoriei did I realize that the Romanian revolution had actually occurred in the middle of the winter. The Ceauşescus were overthrown in December. He and his wife were shot on Christmas day. It was winter and cold. How did that fit with Silviu Brucan's meteorological theory?

If it not was this that he had tried to tell me: that a winter revolution does not really mean anything, that it does not leave anything behind other than a bloody ripple on the surface.

THE SIXTH FINGER

OUTSIDE IT IS FALL, THE DAYS GROW EVER SHORTER. AT DUSK THE green of the trees ascends into an already blue-blackness, and while we are waiting to go to the table the baron tells me about that night of almost seventy-five years ago.

Later that same night, says the baron, I am standing on the balcony of our family's house in Stockerau. My mother is holding my hand. It is snowing. But the snow is invisible in the darkness; I only feel how the snowflakes melt on my face. My face is warm and I feel something wet running down my neck. Out there in the darkness around us, church bells are ringing in the new year.

Now you have to imagine that it is New Year's Eve, 1914, says the baron.

Out there in the darkness there is nothing special to see, the baron goes on, only the bells to listen to, and they keep on ringing. Sometimes the wind carries the sound away, out over the Danube all the way out toward Kahlenberg, but the sound of the bells turns back again toward Stockerau, and the whole time the snow keeps falling and melting on my clothes and my face, and my mother, says the baron, held my hand.

What is that woman doing in the kitchen, anyway, he interrupts himself irritably. What is keeping her?

I was just a child, you know, and she held my whole hand in hers, the baron continues. As if it were not the hand of child but a stiff bouquet of winter flowers to place on a grave.

The baron speaks just that beautifully, and I do not know what I should believe.

Already that night one sensed that it was all over. One sensed it, he says, as if he had read my thoughts.

And there stood the two of you together, out on the balcony, I say.

In the next room the maid is setting the table for dinner. The chairs scrape against the floor, the glasses brush one another with a muted clinking sound, and I wonder about the role of this "one" who sensed the end.

Who is this "one"? Where does it come from? I suspect that it belongs to a later time, and that many years later, the baron must have sent his "one" back on a journey to his past, to the year 1914. It is quite possible that this "one" might find a child on a balcony, and a whole lot of snow and church bells besides, but it would hardly find the presentiment that now, on New Year's Eve, 1914, everything would be finished and past. The baron's "one" probably had that presentiment in its baggage, like a toothbrush or a comb, so that he could take it out of his suitcase upon arrival.

Isn't everything in this household approaching its end? I ask myself. And like an auditor responsible for overseeing Time the baron's "one" has the assignment of applying an eraser occasionally to the books, but just so that they balance, more or less, so that the debits and credits cancel out, at least if one does not ask for too much precision.

That is just how careless I imagine the bookkeeping in this household to be.

A bell tinkles in the next room.

Let us go to the table, the baron says, making an inviting gesture with his right arm in the direction of the next room.

Perhaps Helga baked a strudel for us.

The child at that time must have been exactly as old as the century, I say.

What child?

Fourteen years old, I say. You, yourself. Almost.

Whom do you mean?

The child on the balcony, I say. But really I am wondering about what "one" was sensing at that moment.

The baron shakes his head.

I do not understand what you are talking about, says the baron to me. You express yourself so unclearly. I do not understand what you are getting at.

It is stuffy in the dining room, and a clock begins to strike somewhere, but in another room, farther back in the house. The clock strikes hysterically, shrilly, time after time, incessantly, as if there could not be enough hours here in this house, since no one cares to count them anyway.

We sit down at the table. We eat the soup with silver spoons. They are equipped with the family seal, an animal under a crown, and the ones we are eating with are the only ones left, the few that the Russians did not stuff in their pockets when they made a field hospital of the baron's house during the war. The soup is green and lukewarm. The spoons were made for an extinct race of giants, and from the other side of the table the baron is looking at me over his soup dish with his childish blue eyes.

Here in the dining room they operated and cut people up, says the baron.

On my dining room table, he says. I'm telling you this so you will understand what kind of house you are in.

The baron slurps loudly every time he sticks his spoon full of soup into his mouth. On purpose, it seems to me.

They lit the stove with my books, says the baron. They burned my whole library. Nothing burns like books, it doesn't matter who wrote them. In less than three weeks all of world literature burned up in my house, and I showed the Russians how to open the register—they weren't acquainted with such refinements.

All of world literature, slurps the baron. Bound in leather.

We threw it all into the oven, though out of consideration for my guests, I wanted to at least rescue Turgenyev and Merezjkovsky. But they just kept screaming at me, *davaj, davaj*, that means give it here, in Russian, and I did as they said. There was no firewood, you see. Have you read *A Hunter's Diary*, by chance? We did not have any firewood in the house, you see, says the baron.

At night they drank up whatever they could find in the wine cellar and played the accordion. They played beautiful melodies from places you've never heard of. Or perhaps you have heard of them? Orel, for instance? When they were sober, they were well behaved and sad people. In the morning I used to rake out the stove for them while they were sleeping, they did not have any understanding of such things. But not all paper burns equally well, there are books and then there are books, and one morning I found a half-page that had not burned up, though it was sooty and black at the edges.

It was Cervantes's horse, the baron says. The horse had not burned.

The horse that did not burn is now joined, during the soup course, by other horses, a whole hippological report about a great number of horses the baron has met or sat upon, while I wonder if it is really worthwhile to go on missing a house or a balcony for the length of a lifetime.

Our spoons scrape against the bottom of the soup plates.

They never had a renaissance, says the baron. Did you know that? In Russia there are millions of people who have never heard of a stove with a register. It's the same with electricity.

There are no registers in Russia, says the baron.

Where is that woman hiding? he says and puts down his spoon.

In the kitchen, I think, I say.

Everything just disappears, continues the baron. One imagines that one's drawers and closets are in order, but as soon as one opens them, everything is gone. One fine day there is nothing left. Not even a register! That is the kind of people they are.

What did you mean a while ago when you said "one," I asked. When you said "one" sensed it.

Their literature, on the other hand, says the baron, is grand. One has to give them that.

Yes, I say.

What have you read, by the way, asks the baron. You look like someone who reads. What is the best book you have ever heard of, I mean really immortal literature?

The maid enters the dining room.

What are you up to in there, Helga, says the baron angrily, turning on her.

Such a question is worth consideration, and I hesitate between something French and something Russian while the maid is serving us *Tafelspitz* from a large platter, and the meat gets stuck between the baron's teeth. He grimaces, forgetful of his guest, and the baron's grimaces bare long, yellow teeth which, if they had not been his own real teeth, could have been keys on a harpsichord that has not been used for a long time. The forks on the table could have been used as pitchforks and the knives lack the family seal; they are rusty and dull, and on close inspection, everything in this room is in the same, worn-out condition. Much of the family silver has been lost, the spoons have already disappeared, though that was long ago, and the baron himself has moved back and forth between his various times and lives so long that he probably can not separate them in his own memory.

If I look around, I see that the whole house is not much different. Whole continents are coming loose from the globe. America's blue lakes have blackened, Africa is rolling away from the Gold Coast like a roll of wallpaper, from west to east, and if this keeps up, all six continents will soon disappear, so that the only thing left in this house will be a completely bald globe, without mountains, rivers, or cities.

In the end even Vienna will disappear as the rest of the world already has.

Helga takes the plates away and the baron asks for a toothpick; there are no toothpicks out on the table.

You look pale, says the baron, holding both of his hands in front of his mouth. As if you were thinking of something disturbing.

I can only hear him indistinctly.

No, I say, this is just how I look.

So that is your usual appearance, says the baron.

Yes, I answer.

Well, in that case, says the baron. One never knows.

In the middle of the dining room table stands a crane in gilded bronze, and the bird has placed his feet on the back of a turtle, also gilded. In his beak the crane holds a gilded candleholder, but the candle is not yet lit, though it is already dark.

Do you smoke, asks the baron.

No, thanks. I've quit.

The baron must have dragged all of the requisite items from his past in portmanteaus and chests through two wars to be able to furnish his rooms in this house with what actually belongs to another age, but none of it has helped. For years all of his things have been turning away from him and bidding him adieu: his suits grow, his wine no longer tastes good to him, the leather in his shoes splits, his parakeets' beaks crack, his shirt collars no longer find his throat, his matches fall from their box and scatter on the floor, and if his house had had a balcony, he would no longer have been able to find his mother on it. Even she has left him, and with both hands he holds on tightly to the edge of the table in his own dining room and asks me what kind of dessert I prefer, pound cake, perhaps, or strudel.

I like both of them equally, I say.

We'll soon see what Helga has found for us, says the baron, and he pronounces the word "soon" so that I understand that the word itself is more important to him than pound cake or any other dessert; that with the help of this "soon," he is trying to lay claim to yet another piece of future for himself, and the baron uses the word so that I can tell that he desires a future more than any dessert here in this life, and with no thought of sharing it with me, just the cake or the strudel Helga soon, in a moment, will be offering us.

He will share the cake or the strudel with me, but nothing more.

On an evening like this, says the baron, one's whole life returns. Not yours, but mine. I see my whole life before me. I look out through the window and see my life, though you believe that what I see is the garden there outside, but in the garden I see only my own life. I see it out there in the garden while I sit in here with you.

I do not see you, says the baron. Don't think that I see you, you are perfectly indifferent to me. You are only here to remind me of the people who are no longer here, and you help me see them, though you yourself are perfectly indifferent. Therefore I am grateful to you.

Do you understand? says the baron.

Yes, I answer.

No! You do not understand! You can not understand it, says the baron, nor do you understand that what I am telling you is not actually intended for you, but for me, that I do not want to communicate anything to you by telling about my life, I only want to entertain myself for a while in the company of those I love and who no longer exist anywhere but in my memories. Do you understand? No, how could you understand? It is a lie that we live on in one another. We only live on in the tales about us, tales in which we are together with the others, and when we die we are gone forever if we do not exist in a tale that seems to be about the others, but is really about us.

Everyone is dead, says the baron, and the maid bends down to pick up his napkin, which has fallen on the floor.

One knew it, says the baron then; now at the end of dinner he once again stands on the balcony.

It was all over already, and it lay in the darkness out there. The snow and the church bells. One sensed it even then.*

The baron lifts his wine glass filled with water, and it is then that I suddenly see it: his right hand has not five, but six fingers.

On his ring finger is another finger, a shrunken one, tender and white as a head of asparagus, a sixth finger that grows out of the larger one in its very own crooked direction, as if it did not want to have anything to do with the rest of the hand.

Somewhere far back in the house the clock strikes again, too many times. But even the baron's own clock seems to be out of order, it has fooled all of the juices of his body so that it is not easy to tell what is working within him, whether it is life or death. They have mixed up their assignments to such a degree that new fingers have begun

---

*Later that very same year the war broke out and everything was over.

sprouting on the baron's hand, a right hand that belongs to a body that no longer has any mission to carry out in this life.

I see that the sixth finger has its own nail, no larger than the head of a nail, and that the baron lets all of his nails grow without clipping them, perhaps in order to shorten the life that so unexpectedly has emerged from his body.

And his body's disorder is like the disorder here in the house, and I wished that he had asked me to step out onto his balcony, though we are here on Hohe Warte in Vienna, not in Stockerau, but instead the baron asks me to accompany him to the salon, where the parakeets twitter as best they can with their cracked beaks.

He places himself with his back to the open fire and observes me with his light-blue eyes. The baron slumps, with both hands behind his back.

If he were now to clasp his hands behind his back and knit his fingers together, this knitting would consist of not ten, but eleven fingers, and I believe that it is the eleventh finger that gives him his mocking countenance, as if he had played a trick on death itself.

There is a crackling from the fire in the hearth.

You know, of course, the name of that horse, says he.

IT WAS A STRANGE COUNTRY, ALBANIA. ALREADY AT THE AIRPORT there was a man in a dark suit standing under a palm tree, and though I was almost completely certain that I had never seen him before, he said *welcome, my friend*, in English, took me under the arm and led me into a special room, to the left of the arrivals hall, and asked me to sit down in a large armchair; one of its legs stood in a glass ashtray.

I sat down. An electric fan was humming in a corner of the room. Two other men in dark suits already sat in the room, sunk into their own armchairs; only our heads stuck up over the worn chair backs. A fourth person, about my age, sat on a plain chair. He was introduced as my interpreter. I immediately noticed his large, round face, looking as if it were rolled out of lumpy dough, a face in which the need to stay awake seemed to hold back, but only with difficulty, the strong urge to fall asleep on the spot.

The interpreter gave his name.

"I am going to call you Sali," I said.

"*My friend*," said the first man in a dark suit again, and as if that were not enough he went even further: I was *a friend of his country*, and the two other men in dark suits, who each sat with a coffee cup in his lap, looked at me and wagged their heads like two porcelain dolls, sideways, from one side to the other, which in this country meant that they were of the same opinion.

They balanced their little coffee cups with the tips of their fingers. They, too, knew that I was a friend of their country. Only for me did this friendship with a whole country come as a surprise.

"*My friend*," repeated the first man in the dark suit, smiling at me.

The interpreter smoked and said nothing. There was not much to say to that; *my friend* hardly needed to be translated. The only remarkable thing about it was that the man in the dark suit had made me *his* friend, when he could have satisfied himself with a less defined and more impersonal friendship. This *my* carried the risk that I might later turn out to fall short of expectations, despite the fact that I had been so carefully tested. I had drunk coffee for years in my hosts' embassies in both Stockholm and Vienna before a visa, which took up a whole page, had been glued into my passport. How could he know that I was not going to disappoint them? The man in the dark suit had really taken a risk, but a calculated one—if, during my visit to his country, I should meet or even exceed expectations, he would perhaps be able to benefit not only from so unconditionally having supported the summing up of my person by higher authorities, but also by privately having so early committed himself with his *my*.

His *my* also said something about power. This person—whom I could not remember ever having met—had allowed himself to express his personal opinion of me, and in the presence of several witnesses. He had taken a position on a matter that would not be decided officially until later, when I had left his country, and that he had gone on ahead of events made me guess that he had a higher rank than the other two men in the group, despite the fact that his dark suit did not differ from theirs in any way.

The man who called me *my friend* leaned forward and offered me a cigarette. When he offered me the pack I saw that the nail on his little finger was painted a dull blue, and that it was longer than the other nails.

The interpreter, Sali, also continued to smoke. He swallowed the smoke right down; it disappeared inside him.

The three men and Sali drove me into the city. We passed through crowds of sheep and people who walked down the middle of the road, and in the center of the city the car stopped in front of a broad staircase that led up to the hotel where I was going to be staying as a guest of the country. We took leave of one another at the reception desk. While we were standing there, shaking hands and exchanging pleasantries, my baggage arrived in another car; I had completely forgotten it.

"Room thirty-two," said one of the men in a dark suit to the receptionist, before he drove away with the others in the same car we had come in.

Before I went up to my room, I wanted to inspect the hotel. It was large and gloomy, and the first thing I noticed was the cages with songbirds in the lobby and in the hotel's dining room. It was unclear what the birds were doing there; I had read that there were no dogs in the country, and the only animals I had seen on the way in from the airport were sheep and three mules.

The hotel's birds were little and yellow, but they did not sing. What was supposed to be their song was really not more than a chirping, like a fragment from a much bigger song that could no longer be heard; just this short, indistinct twitter was left for the ear, and now, toward the end of the afternoon, it added to the sleepy atmosphere of this building.

The caged birds reminded me more of the Orient than Europe. But soon enough I would become used to them. Usually they sat silent and still in their cages, cages that were nests for the birds, protecting them from diverse dangers with their bars. At that time— almost twenty years ago—it looked as if the hotel's songbirds were both well fed and contented, so the hotel guests had good reason to believe that it is an entirely different thing for animals to be caged than people.

But they did not sing.

Still I was captivated by them. In all of that dark and gloom they were a splash of color, small balls of yellow life. They did not even seem to miss the freedom to fly around; free flight might look beautiful to a human, but for the bird it is not much more than the arduous choreography of the hunt for food. The maids stood on tiptoe and cleaned the cages with small brushes, and the birds twittered so softly and so rarely that it sometimes happened that I did not even notice them in their cages, where they sat motionless.

Adjacent to the reception desk was a little bar. Straight across from the bar, on the other side of a long corridor, lay the dining room, where every evening for two weeks I would sign bills that I never saw again. I signed them, they were taken away, and at that moment they disappeared for good. While I ate, strange men peeked into the door of the diningroom, took a few drags on their cigarettes and disappeared again.

I ate *ferghes*, a liver stew, or *shashlik* with cheese, wrapped in paper.

In the bar on the other side of the corridor, the counter was made of dark, fine wood, and elegantly bent, a soft curve almost running through the entire room, equipped with a bar of yellow brass as a footrest. There were no stools along the counter. All of the guests stood or sat at one of the four low tables along the walls.

At one of them sat an older, Egyptian author who had come on the same flight as I had; probably he too was one of the country's friends. The Egyptian had black sunglasses which almost covered his entire face. At his table sat three men in dark suits.

All four of them smoked.

"Do you play tric-trac in this country," asked the Egyptian.

Only seldom was anything other than coffee drunk in the bar, and the crowd was made up of men, strikingly short ones, as if they all belonged to a delicate race. Their shortness made it tempting to imagine that they were especially meek and mild by nature, free from all aggression. All of them seemed to know one another. They were veiled in a cloud of smoke that lingered under the ceiling, even when the bar was aired out in the mornings. The guests of the evening had disappeared by then: only the smoke remained.

Usually they stood or sat in the bar with their coats on, as if all of them were planning a sudden departure or were afraid that their coats would be stolen if they parted with them. But where could they have hung them? I could not find any coat-check; rather, the guests came and went as if the bar were a railway station, but without seeming to be on their way anywhere. Their only wish seemed to be to drink a cup of coffee and stand together for a little while in the cigarette smoke in there.

In the dining room there were few guests. On the short wall by the kitchen there was a painting depicting a kitchen mortar, some green fruit that might have been lemons, and two dead fish. There was also a dead bird hanging in the painting, and a bottle with an exotic label. Breakfast was served here in the mornings; the waiters at that time had not yet put on their black jackets and ties.

Their boss was Mister Miri, or perhaps he only acted as if he were their boss. Suddenly he stood there in the door to the dining room; only Mister Miri could walk through the room without making the parquet floor creak. Mister Miri was always well dressed. The trousers of his dark suit were creased, the only creases in the country, and he wore a vest, even in the middle of the summer. Now it was early in the morning, and Mister Miri was already impeccably dressed and combed; and it would have been no different if I had run across him at lunch or dinner instead of in the morning.

In a country other than his own, Mister Miri would have been a welcome guest at a funeral with his discreet participation, his willingness to taste all of the cakes, and his readiness with a word of comfort for each and every person would have been indispensable. But here in this country such talents were wasted. They did not come to any use here.

No one called him anything other than Mister Miri. I thought that it sounded like a cat's name, and indeed: his eyes and the small bridge of his nose—like a thin line—drew a face, along with his mouth, that could have been stolen from a cat.

Mister Miri clapped his hands. He was even smaller than the shortest of the waiters. Early in the morning they were half-dressed and arguing with one another, as if the hotel belonged to them as long as the guests and the birds in their cages had not yet awakened.

Did the waiters sleep in the kitchen? I admired the way the older of them handled the silverware and tablecloths as if they had always worked here.

"*Good morning,*" said Mr. Miri. "*How are you today?*"

Every morning my interpreter, Sali, came to the hotel and sat down at my table while I ate breakfast. Sali was bigger and heavier that his compatriots and moved as if his size caused him discomfort.

So much body at once! I saw in his big, round face that he was still sleeping, though his eyes were open. He leaned over the table, lit a cigarette, and began blowing smoke at me. With a few, indistinct words he presented the day's schedule while he took and ate the black olives from my plate; distracted, as if asleep. While he was stuffing them in his mouth he continued to smoke and talk and swallow the olives along with the smoke.

I asked him if he were hungry.

"Do you want me to order something for you?"

Frightened, he straightened in his seat. He had awakened, he looked at his cigarette as if he were just now discovering its existence, and he put it out in the ashtray. The ashtray was of white porcelain and full of butts. It advertised the country's tourist agency, though almost no tourists were allowed to visit.

Every day after breakfast Sali and I left the dining room together, and out in the hall one of the three men in a dark suit was waiting. He was visible from a good distance. While he was waiting he paced the hall and smoked or leaned over the receptionist's desk and talked to Mr. Miri. Mr. Miri smoked, too, and in the hall the yellow birds had begun to wake up; from their cages a faint twittering could be heard, but it soon stopped short.

"*Good morning,*" said Mr. Miri. "*How are you today?*"

"*Fine, thank you.*"

I spent the whole day with Sali and one or two of the men in dark suits. Together we visited factories, schools, art museums or museums of the country's recent past, collective farms, day-care centers, or ministries, where the staff was already sitting in a row and waiting for us when we came into the room. One of them rose; that was the minister. Everywhere we drank coffee. "May we offer you a cup of coffee?" It was even more usual that they did not ask, and the coffee was simply brought in. The coffee was brought in while Sali translated, so that I got the feeling that the coffee had more to do with him than with the foreign guest.

We visited farmers, engineers, authors, and people who had made some kind of a mark, and the men in the dark suits stayed in the background and ensured that I would become acquainted with their country in this way and would be able to get a true picture of it.

We also visited towns besides the capital in an old Volvo, with a thin, quiet chauffeur who handled the car as if it were his own donkey, and who, when he was not sitting behind the wheel, polished the car, smoked, and waited for us. Every day we traveled together to some new factory or city, from the north to the south we drove through the country and then back again, the roads were empty and the men in the dark suits stayed in the background and expressed the hope that my friendship with their country would be deepened the farther we went, and the more I was given the opportunity to see.

After an especially long day, I wanted to give the chauffeur a pack of cigarettes. Frightened, he recoiled. I put the pack back into my pocket.

Much of what I saw out in the country was odd, and every evening we returned to the capital together and to the hotel, which I had begun to consider a second home. In the dusk the Volvo stopped in front of the steps, and if Mister Miri were not standing there, I was sure to meet him in the hall, right near the door, busy talking to some other short person in a dark suit whom I had the feeling I had seen before.

"*Did you have a nice day?*" asked Mister Miri.

"*Very nice,*" I said.

In the evening I sat at my table in the dining room and looked at the painting with the dead fish, happy to be alone. The dining room was nearly empty, as usual, but at a table near mine the Egyptian author sat alone, too, without touching the food on the plate in front of him. At a third table sat two young people from a Scandinavian country in sandals and cotton shirts, also friends of the country. They ate olives with sheep cheese and did not speak to me; I was from the wrong newspaper. I suspected that one could show and tell them whatever one wanted and that they would be convinced even of things that their hosts did not themselves believe. I drank another carafe of wine and signed the check. As I left the dining room I greeted the Egyptian author and he returned my greeting, or at least he happened to nod just slightly at that moment, sunk in his own thoughts behind his sunglasses. There was a greasy piece of paper on the plate in front of him.

Up in my room I took out my notes from the day.

I read through them once and then once again without being satisfied with what I had written. It seemed to me that what I had set down did not do justice to a long and eventful day. The images of the day that were still in my head did not correspond to what was on paper. The images were different from my notes, more interesting and alive.

Had I written down the wrong impressions? Had I happened to get hung up on things that were not so important in conversations, written down a fact or a sentence that really was irrelevant, so that my harvest for the day consisted of observations and information that had nothing to do with this country?

I took out my older notes, the ones from the week before, in the hope that they would prove livelier. Perhaps my eyes and ears had begun to tire during the second week, so that what I saw and heard no longer did the country justice and never should have been committed to paper? I read through them. There was no difference; the first week was just like the second in my notebook.

Everything was wasted, the men in the dark suits had exerted themselves in vain!

Now at the close of the day what was written in my notebooks seemed so meager that I feared that I might not even be able to use them. My notes made me suspect that as soon as I tried to get this country on paper, it disappeared; and I did not know if it were my fault or the country's.

Most of what I had noted were figures or years—the price in the country's currency for a dress or a loaf of bread, the date of some important event in the country's history, how many tons of chromium had been mined the year before, the weight of the little tractor

that was manufactured in the capital with the help of foreign tech-
nology, as well as the number of those tractors that was produced
every month. Or I had noted what had been especially emphasized in
conversations. I had quoted sentences like "We depend on our own
strength," "History is on our side," or "We would rather eat grass
than give up our independence."

Yet again I read through the figures for the day. I re-read sentences
like "The Vatican is supporting our enemies," and I saw that this
could not be the day I had just experienced, which was now nearing
its end, and that the remains of the day that were still in my head had
nothing to do with so and so many tons of crude oil or kilometers of
cotton fabric; that there was nothing in my notebook of the day that
had been really worth remembering.

This troubled me. I went out into the bathroom and splashed my
face with cold water. On the shelf under the mirror stood my razor,
shaving brush, styptic pencil, and toothbrush in its glass, nicely
organized. Alone in my room I would not get any wiser about where
my day had gone, so I went down to the bar.

As usual, it was full of smoking and coffee-drinking men. At the
counter stood the Albanian author I had met for lunch that day,
whose novels were going into multiple printings in France. Along
with a man in a dark suit, we had eaten lunch that day at the hotel,
in a *chambre séparée* off the dining room. The door to the room had
been locked. At lunch he had told about a meeting with Chinese
authors in Shanghai. The author was short, had thick glasses and an
enchanting little mouth, just made to kiss a person right in the
middle of the forehead.

Now he was standing at the counter, smoking and drinking coffee
like everyone else. He greeted me and asked how the day had been,
and I told him how it had been: I had lost it.

He looked at me with interest. The thick glasses magnified his
brown eyes and made him look like an insect.

"I am here, after all, to try to understand you," I said.

"You will come to understand everything," he said soothingly.

"But with whose help? You eat lunch with me and tell me stories about China. And everyone else I talk to gives me figures that I have no use for."

"You haven't studied them carefully enough. Talk to ordinary people."

"I try," I said. "But it doesn't work. Wherever I go there is somebody in a dark suit with me. It's not exactly calculated to inspire confidences from ordinary people. But I wouldn't be able to understand them, anyway. If I were alone with them, I mean."

"This country is like reading an open book," he said. "You don't need to know a single word of our language. All you need is eyes and ears."

"I know," I said. "This morning I saw an old woman in a corner of the square. She was trying to sell an egg."

"That is possible," said the author.

"Do you understand? A single egg, I saw it myself."

"It is also possible that it was not an egg."

"No? But I saw it myself."

"Then it must have been as you say. But it was not necessarily an egg."

"How do you sell an egg that is not an egg?"

"It is entirely possible here," he said. "Perhaps she was just sitting there with an egg in front of her. An old woman, you say? Are you sure about that? Perhaps she did not want to sell it at all. Did you buy the egg?"

"No."

"There, you see," he said.

He lit another cigarette. "Buy whatever you can," he said. "If it is for sale, that is. We have many beautiful souvenirs here in our country. Just buy! That's my advice to you."

The author excused himself, and soon he was having a conversation with someone else at the other end of the counter; it was my chauffeur.

After the conversation in the bar I was relieved to find everything in my room as I had left it. In the bathroom my razor, shaving brush, styptic pencil, and toothbrush in its glass were still there under the bathroom mirror. This calmed me. A toothbrush is perhaps not much to hold on to, but if even a single egg can set the universe spinning, a toothbrush is at least something of a comfort. Here in my room there was, despite everything, a kind of hidden order; something tangible and graspable that was not a mirage, something that was there no matter what happened or did not happen, just like Mister Miri or the birds in their cages.

BUT THEN THE BIRDS DISAPPEARED, TOO. IT WAS STRANGE. COMPARED to other animals, caged birds can be distinguished by their extreme predictability. It is true that the hotel's yellow songbirds did not sing, but even in that respect they were predictable, a part of the hotel's own sense of order. They did not sing, they sat motionless in their cages, but they were *there*, and when they were no longer in place, it could not be interpreted as a good sign, in any case not by a regular guest of the hotel.

When did the birds actually disappear from the hotel?

Was it five or ten years after my first visit to the country? Or perhaps not more than three? It irritated me that I had not noticed it, that one day it just suddenly struck me that they were no longer there, though I could not say if they had still been in the lobby or the dining room yesterday or at least at the beginning of the last week. The more I tried to figure it out, the more uncertain I became. Were the birds even there during my very latest visit to the country, a little less than half a year before?

I did not know, I had not made a note of it. There was nothing in my notebook about the birds.

It irritated me especially that the birds' fate had escaped me since everything else seemed to be completely the same, year in and year out, so that perhaps the only thing of any real importance that had happened here for a long time was just that the hotel's yellow songbirds, along with their cages, had disappeared.

Everything else was the same. The men in dark suits waited for me just as they had ten, five, and three years before, Sali translated, all of the dates and figures were the same as before and in the museums the same objects were being shown that were there ten, five, and three years ago: a Bible with a space between its covers for a radio transmitter, a saint stuffed with straw, flags, yellowing flyers, a revolver side by side with a fountain pen, and when the day came to an end, Mister Miri asked me how it had been.

Even the bar was the same. As usual it was full, and at the counter stood the author with the multiple editions in French, smoking. In the crowd I could recognize ministers and chauffeurs speaking to one another; I knew which was the minister and which the chauffeur only because one of them had driven me to a meeting with the other at some point.

As usual the coffee beans were ground in a little Italian machine behind the counter. The humming of the machine and the murmur of the guests did not quiet until late in the evening, when the coffee was all gone and the doors to both the bar and the hotel entrance were locked. The coffee was served with water, and I asked Sali why he never touched his glass of water; he just looked at me in amazement.

With the years his face and everything in it had grown even larger. Only his eyes grew smaller, until gradually they were nothing more than two diagonal slits in all of that dough. A dirty dough; his face was full of black spots that did not seem to wash away.

I was almost always the one who paid at the bar, or rather I signed the check that then disappeared for good, while Sali and the others I had treated began digging through their pockets and looking distressed and relieved at the same time; none of them, not even the ministers, had much money to spend. All of them seemed forced to rely on whatever they happened to have in their pockets, which most often were empty. Even their gestures seemed muted, as if they were obliged to conserve all of their resources. Only rarely did it happen that one of them allowed himself to throw away a smile, a distorted one, almost like a spasm, and sometimes I had to wait several years before it turned up on the same face again.

In the bar I bought a coffee for a former ambassador, whose face was completely eaten by eczema. We spoke of the war; the ambassador told about how he had taken part of the liberation of his country as a partisan, and I asked if the occupying army's retreat hadn't helped them get their efforts off the ground, since the enemy was kept busy trying to shorten their front. Insulted, he turned away; I was not used to such strong expressions of emotion in this country, but perhaps it had more to do with the sanctity of his memories of youth than with a long-forgotten war.

"You ought not to have said that," said Sali, when I told him how the former partisan had turned away from me.

Sali rested his head in his hands. He was sleeping again.

"But it was true."

"You ought not to have said it," he repeated.

In the years that followed I saw the ambassador's rough face here and there in the crowd, but always at a distance. The ambassador ignored me. The cigarette smoke seemed not to have any damaging effect on his face; instead he seemed younger than before. Sometimes I also got a glimpse of his mouth. It was moving in the midst of all that roughness, but in the murmur of voices I could not understand what the ambassador was saying; it was something that was, in any case, not directed to me. Despite the quiet murmuring in the bar, it was the same with mouths as it was with everything else here; they were used with great economy, in order to say something very clipped, most often not more than a *po*, or to drink coffee in small sips or munch on a piece of sticky baklava.

In this bar neither the nose nor the mouth was of much use, despite the Italian machine that ground coffee every night; it was the eyes. Only the eyes moved quickly and nervously in all of that motionlessness, just as suddenly and incalculably as the songbirds hopping suddenly from one bar to another in their cages.

The eyes were important. The author with his cigarette at the counter was right—his numerous French editions were really no accidental occurrence. I looked around for him. He would have been the right person to ask about the birds.

It was easier to make chance acquaintances in the bar than in front of the hotel. The other guests asked me questions, though not about my impressions of their country, or even about my own country, their questions were much more specific than that. They wanted to know what it was like on the floor above the bar, in my hotel room; they themselves were confined to a lower plane, the first floor.

"What do you actually do all day in your room," asked Sali.

"During the day I'm with you."

"Yes," he said. "You have a room and you are almost never there."

Is there running water in your room, they asked me. I answered that there was both hot and cold running water. They asked me how often it was turned off. I answered that it seemed never to be turned off, anyway I had always had warm water every time I needed it and turned on the proper tap. What about at night? I could not give them any information about warm water at night. Why not, they asked, and I answered that I did not take baths at night, I slept, but I had no reason to believe that the water was not just as warm at night as during the day, and at this they shook their heads sideways, but I could not grasp what they wanted warm water for in the middle of the night.

"You just turn on a tap," they said.

A little group of interested coffee drinkers had gathered around me.

"At any hour of the day?"

"Yes," I said.

"Try to find out how the water is at night," they asked me.

But water could not count on the same level of interest that was reserved for coffee here in the bar. As long as each and every person had a cup of coffee in his hand, it was of little importance who was a minister and who a chauffeur; it was only without coffee that such a distinction could become important, only when not even the least little drop would run out of an overturned cup.

"*Do you like our coffee?*" asked Mr. Miri when he looked into the room and discovered me standing at the counter.

I offered him a cigarette. Mr. Miri weighed his choice for a long time before he took a cigarette in the middle of the case; I thought I saw a paw instead of a hand. He lit the cigarette with a lighter that glistened in the glow of its flame. With half-closed eyes he carefully blew the smoke out through his nose.

"*A very fine cigarette,*" said Mr. Miri.

"Do you like your room," he asked. "Let me see, it's room thirty-six, is it not?"

"Thirty-two," I answered.

"*I am sorry,*" said Mr. Miri.

"Thirty-two," I repeated.

Mister Miri looked as if we ought not to let ourselves be bothered by this confusion of thirty-two and thirty-six.

I assured him that I was satisfied with the room. He nodded, with a slight bow of his head instead of moving it sideways; this was, after all, the country's very finest hotel, almost exclusively intended for foreign guests.

Mister Miri looked out over the crowd in the bar and the smoke from his cigarette rose toward the ceiling.

"And your work?"

"Thank you," I said. "It is proceeding nicely."

Mister Miri bowed slightly once more, perhaps a bow of respect for me and my work.

"Yes," he said. "Number thirty-two is our very best room. *A very nice room.*"

Then he excused himself. Another guest was demanding Mr. Miri's attention and I, who would had wanted to ask him about the birds and when they had disappeared, was left in the bar. But the first disappearance must suddenly have reminded me of a second, since disappearances rarely occur singly; it struck me that the ice cream, too, had vanished.

Where had the vanilla ice cream gone?

Ten, five, or three years ago ice cream had been served here topped with grated vanilla bean; the Italians had been here not so long ago and left behind not only their dead soldiers' bones, which the author with the many French editions wrote about, but also the beginnings of a real cuisine. But now the ice cream, speckled black with grated vanilla, was gone, and I had made no note of that, either, so that "now" might as well have been yesterday or ten, five, or three years ago.

The vanilla ice cream had vanished!

"Mr. Miri!" I called, but he was already gone.

"Mr. Ramiz," I asked the waiter at dinner, "how about that ice cream?"

"No ice cream."

"I know. The ice cream is gone. But since when?"

"No ice cream. There is *crème caramel*. Would you like some?"

"No, thank you. I do not want any *crème caramel*."

The waiter wanted to leave my table. Just like Mr. Miri, he was already on his way somewhere else when you really needed him.

"Mr. Ramiz," I said, before he had managed to leave. "I know that there is no more ice cream, but I want to know since when. How long have you not had vanilla ice cream?"

"Have some fruit," said the waiter. "There are oranges today." Without waiting for my answer he disappeared and soon returned with some grapes on a plate.

I put the grapes in my pocket and went back to the bar to drink an after-dinner cup of coffee. The bar was full of smoking and coffee-drinking guests, and as usual my hotel room gave them no peace. I was forced to describe in detail my bathtub to an older man, a head higher than the others, who seemed to me to be the missing link between ministers and chauffeurs. On an impulse that was not entirely clear even to me, I did not say anything about the plug and large pieces of mosaic in green tile that were missing from the tub.

He listened attentively to what I had to say about the bathtub, his large, hairy ear pushed close to my mouth. I told him everything I knew.

"So it is the Italian ones, the Italian ones," he mumbled, straightening up.

What was so interesting about a hotel room? Mine was not much more remarkable than any other I had stayed in, just simpler and with more cockroaches in the bathroom and on the walls. But every day it was cleaned carefully by two maids in light-blue dresses and white, stiff aprons; if my hand towels happened to fall on the floor in the bathroom, they were already changed that same evening, or neatly hung up again. If I was in a hurry in the morning and left dirty clothes strewn around and the bed unmade, there were no other consequences than ironed underwear and shirts lying on a chair and new sheets on the bed when I came home.

It was like a quite ordinary hotel; I could count on them taking care of my room even when I was not there myself. A green tag left on the doorknob was enough. And if I forgot to hang it out, it made no difference. When I came back, they had been there anyway.

Everything was in perfect order. On the shelf in the bathroom stood my razor, my shaving brush, the styptic pencil, and the toothbrush in its glass, and I could count on being left in peace in my room, besides. I could retreat, still occupying this strange country, it is true, but only subject to my own rules and demands; if I went down to the dining room I could eat and drink things that I had begun to suspect—was it ten, five, or three years ago—actually did not exist, in any case not outside my hotel, and the only thing I needed to do in order to have it all placed before me was not to leave the hotel. In the dining room I could then consume cheese that did not actually exist, drink wine that did not exist, and eat my fill of meat and vegetables that did not exist.

My room had a single table, and on it I laid my papers and

notebook. I used to sit there in the evening and try to work. If I raised my eyes I did not look out a window, but instead saw myself in a large mirror on the wall, just as there had been a mirror in each birdcage, just a smaller one, for the birds to look into and keep themselves company.

I would have liked to have eaten in my room as well, but no matter how often I pushed the white, green, and red buttons, the result was always the same. Nothing happened.

The hotel's room service was not working.

This made my work more difficult, since the hotel room was my office, after all, and a functioning room service was almost as important as my newspaper clippings or typewriter.

But nothing happened, and every visit to this country was like the others. After a long day of work I returned to the hotel, the men in dark suits took leave of me and promised to pick me up the next morning at a quarter after eight, and I asked for my key at the reception, number thirty-two.

"Did you have a nice day?"

The little feline nose, the eyes, the servile look; Mr. Miri stretched out his hand for the key and found it without having to turn around.

In the room I read through my notes for the day, all the figures, dates, and quotes, like "we are building a second Albania,"—as if one were not enough—and the names of the people who had said these things were written down with the quotes. Every evening I returned to the hotel with a new crop of such sentences, and the only thing that happened over the years was that I no longer thought of them as the words of my interviewees, despite the fact that I had heard them come from their own mouths, in the presence of some men in dark suits. Instead I began in time to think of their words as phrases that had been placed in their mouths, so that our conversations were more like interrogations, in which they parroted their memorized lines.

While they ground out their lines, I sat silently across from them and wrote down what they said, but mechanically as if it were they and not I who moved the pen across the paper; in my notebooks their lines were reproduced quite exactly, just as exactly as the image of myself when I lifted my eyes from my notes and looked into the mirror in my hotel room, and this conformity would have been almost perfect if something had not been missing from the notes, something I was reminded of every time I happened to look up from them—myself. It was I, myself, who was missing in these notes. That was why the notes had nothing to do with this country, either.

It was my questions that were wrong, not their answers.

But when had I realized that? Ten, five, or three years ago? And why not on the very first day in this country?

A few isolated times I had managed to sneak away from my keepers, but the people I then tried to interview were so frightened to see me on my own that they fell mute. Or else they had nothing to replace their phrases with, so that what I had to read in my notebooks that evening were just more words that were not their own, and I read them again and again, no longer to remind myself of what I had written, but in the hope of discovering just one of their *own* words, like a loose tooth that would betray that all was not well here.

In vain. I went into the bathroom. Was it really I who had set the toothbrush on its head in the glass? And the styptic pencil was gone; I looked for it on the floor, but in vain.

Things could not keep on going like this. In desperation and disgust I took courage and devoted myself to a new kind of interaction on my official visits. It was an unconventional style, almost impolite, but I was less ashamed of the new style than I was of the fact that it had taken me more than ten, or was it five or maybe three years before I had begun to put it into practice.

So: good-bye to everything that could be weighed and measured! I stopped asking about harvests. I did not ask anymore about the number of privately owned sheep, pig iron, or their diplomatic relations with neighboring countries, since such questions—even if I did not know the answer to them—only distanced me from myself, from my own curiosity. Such questions only provided me with answers that surprised me just as little as my questions surprised those who were instructed to answer them.

Instead I started to ask questions that had nothing especially to do with this country. As long as I did it politely and with an innocent expression, I surprisingly enough often got answers; Sali hurried to translate, wearing the same innocent expression himself. Perhaps he was just as interested in their answers as I was, and the men in the dark suits were caught napping.

And the interviewees? People had nothing against telling their own stories. The stories could seem petty and banal, but they were *theirs*, and since they were the ones narrating and not I—it was my task only to write them down—they were neither petty nor banal. They preferred their own fates to the country's; so selfish were they, in fact, that their wife's doings interested them more than the wheat harvest, and their country's isolation helped me get them started: the people I spoke to could not be quite certain of how normal or abnormal my questions were, closed off as they were from the world. For safety's sake, then, they answered them all. Out of pure politeness, or in the secret supposition that my world was, after all, more normal than theirs.

Or they might have been more confused by my new questions than interested in them. They were not of the type they had been trained to identify as malicious, products of an enemy of the people, questions which they were prepared to parry. And so I actually managed to find out one or two things. Sometimes I had the impression that my interviewees were even relieved—that for once they were getting a completely ordinary question, a question that concerned something they themselves had pondered; and since my official caretakers only squirmed in their chairs and I myself, the stranger, looked at them with so much sympathy, they answered quite willingly. And so I was free of the dates and figures, and instead of phrases I came back to the hotel with real answers like "two times a week," "a person cannot have an opinion about that," "there could have been more," or a pure, unadulterated "yes."

With every answer like that it was as if I had conquered a piece of this strange country, and I returned elated to the hotel in the evenings. The men in dark suits were perplexed. They seemed not to have any instructions on how to act in a case like this one, and our leave-taking at the reception was longer than usual.

"Were you really satisfied with the answers you got today?" they asked.

"Very," I answered, and they must have been able to see that I meant it, because they looked at me suspiciously. But they themselves had neither questions nor answers; they hurried with their good-byes, exchanged a few hasty words in their own language, and there was Mr. Miri again.

"*Did you have a nice day*," he asked.

"*Very nice*," I answered.

Mr. Miri smiled and reached for my key.

"Mr. Miri," I asked. "May I ask you something?"

Mr. Miri continued to smile.

"Do you believe in God?"

Mr. Miri looked at me. He smiled, it was the same smile as before, but the smile that had gone so well with *a nice day* did not at all suit his present silence. But still Mr. Miri kept smiling, just like a cat, who is not capable of more than two or at most three expressions, anyway. Mr. Miri could not get rid of his smile; it was glued to his face like a mask.

Back in my room I put my notes down with the ones already out on the table. Inspired by all of the new answers, I had started writing something coherent about this country. I counted the pages; it seemed that some of them were missing.

I ate breakfast earlier than usual the next day, and before Sali showed up I had a visitor; the parquet floor had not betrayed his presence, I only caught sight of him when he already stood right next to my table. It was Mr. Miri.

"*How are you today?*"

It was early in the morning. The two of us were alone in the dining room, and I asked him to sit down. Mr. Miri sat. Without seeming to be embarrassed at my presence, he began to adjust his white shirt cuffs, which protruded from his jacket sleeves. Mr. Miri's cuffs were white and folded; carefully he polished his cuff links with a napkin.

"How is your work going," he asked.

"Thank you, very well, it's progressing."

Mr. Miri looked around as if he were seeing the dining room for the very first time and was quite content with what he saw.

"And yesterday," asked Mr. Miri. "Did you have a successful day yesterday, too? *Did you see or hear something interesting?*"

"*Very interesting,*" I said.

A waiter without a bow tie or jacket pushed open the kitchen's swinging door, but then disappeared immediately into the kitchen again. Mr. Miri regarded his cuff links.

"*Very good,*" he said, and got up from the table. "*Very good.* You know that you can always count on my help. At any time. If there is something you do not understand."

He smiled at me and it was the same smile as the evening before: a mask's smile, but out of the mask's eyeholes a watchful gaze was directed at me, at a friend of Mr. Miri's country.

BUT EVEN THE MASKS WOULD DISAPPEAR, AND WITH THEM, MR. MIRI'S smile.

But first the coffee disappeared.

Or rather: the guests in the bar disappeared, not the coffee, and it was American dollars that chased them out into the street. For a while the old guests wandered around the hotel along with the beggars and dogs which had not existed before, but which now existed in abundance; one or two of them continued to stand there outside and looked into the windows in the evening so that he no longer resembled a minister or a chauffeur, but only a dog. Not even the ministers had imagined the end of their country's isolation like this.

[192]

None of them had any dollars, and when the coffee in the bar suddenly had to be paid for in foreign currency, the Italian machine stopped humming.

It was American dollars that had taken their coffee from them, but first statues had been toppled, glass had been crushed, and the Bible with space for a radio transmitter had disappeared from the museum, so that my worries about the songbirds and vanilla ice cream seemed ridiculous and offensive, at least for those who were engaged in toppling statues. Their attention was now focused entirely on the statues, and when the largest of these was forced on its end and proved to be hollow, they claimed that they had always known it, and I was silent, though there was something completely different written in my notebooks; just about the birds and the vanilla ice cream there was nothing.

My notebooks had become archaeological records, and I had put them aside, but since the statues soon were joined by other things, things that people had valued here and now had disappeared, the country's people began to be interested in what I had recorded over the years. Together we marveled at all the things that once had existed here in their country: mineral water, folk music, street cleaners, at least *one* egg, and coffee at a fixed price in the local currency.

One of the taps disappeared from my sink in the hotel room, so that I no longer had the pleasure of warm water, and in the dining room Sali stuck his hand into the ashtray to pick out the largest butts; the olives had already disappeared. For the waiters, this price for freedom was all too high, freedom should at least have been kept out of the dining room, and Sali's face was bigger than ever, yellow at the edges and swollen. Some grave disease must be eating him from inside, and even diseases like that had been unknown before, they were not allowed to exist; Sali's, too, must have had something to do with this freedom. The new freedom was hard on everyone and liberated everything without distinction: diseases and bitterness, people that had been exiled to the interior of the country, whole families—and so much liberty at once tired everyone out, so that they soon did not have sufficient energy to be happy about their freedom.

New guests turned up at the bar. A juggler, a one-legged girl on a crutch, a man with a sculpted eagle on his shoulder. Spartak, the juggler, provided me with new figures. For over eighteen kilometers and one hundred and six meters he had held a football in the air without dropping it. The waiters tried to drive out the new guests, but not very energetically. The waiters were accustomed to the old order and were afraid of the new one because they still had not figured out their places in it. Their arrogance was on the decline. They had thought that the world outside the hotel would one day perhaps become like the hotel's world; it had turned out precisely the other way around. In protest they had begun to eat up the food in the kitchen themselves instead of serving it to the guests. The new guests begged and tried to sell one thing or another, Sali poked around in the ashtray with his fingers, he coughed, and I took out my notebook to ask him about the birds; it was a Friday, the freedom was only a few weeks old.

"What birds?'

"The songbirds in the cages," I said. "When did they disappear from the hotel?"

"There have never been any birds here."

"The birds, Sali."

"There have never been any birds here."

"Do you remember Gjergji," I asked.

"Gjergji? What Gjergji?"

"The farmer we visited who believed in God. What happened to him?"

"He must have died. Probably drank himself to death. Too many foreign delegations to toast."

He smokes too much, I thought. Even if it is only butts.

"And the vanilla ice cream?"

"There has never been any vanilla ice cream here," said Sali.

"Why were we always friends," I asked. "Why was I forced to be a friend to a whole country? Was that really necessary?"

Out on the street, cars pass slowly by. The drivers honked, flags were waved in the air, a piece of a statue was being dragged a bit over the asphalt. The people screamed straight into the air. Where did the cars come from? There had never been any cars here. I could not understand what was being screamed out there. The noise was deafening.

On the steps we embraced, and I stuck a pack of cigarettes in Sali's pocket. He pretended not to notice; close up, I could see that his eye whites were yellow, and when I turned to go back into the hotel, Mr. Miri stood on the steps. He stood in his usual place inside the door, observing the cars that drove slowly from the great square to the university, a long line of cars, and people were leaning out of the cars, screaming or swinging flags in the air.

"Mr. Miri!"

I was honestly glad to see him, not everything could disappear, though Mr. Miri was not quite the same as before; the dark suit had been exchanged for a short red jacket with white arms, a much too tight jacket, so that his torso seemed bound, and the jacket almost lifted his arms from his body.

"*How are you today?*" asked Mr. Miri.

"*Fine, thank you,*" I answered.

Mr. Miri told me that he was no longer with the hotel. Now he was working for a private electronics firm, a business of the future. He smiled at me and carefully licked his lips; the tongue that disappeared between his lips was red and pointed.

"New times have come now," said Mr. Miri. "Do you understand? And I have my old mother to take care of."

"You have a mother," I asked, astonished.

Mr. Miri looked at me, and in his face I saw the same astonishment that he must have seen in mine.

"Yes," he said. "Don't we all have mothers?"

"Yes. I suppose so."

"Ninety-two," said Mr. Miri. "This summer she will be ninety-three."

He zipped open his jacket and took a business card from his wallet and gave it to me. On the card was the name of the electronics company and a telephone number.

The cars had turned at the university and were on their way past us again; the people were screaming and honking. The statue's severed legs slammed against the asphalt. The noise was really quite deafening. Together we looked out over the open square in front of the hotel where the men in dark suits used to drop me off in the evenings.

"The children are not going to school anymore," said Mr. Miri.

The demonstrators who drove back and forth on the street in front of us in that deafening noise could not have been much older than the children who no longer went to school.

Mr. Miri excused himself, a customer was waiting for him.

"If anything comes up, get in touch with me," said Mr. Miri. "At any time. I will always be at your service."

He bowed, hurried down the steps, and on the back of his jacket there were two nines in blue along with the name of an American sports team, baseball or hockey.

AN ALTERCATION BOUND ME TO M., THE GREAT HUNGARIAN WRITER; at the cost of considerable personal humiliation, a mutual friend had managed to wring from him the promise of a dedicated copy of one of his works for me. M. promised him that when he got the chance, he would give me one of his books.

At that time we did not even know one another. M. was famous for his spare style and for never writing any dedications in his books. Our mutual friend was forced to serve as our go-between, caught between arrogance on both sides: the poet's Olympian and mine preoccupied.

After our friend's intervention, the book was handed over to me in Vienna by M. personally. It was my very first meeting with M., who was stopping over in one of the Austrian Literary Society's guest apartments on a trip between the East and the West. A narrow elevator, filled with the smell of cabbage and cleaning fluid, carried me up to an apartment with dirty walls, almost completely empty of furniture. The book with a dedication was a kind of letter of introduction that our mutual friend had provided for me. Anything more would be my affair. M. wrote the dedication with a leaky fountain pen after inquiring after my wife's first name. With a grimace, he handed his own book over to me. When I was ready to go and standing in the doorway he said—as if it were a matter of reminding me to pick up a quart of milk—that our mutual friend was suffering from chronic headaches and from his marriage, and that he probably was dying, besides.

Dazed, I tumbled out into the winter night. It was snowing. A light and dry blowing snow; the winter was as yet just trying out its repertoire, and I had to walk all the way down the street to the Café Eiles to get a taxi. So much ink, death, and snow. And all of it at once!

When I got home and stamped off the snow, I put the book away.

I thought I was done with it for good; I did not have the slightest idea that I would soon take it out again. My wife's name was written on the flyleaf. Her name was misspelled. On the book's cover M.'s own name was printed in grand letters, in black with all of the dots and accent marks in perfect order. One glance at the pea-green cover sufficed for me to be reminded of disease and mockery.

In Budapest M. was considered a Francophile and an extraordinarily beautiful man. He has a name in Paris, they said in Budapest. He himself loves Paris and French culture; most of all he would have liked to be a French poet. That he is Hungarian is not his fault. Everything about M. is beautiful. His profile, teeth, and eyes are beautiful, and precisely like M.'s gestures, this beauty has spread to his texts. It has absorbed his art, which is admired even by his enemies and his critics. In the company of others his beauty seems to rise up, unbidden, to his surface, so that it covers everything ugly and half-finished within him.

To me it seemed that this beauty was a natural part of M. It was a part of his being, and I was sure that I would have been able to discern it even in the little boy M. in his sailor outfit. His beauty had been given him as a gift, just like the little sailor hat with its blue anchor of his childhood; but while M. had gradually grown out of his sailor outfit, he had, later in life, just as naturally grown into his beauty, until it no longer could be distinguished from M. himself, but fit as if it had been tailored just for him.

He had begun his career as a runner. M.'s beauty was that of an animal. It had to do with speed and legs, but such a beautiful body belonged to those legs that one really could speak of harmonious perfection. When blank paper became more of a challenge to him than the tape at the finish line, it was a trained athlete's body that took its place behind the writing desk. But M. wrote much more slowly than he ran. His books were few, but his beauty was such that it would have done fine even without books, and that his books happened to be few and rather thin only emphasized the unique beauty of both them and their creator. As a runner, M. had learned to husband his strength. And thus at that writing desk there was no lack of either stamina or conditioning. M. had the strength to wait for the right words—the fact that they appeared at such great intervals did not make him lose his head.

I wondered if so much beauty at once might not be a danger which threatened to destroy him. He must have been reminded of it all the time; it never left him in peace. Shouldn't he try to destroy all that beauty before it turned on him? Shouldn't he try to kill it for the sake of his art? Destroying one's own beauty ought to offer the possibility of salvation, and I could see how his beauty played tricks on him: when M. lit a cigarette for one of his admirers, this gesture was so perfect that no one noticed when the cigarette was not properly lit, and then it went out and had to be lit again. It was irritating. His beauty did not allow him to simply lift his hand and light a cigarette like other people, but his movement had to be at the same time a model, so that no one else was able to light a cigarette without having the image of M., lighting his, before their eyes.

When we met in Vienna I was fully occupied with just looking at him. M.'s beauty was of the devastating type. Our eyes met. In my eyes, M. resembled a dangerous, though quite content and somewhat simple, beast of prey.

I did not move a muscle. He stopped in front of me where I was sitting on the sofa, took a step closer, and let an ash fall from his cigarette into my lap, as if by chance.

Then M. began to walk back and forth through the room, but not restlessly, not as if the unfurnished apartment with its dirty walls were a cage, but as if he had just awoken in his own jungle and was now prowling around a smaller animal that would be just right for breakfast. I sat on the sofa and stared at him. Back and forth he went, across the room. A Hungarian beast of prey! The floor creaked under his feet, but not even the noise of his leather soles against the parquet floor took away the feeling that I actually was in a jungle, and no longer in Vienna.

At first I did not even want to leaf through the book he had given me that winter evening. I was afraid to meet with the same beauty there as I did when M., standing before me in the middle of the room, had lit a new cigarette and opened both eyes wide—they were blue—to listen to something he allowed me to say.

But in the long run I could not withstand the temptation. A few months later I opened the book to a random page. It was page fifty-six. What I found there was really the same blinding beauty the author possessed; between the covers of a book it seemed a bit cooler, more like marble than meat. I read a bit farther. My eyes glided over the pages without being drawn to anything in particular. To protect them from so much light, I slammed the book shut. For the second time I put away M.'s book, this time for good.

Out of pure envy.

Envy? Yes. Why should I deny it? It was pure envy, though I pretended that I had opened his book to convince myself that so much light and beauty were harmful for a poet, and that a poet afflicted by them would have to be led down false paths. But no shadow fell over what M. wrote. Without the slightest shelter, all of his words stood there in the middle of the merciless light; I had paged back and forth to see if there were not some dark corner, a place where the things that could not be shown were forced to congregate. I turned the pages and searched. Out of concern for M., of course, for the sake of his art! If I had found something ugly or simply unsuccessful, it would have made the glory of his art that much more obvious.

But without success; I found nothing. Besides, I was lying to myself. I did not do it on behalf of his art. What really disturbed me was that M. had been gifted with so much beauty; and on top of that, he was a person who—one only had to cast an eye at any of his book's pages—could write.

But despite everything I managed to discover something ugly in him. M. did not have any lips. When he fell silent, his mouth disappeared from his face. Then only his eyes and nose were left. Only when he began to speak did his mouth return, but as a thin, bloodless line, as if M.'s face had been slashed with the quick cut of a razor to open a place for a mouth.

I knew that I had hurt him by not reading his book and never thanking him for it. I had not even written about it in a few lines in a letter. But it was all of this beauty that came between us, and I avoided him. Still, I knew that we would not be able to escape one another in the long run; Vienna might be able to get along without Munich or Zurich, but not without Budapest or Klausenburg. We were doomed to run into one another again, and when finally, several years after our meeting in Vienna, it could be avoided no longer, the two of us were just as unprepared.

IT WAS AUTUMN, AND IN BUDAPEST THE GREAT AND SOON-TO-BE-great had gathered for a few days in order to discuss Europe and what Europe is, and there was M., too, in the same leather jacket he had worn in Vienna; only his hair was no longer silver-gray, but white. This did not make him any less beautiful. For this European meeting he had, perhaps because he felt that he was one of the hosts, prepared an address in his own language, and at the moment it was his turn to speak, his mouth appeared in his face. There it was again! But smaller than I remembered it, and the only thing the assembled European intellectuals could hear and recognize out of this mouth was *Guevara*, and this they did not understand. M. did not understand either; that he was twenty years too late.

Che Guevara.

Each time he uttered it, this *Guevara* sounded like an ingratiating concession to the incomprehensible mass of Hungarian words. Again and again the name of the dead Cuban sounded from M.'s mouth, and I ought to have whispered a warning to him. Any other name would have been better, even Guerlain, Goodyear, or Godiva would have been better names, but the assembled intellectual elite had already begun to whisper to each other so that M. finally fell silent and remained standing there in the middle of the floor, mute and alone. His mouth must have completely disappeared from his face at that moment, but I could not see it. It was already late in the day. The afternoon sun's slanting rays fell through the two windows behind M., filled the entire room, and blinded me. In the direct light, only M.'s Olympian profile could be distinguished.

M. remained standing in the middle of the floor. All around him everyone had begun to speak of other things. Why did I not go to him immediately? Shouldn't I have tried to do something about his solitude and my own embarrassment? He was stretching his neck a little; there was the beast of prey again, but now it was wounded and not so sure of itself. M. must have been offended by the lack of attention from Samstag, Trash, Enziansberger, and Fleckenmaul, who did not seem to understand why a Hungarian poet insisted on reminding them of someone they almost had managed to forget and no longer talked about.

But M. knew nothing of that. Not even his love for Paris would have helped him in this situation. It was too late. M. did not know all of the new names and words, and his own Hungarian words were of a completely different nature. He had had to wait a very long time for each and every one of them, words that had nothing to do with what the latest fashion prescribed; they were not there to be traded for just anything that came along.

Where had he come up with Guevara? I think he got it from an image. I think that he had allowed himself to be seduced by a poster: the one with the Cuban's face framed by his hair and beard, like a wreath of black flames, and with a gaze that does not meet the viewer's, but instead is turned toward a distant point over the viewer's head. Guevara's black leather jacket. The zipper chastely closed, all the way up to his throat. The beret with the solitary red star. Everything there pointed toward the future, not the here and now.

What M. saw must have spoken to him, though the Cuban had kept the beard that he himself usually shaved off each morning. But with a total lack of caution, M. had dared to go too close. Eye to eye with the Cuban he must have recognized himself—the same perfection, the same blinding beauty, a beast of prey like himself, but from a much more dangerous jungle than his own. From the other side of the grave the Cuban beast continued to rule his territory, and M. must have been one of his very last victims.

M. remained standing in the middle of the floor all too long, out of incomprehension or defiance (I hope it was defiance). Afterwards I was the only one who went up to thank him. It seemed as if he appreciated that, even if I had not understood more than two words of what he had said and did not understand why he wanted to talk about Che Guevara. But no one had told M. that everyone had stopped talking about the Cuban, this had escaped his attention, and that he did not know it had to do with Budapest; with the city's dark and moldy apartments, with its decaying floors, the rats and the corridors, with the smell of sweat and latrines.

I took his hand, though I had never read his book, despite his inscription. I saw that he was relieved that someone talked to him, anyway, but I also saw that his eyes took no notice of me; it was as if they were blinded by the disgrace that had just befallen him.

"*Merci*," said M., though he did not have especially much to thank me for, and we usually spoke German to each other. But *merci* proved to be a better word than *Guevara*; with the French word he won back some of his composure; he has, after all, a name in Paris. M. blinked several times as if he were just waking up from a troubling dream. He brushed both hands through his white hair, but when his mouth appeared once again in his face to form more words, not more than a single one came, the same one as before: Merci.

THE NEXT TIME WE MET IT WAS IN PARIS.

For my own part, I was escaping Eastern Europe. I had had enough of the depressions and all the things that did not happen, and I wanted to save myself from what was threatening to destroy me. Perhaps I exaggerated. But I had sought out Paris to lick my wounds and rest, and I felt that I had earned it. This soon proved to be a mistake. One does not rest in Paris. Here you are forced to be interested in everything that happens, even things that are completely uninteresting, and not only that, you are also supposed to have an opinion about them, an opinion that no one listens to.

How innocently I approached Paris! At a distance the city seemed to satisfy my requirements. From the perspective of Vienna, I had taken measure of Paris like a tailor, planning to cut a fine suit for myself; with a French suit in my closet, along with the Swedish and Eastern European ones that already hung there, I imagined that I would be fitted for any kind of society. This was yet another mistake. You do not make use of Paris. Paris uses you, or, more often, it does nothing with you at all. The mere thought of taking measure of this city—as if there were something you could measure it with—was a mistake.

Paris exists for its own sake. This city was its own measuring stick, and what existed outside Paris existed only to the extent that Paris allowed it to exist. For example, Berlin existed only in the image of Berlin that Paris had created and had nothing to do with the real Berlin (why should it?). This disoriented and confused the Parisian who, not content with a mere image, visited the real, existing Berlin, only to find himself completely uninterested in the Berlin that really existed, which he had taken the trouble to visit. The only question the Berliners might ask of him was *why, really?*

The Parisian, irritated by the Berlin that did not conform to his Parisian image of Berlin, soon asked the same question as the Berliners—namely, *why, really*—and returned to Paris in a mental state that only strengthened the Parisian image of Berlin at the cost of the real, existing Berlin. And with that the Parisian who had taken the trouble to visit Berlin was satisfied.

And so everything turned out for the best. The world—that is, the Parisian one—was in order.

Occasionally it did happen that Paris revised one of its images. One such Parisian image, for example, was that of the Hottentot. The Hottentot was painted in broad strokes and glaring colors; it was, in short, a magnificent image of an especially terrifying savage, with boars' tusks stuck through his nose and earlobes (though there were no boars in Namaland). Here was the perfect and complete barbarian, armed with an assagai. This was the very incarnation of the Hottentot, and it was not worth the trouble for a foreigner in Paris to point out that this Hottentot image was not only quite out of date, but completely false; the Hottentots had long since started wearing shoes, walked around in white linen suits, and could blow their noses as well as any Frenchman, without any animal tusks getting in the way.

To point this out would not have been worth the trouble, not in Paris, where the Hottentot's image trumped the real, actually existing Hottentot, who had long since taken up a nail file instead of a spear, and when I finally realized that—that I had worn myself out to utterly no avail in the cause for African development and emancipation—Paris suddenly produced a new image of the Hottentot: in a white tie and tails, newly voted into the French Academy, which will now soon be populated only by Hottentots, and Hottentot poetry began to conquer the world, that is, the Parisian one.

The old Hottentot image? It was put into the fire. It had disappeared under the bridges; nowadays it is used only on wrappers for oranges. In any case, it never existed. What had, however, always existed, was this Hottentot in tails. In a top hat and with a laurel wreath on his brow.

I had wanted to contribute something to Paris in exchange for that fine suit I was counting on. I had wanted to share something about life in the East, the real, existing life that no one in Paris wrote or talked about. But Paris only wanted to hear its own voice. Mine did not count. Although Paris knew nothing whatsoever about Eastern Europe, the city preferred to invent every possible Eastern European thing on its own instead of listening to me, and this refusal to take what I said into consideration was the most humiliating of all punishments because it was not even pronounced out loud, and yet carried out to the letter.

But I have a voice, too! Not an especially strong one, perhaps, one that belongs among the voices of the great chorus, but still unique enough not to be confused with any other.

One day in the Marais I found one of M.'s books in French at a secondhand book store. Of course I knew that he had been translated into French. But still it surprised me to find the book there on the shelf, and I put it back without looking at it. The most surprising thing was that M. was actually there, in Paris. He *existed*, though there was nothing about him in the newspapers, and neither of us was allowed to participate in the Parisian discurse. Neither were our countries, Hungary and Sweden, allowed in. The Parisians did not even care about those who were more important than M. and me. Not our politicians, statesmen, or poets laureate. We did not exist. We only appeared in the weather report: a low pressure center that pushed a mean little drizzle before it. But soon the sun would be back, and our countries would disappear again, and we along with them.

Every day I tried to read the French newspapers. I sat in one of the cafés in my neighborhoods around Rue de Varenne. *Garçon*, I called, and ordered a *café au lait*. My pronunciation was good and made me seem in some ways more Parisian than those who were African or Asian in appearance. I read the newspapers from the back in the hope that they might reveal something from that direction, from the other side, so to speak, before I found myself on the first page, where the articles and headlines meant nothing to me at all. Only the occasional news item in the French papers was comprehensible. The Bulgarian corn harvest or a strike in Poland I could understand, the same with a flood in China. But not much more.

All of my mistakes had made my position in Paris untenable from the beginning. Paris had not summoned me. That I had then forced myself in on my own initiative did not improve matters; it was impertinent, and Paris allowed foreigners like myself to play only the role of the admirer. Our task was to admire this city, and for the person who wanted to stay here it meant subjugation. Paris expected the foreigner to fall on his knees and kiss the hem of the city's skirt, to make his obeisance to all the local house gods and touch even the most disgusting totems with reverent fingertips. The more we were mocked and humiliated, the higher praises of Paris we ought to sing, and the obvious greatness of Paris lay not so much in what we praised the city for, but in the fact that no one escaped kissing the hem of her skirt.

For all of this, Paris did not ask for the conviction of our hearts; our hearts were already lying with our other organs on a plate, marinated and strewn with rosemary (served up with *frites*). Paris only demanded of our hearts that they pretended to respect and love, that the foreigner act as if what Paris announced as the latest truth really were the truth, and in that respect "Paris" was like any other ideology. What we really thought did not interest the city. Nor did Paris ask where you came from, or what you had done (which was completely irrelevant, since you hadn't done it here), or consequently about any of your views, which might well be the complete opposite of those that were valid in Paris. The only thing that was demanded was that you kept them to yourself.

What Paris was out after was an unconditional surrender, and one of my first lessons in this regard was about fish. We were eating fish. The Parisians praised their own fish. I tried to convince them that ours was better. Cold water is better than warm for fish that is going to end up on a plate. Warm water makes a fish dry and tough; all warm-water fish taste the same. My water was colder, but Paris explained that my fish tasted worse.

Had they ever tasted my fish? What kind of fish? Mine! Taste your fish? What a bizarre idea! Only for our salmon would they make an exception. But they only had flatfish here, I said. Flat? I stood my ground, but in vain. They did not listen to me and kept eating their own fish. I became loud and coarse. All you have here is flatfish from warm water, I said. Only ray, *la raie*, was worth eating, and that Paris for centuries had regarded its only worthwhile fish as cat food and poor man's fare was a secret satisfaction to me, the foreigner.

The ray is your only fish! But how could a foreigner like myself embarrass Paris? Every day the best fish in the world was eaten here. My fish quite simply could not be better than theirs; if it were, it would be here, in their water, and once I had fallen silent in my wrath and took a bite of their fish it was of course worse, even the ray, all of it was fish from warm water that had become so dry and tough that it had to be rescued with a sauce, but convinced that they had the best fish in the world on the plates in front of them, the Parisians were satisfied with just a little lemon. It was part of the Parisian passion to gulp down a really miserable flatfish as if it had been the very best flatfish ever to have lain upon a plate.

Paris wanted surrender, and all of us had to eat warm-water fish. That was the city's way of dealing with foreigners. Our only task was to admire this city as loudly as possible. Many put up with this, but so that they would not be completely humiliated, they magnified and gilded the things that no longer existed in Paris, but which once really had existed there and had been worth admiring. They named a painter who had composed his paintings with just little dots of color. They named a leg, lifted straight up into the air, and it was important to know the name of the artist (almost legless himself) who had painted it, and preferably also the name of the coquette who had once owned the leg swinging into the air.

The coquette's name was Ko-Ko or Kri-Kri; whole books had been written about her. In this way, Paris made herself admirable. But wasn't so much hysterical admiration dangerous for the city in the long run? What was Vienna's meanness and falseness next to this? Or Prague's mute, carp-like gaze?

I tried to free myself of the compulsion to surrender to the city by taking long walks. It was a way of reconciling myself with Paris; in my arrogance, I gave the city one more chance. But the implacability with which Paris demanded surrender of all who were foreigners here seemed to me to be reflected in the very lay-out of the city. It became an *idée fixe* that occupied my mind as soon as I began drifting through the Parisian streets.

The precisely straight allées in the Luxembourg Gardens or the

Tuileries: whips to beat me with. Place de la Concorde's strict geometry: not a fine suit, but a straitjacket. The boulevards that radiated from L'Arc de Triomphe: a wheel to be broken upon. The Eiffel Tower: an awl to pierce me.

Wherever I walked it was always the same, nothing but this grim self-absorption, disguised as beauty!

Paris was perhaps the capital of the world, but it was also a house of correction, and to my astonishment I discovered that I was not alone in that assessment. Other foreigners suffered here, too. They were suffering, though they did not want to admit it. They had decided to act as if the city heard and saw everything they did, as if Paris were watching over them and had the power to punish them for everything it registered and did not like. But even among themselves the foreigners of Paris avoided speaking about how they had surrendered to the city and how many humiliations they had already experienced. They allowed themselves to be whipped, and suffered in silence. Paris had gotten under their skin, but they preferred to wear their wounds like medals. Perhaps they were sometimes ashamed of it. But they did not want to talk about their shame, either, since they then might have been asked what they were doing here, anyway, and on their knees, to boot.

The time I stood in line in front of the prefecture during the cattle calls organized for extending residence permits, along with all of the others who did not really belong here in Paris, was the first time we were united and related to one another as foreigners: we had all fallen on our knees before Paris, but we tried not to let on.

No foreigner in Paris wanted to rise up against a city that he had—in full possession of his senses—decided to worship, whose attentions, it was true, he could not depend on, but where a hope lived on that he might be allowed to stay in some dark corner if he did not make too much noise.

I met many such foreigners and wondered what they needed Paris for. I myself had begun to think of leaving. It felt as if I were the only one trying to defend myself against this city. Was it out of pride? Out of arrogance; that is what those who had no intention of abandoning Paris themselves thought, and who therefore considered me an idiot. I did not protest. What I finally decided upon was of course both arrogant and stupid, but there was much too much at stake; in my situation I was forced to make use of both my stupidity and my arrogance. For if Paris had won, the city would have finally humiliated me so much that I never would have been able to recover. I would become like the other foreigners here; like one more Parisian life to be piled up with all the others.

I decided to withhold my admiration from Paris. I would decamp, just as I once had already decamped from Eastern Europe. I wanted to return to Vienna. Of course I cut a ridiculous figure, and Paris took as little notice of my decampment as it had of my arrival. The other foreigners saw my longing for Vienna as my total defeat. They began to treat me with contempt or pity. As I drifted through the streets with my head filled with the grim images of the beauties of Paris, the city could have taken me for any tourist or flaneur, but I knew: here there was only a choice between destruction or flight, and I fled—soon I would leave Paris for good, only three months after I suddenly detected M. among the throng during an evening walk on the Boulevard Saint Michel.

IT WAS A WET BUT MILD EVENING IN OCTOBER. MANY PEOPLE WERE out and about, and M. was alone; he did not see me. With the feeling that I was doing something forbidden, I began to follow him in the crowd. M. walked slowly, as one does who has no destination. For two blocks on the way down to the Seine I was able to study him secretly, as ashamed of not having announced myself as I was attracted by the forbidden.

M. stopped outside a restaurant. In the restaurant's window was an aquarium. Bubbles rose to the surface; the fish that still had not ended up on a plate pressed themselves against the bottom. M. regarded the fish. In Budapest there were only carp and pike perch. M. could not know that he himself was also being observed, and without an audience his beauty seemed to be at rest, as if it was not used when it was not needed.

Slowly M. moved through the crowd and I followed, close behind him on the sidewalk. I spied on him, and Paris was my keyhole. It was Paris now that gave me the chance to find out secrets that I never would have been able to trace in Budapest or Vienna, and what I saw was an Eastern European: a visitor in jogging shoes from the European provinces, who looked into the brightly lit cafés without going into a single one; a person who awkwardly stood outside the department stores, picking through the boxes of plastic-wrapped, remaindered books, without buying a single one; who shyly turned to look at the other evening wanderers without speaking to a single one.

I spied on him. I saw that M.'s movements had lost the surety of Budapest or Vienna, and that here in the crowd there was no one else who would notice this but I, another foreigner, about to leave Paris for good, and in order not to commit an even more unforgivable crime than the one I had already committed, I called his name, not once but several times, but the indifference of this city toward M.'s existence was so great that it did not even allow him to recognize his own name.

Only when I laid my hand on M.'s shoulder did he turn around, terrified.

"Oh!" His first words were something in Hungarian that I did not understand. Immediately he corrected himself with a *mon Dieu*. Purple and yellow neon light fell over his face; the furrows in it were deeper than I remembered them from Vienna or Budapest. It was a face on its way to drying out, an old man's face.

M. embraced me. It was for the very first time—we had never been so close to one another as in this embrace. He held me tightly in his arms, and this embrace would not have been possible if it had not been for the Paris he loved, a city which for me no longer meant anything at all.

In the middle of the Parisian crowd we stood there and held on tightly to one another, two foreigners who wanted to protect themselves from what was even more foreign to them, and from the warmth of his embrace I realized that he was a disappointed lover; that Paris took as little notice of him as of me, and that he knew it.

My happiness at this embrace was so great that I did not want to share it with anyone, not even with M. I excused myself. So sorry. I was in a hurry, I was on my way to an important meeting. I was already late.

I could see that this was a disappointment to him.

But what I had said was not true. Instead I went alone to Vagenende to eat oysters. I did not offer to treat M., though I was sure that he had only a few francs in his pocket and would not have been able to afford even half a dozen; not even of the very smallest ones.

THOSE OF US WHO DO NOT PLAY THE PIANO LIKE TO IMAGINE THAT pianists are equipped with long, slender fingers, and we are amazed when we learn that a pianist needs a broad hand instead, with short, strong fingers.

Probably we make that mistake because we so seldom encounter pianists in person these days—even piano lessons at home have gone out of style—we only hear pianists. But I do not have that excuse. I really *saw* Miss Maria. For an entire afternoon she sat on the sofa across from me, and still I did not notice the one thing about her that would have been important for me to see.

It is true that what she was telling me interested me to such a degree that I blinded myself to everything that did not have to do with her story, so that only afterwards—when it was already too late—did I realize that her story was really incomplete without what I did not see. But that is not a sufficient explanation, either, and I cannot even blame it on the table. Yes, it did stand there between us; the table hid everything from her waist down, so that what we actually saw of one another was not more than our heads and torsos. But now and then she must have reached for her coffee cup on the table, even lifted it to her mouth.

With which hand did she reach for the cup? Her right? Or was it perhaps with her left? I did not see it. Is Miss Maria right- or left-handed? I do not know.

One has to lift a coffee cup with one hand or the other; even Miss Maria. But the thought that continues to plague me is that even if she had happened to lift her cup in both hands, I probably still would not have noticed the one thing that was important for me to see.

Yes, I know: Miss Maria was nervous, and it is possible that her nervousness infected me. Miss Maria was very nervous. Even though she no longer had to think about being punished for what she confided to me, she seemed almost afraid, and Miss Maria did not mean to let anyone take her fear away from her so easily; I had the feeling that she was holding on to it as hard as she held onto the purse that she pressed with both hands into her lap, which was the first thing I saw when the doorbell rang and I opened the door to her.

Yes. I saw the purse.

I helped her with her coat, a worn, black coat, and it must have already frightened her that someone now wanted to ask her about her two employers, as if they were still alive. And a stranger, a foreigner at that! Could she be quite sure that they were both dead? And that death had really rendered them powerless? Still, she had decided to tell me what she knew, perhaps because all of us hold fast to what we happen to have. With both hands we try to hold it fast, and what Miss Maria had to hold onto was so dirty and bloodied that it could have stained her as well, though she herself could discover no stains; and in order to be rid of what she could not discover herself, she had decided to tell me what she knew.

But how? What light would be most advantageous for her story? Should she tell her story in the light of what she knew *then* and had experienced, or should she place it in the harsh and revealing light which now, afterwards, seemed to transform so much of what she had then known and experienced, so that she felt obliged to think about those stains again? Which light would be most advantageous for her? Not for her tale, but for herself?

Personally I believe that Miss Maria preferred the first light because she was used to it. She was used to half-light, she herself had never had any trouble orienting herself in it. And—cross her heart—it had never scared her, not then, not in the way it had scared so many others. This new and stronger light, on the other hand, troubled her; not so much because of its intensity but because she was not certain of its source.

And whose light was it, really?

But then she began to tell her story anyway, and the longer she spoke, the more her nervousness began to ease. Finally she could not be stopped. What she had to tell welled forth from her without order or reflection, and the light that fell over her story was neither weak nor strong, but flickering, so that there was never any real order among shadows and daylight, because, I believe—in retrospect—that she no longer knew herself what she ought to think about what she once was a part of: and this is Miss Maria's own story, as it was told to me in Bucharest.

MISS MARIA WAS BORN TO A POOR FARMER'S FAMILY IN OLTENIA. AFTER attending the village school, she got her nursing degree in Craiova, a sad industrial city on the road between Bucharest and Timişoara. In 1954 she was sent to Bucharest to continue her studies at the Party's cadre school, which at that time bore Andrei Zjdanov's name, the man who, under Joseph Stalin, suppressed and liquidated culture in the Soviet Union. At the cadre school she studies Marx and Lenin, but these subjects hardly seem to captivate her, and soon she is back in her old profession, with a position as a nurse at the Party's own Ştefan Gheorghiu School on Boulevard Armata Poporului in Bucharest. At that school, the Romanian cadres of Stalinist Party functionaries, journalists, and propagandists were educated, and it is here that she, by chance, meets the country's minister of health. The minister is kind to her and gives her some advice: get some training as a masseuse, learn physiotherapy. Learn all of these new methods of electric treatment!

Miss Maria does as the minister says.

For ten years she then massages teachers and the occasional student at the Party school, so skillfully that her reputation begins to spread in Bucharest. Even the *nomenklatura* gets word of her healing hands, and in 1965 the door to the inner circle of power opens—that year she begins to massage the wife of the minister of the interior, Marta Drăghici, on a regular basis, and then Ion Maurer's wife becomes her client as well.

Everyone is pleased with her. High ministers begin to call her; at home in her little apartment she gets a telephone installed at a time when there are hardly any private telephones in Bucharest. Miss

Maria has excellent knowledge of both anatomy and physiology, and she begins to develop her own type of massage. Not just anyone is allowed the chance to enter the inner circle. Twenty-three people before her have had the chance to show what they can do, but the ministers were satisfied with none of them. With Miss Maria they are satisfied. The ministers agree that her massages are better than those offered in the Crimea or in Karlsbad.

I was very good at my profession, Miss Maria tells me.

In February of 1968, Ion Maurer's wife is drinking coffee at Elena Ceauşescu's and telling her about Miss Maria. Elena immediately asks Miss Maria to come and massage her; this happens only a few days after the two ladies have had coffee together. In the beginning Miss Maria is hesitant—she is, after all, not a member of the Party, and she turns to Mrs. Maurer for advice. What should she do? It is true that Elena Ceauşescu did say to her on the telephone that all that stuff about the Party doesn't mean anything, the main thing is that Miss Maria should know what she is doing, but she is not entirely convinced. The Party is still the Party, and this worries Miss Maria. During her massage, Mrs. Maurer listens to her and solves the problem.

One does not say no to Elena Ceauşescu, Mrs. Maurer says. She is a very vicious woman, who takes revenge on those who do not do what she wants.

Mrs. Maurer says all of this in confidence to Miss Maria. But Miss Maria likes Elena immediately. At any rate, she likes her in the beginning of the story she is telling me; it is only when the end draws near that a different light falls over the woman Miss Maria massaged for over twenty years. Then she becomes a moody and restless woman who always calls her masseuse at short notice, and has her picked up immediately from her job at the Party school or the apartment where Miss Maria lives alone with her telephone.

The Ceauşescus have their own hospital in the palace where they live, several examination rooms with every thinkable piece of equipment. Most of the instruments and machines come from foreign countries. There is a swimming pool there with a sauna, several different shower rooms, and their own dentist's office. In one of the rooms there is a very special bathtub. When you turn on the tap, the water begins to bubble and boil. In this room, too, the staff wears white coats. Elena's behavior is correct; Miss Maria speaks of her the entire time as "the comrade," and it is meant to be neither ironic nor malicious.

Though she could hardly read or write, she was kind to me, says Miss Maria.

But very soon she discovers that Elena is driven by envy. Elena leafs through foreign magazines that she cannot read and envies the princesses and film stars she sees in the pictures. The pictures of them are more than enough. The very biggest magazines, the ones with princesses and film stars in color, get to be too much for Elena, and she tears them up. Everyone in the palace whispers of her thirst for revenge. And everyone lied to her and her husband Nicolae; it did not take long for Miss Maria to discover that.

In the whole palace I was the only one who spoke the truth to them, and when Elena realized that, she became quite friendly and began to confide in me, says Miss Maria. Though I was only a masseuse.

Even the officers from Securitate, who otherwise only screamed at everyone, so that even the ministers who came to visit lost their composure and began to stammer, were friendly to Maria. Even General Pleşiţă was friendly to her, and the ministers, who otherwise were only seen on television, began to smile at her, though some of them never visited the palace more than a few times, and then disappeared; and they disappeared from the television, too.

In a way I became part of the family, says Miss Maria.

But didn't she feel uncomfortable with the lies and all the screaming? Didn't that depress her? Yes, sometimes. After an especially difficult and worrisome day it sometimes happened that Miss Maria had difficulty sleeping when she got home. She hoped that the telephone would not ring. But at the same time, it did not disturb her all too much, since she knew that she was a person of good standing in the palace.

Even the doctors lied to the Ceauşescus. One of them advised Maria never to tell the truth if the results of their tests were bad. Nicolae, Elena's husband, always called in five or six doctors when he felt sick. After examining him, all six of them had to sign a report, and Miss Maria says that the Ceauşescus were especially particular about doctors' signatures. Nicolae Ceauşescu leaned over the paper and studied the names, which were written in ink at the bottom of the report, for a long time, and it seemed to me that the signatures were more important than what the doctors had found wrong with him, says Miss Maria. If their treatment did not work, he knew who the guilty parties were, and his memory was excellent. Nicolae Ceauşescu was a diabetic.

He even remembered things that others had forgotten long ago, says Miss Maria.

After Miss Maria had been in the palace for several months, Elena begins to come more and more frequently to her for consultations. Maria, what kind of affliction could this be? Elena knows that her masseuse is a registered nurse. She comes to her with her own tests, but also with her husband's. One time the test is for the iron content of Elena's own blood. It is then that Miss Maria realizes that Elena does not have the first notion about chemistry and cannot even read a simple lab report. She cannot interpret it.

Siderurgy, says Miss Maria. That means the study of iron.

At that time Elena Ceauşescu was already the chair of the Academy of Sciences, praised in the press for her groundbreaking contributions in the field of chemistry, and collecting honorary doctorates from universities throughout the world. But in the palace in Bucharest it is Miss Maria who explains the report and Elena who then scolds the doctors.

You swine, you are useless!

Miss Maria interprets, Elena scolds.

With pride Miss Maria tells me that she became in time a confidante in the palace, *o persoană de încredere*, the only one who now and then dared contradict Elena. In the palace there was a Dr. Schächter; a mild and nervous person who had long irritated the Ceauşescus. They had threatened to fire him so many times that Dr. Schächter had become used to being fired in the morning and treating his patients in the afternoon, before he was fired again.

One day Elena comes to Miss Maria with a test and asks if it might indicate some disease. Miss Maria takes a look at the test. It might, she says, have something to do with the liver. Enraged, Elena leaves the room and Miss Maria hears how she scolds Dr. Schächter in the corridor.

You are a liar! You are good for nothing, get out of here immediately!

Two hours later, as it is later rumored in the palace, Dr. Schächter throws himself out of the window of his apartment. In Bucharest there are many people who are supposed to have seen him with their own eyes, lying on the pavement. The doctor is dead. He has thrown himself out of his own window, and in the palace it is whispered that he did not do it of his own accord, but that someone helped him.

Dr. Schächter's death is too much for Miss Maria. A few days later she gathers her courage and asks Elena if it really had been necessary to scold Dr. Schächter about that test; he was such a nervous person that he should have been relieved of his duties long ago. Here in this house he was not treated as he deserved, in any case, Miss Maria is supposed to have said to Elena, and to me she says that no one else in the whole palace could have said to Elena Ceauşescu what she, Miss Maria, felt obliged to say in the Schächter case.

Elena avoids looking at her, she looks out the window. She is angry, but affected. What happened was not her fault. Doctor Schächter had already tried to commit suicide many times before. Everyone knows that certain people will try again and again, until they are successful, sooner or later. What can she, Elena, do about that? Besides, it isn't true that she wanted to get rid of him, the children were used to Dr. Schächter.

My children were all so attached to him, says Elena.

After that there is a rumor in the palace that Dr. Schächter is not dead at all, that he has been seen outside the country. A girl who works in the kitchen claims that Dr. Schächter is supposed to have been seen in Paris, dressed in a fur coat, getting into a taxi.

Nicolae Ceauşescu, on the other hand, was a good person, says Miss Maria.

After taking a hot bath and having his blood pressure taken, he has himself massaged. The Romanians are living in what is called the Era of light, and Miss Maria is kneading the person who is responsible for the light. With Miss Maria he talks about her family. He is interested in everything having to do with farming and what people talk about out in the country. He likes to give her advice about practical things, the kind of weather that is best for sowing or how one ought to help a cow calve, and he gives her to understand that it would please him if she, Miss Maria, took his advice to her family in the country, with a special greeting from him, Nicolae Ceauşescu. He also asks about her parents and their health, and on one such occasion she dares to complain. In the village their private plot of ground has been taken from them. They no longer have any potatoes.

Nicolae listens, lying on his stomach; Miss Maria is busy massaging his shoulders and back. Still on his stomach, he promises to fix the problem. Shortly thereafter Miss Maria's parents have their land back.

Did she ask for favors from Nicolae Ceauşescu for anyone else? No. Miss Maria shakes her head. That would not have been right. She could not bother him with such things, he already had so many other problems to take care of. She had asked Elena, on the other hand, to help her many times, but in vain. Elena did not lift a finger for her.

He was a very busy man, says Miss Maria. Oh, how he had to work!

Miss Maria was paid for her massages in the palace by the Ministry of health. Once she got a tip of two thousand *lei* when the Ceauşescus were especially satisfied with the treatment Miss Maria had given their son Valentin; Valentin had broken his leg, a complicated break in several places. Two thousand *lei* was a lot of money at that time, says Miss Maria. She seldom received gifts, almost never. She can only remember getting a piece of cloth for an outfit.

Of Nicolae Ceauşescu's problems, there was one that was especially difficult to treat and gave him a great deal of pain: he could not keep down what he had eaten. Nicolae Ceauşescu ate very little; a bit of lean meat, just yogurt in the evening, but everything came up again. As soon as he had eaten he had to go to the toilet, and that was not at all nice, says Miss Maria, everything came up again.

Even what he drank came up again. Red wine was what he most preferred, always in moderation, but after even half a glass he almost immediately vomited, so that the doctors, who of course could not be trusted in any case, wanted to put him into a real hospital. It could simply not go on this way. Nothing but his stomach was important to him now, and he no longer spoke to Miss Maria during his massage, he was only interested in the two hands that kneaded his stomach. He was silent. But no longer could she help him with her hands, and even today, says Miss Maria, it makes me sad to think of it, that he had those terrible cramps in his stomach and I could not do anything about it.

Instead of listening to the doctors, Elena consults with Miss Maria. If the massage won't work, they have to find something else to help him, just not a hospital. What does Maria think about the case? For her own part, Elena is convinced that her husband's stomach problems have to do with his nerves, his nerves are quite simply too bad. Miss Maria also tends to think that it's his nerves. She suggests a decoction; a tea with lemon peel prepared in a special way, an old recipe from her village back in Oltenia.

Miss Maria is convinced that nervousness resides in the gall bladder. It is there that it must be attacked, and with her special lemon peel; it simply will not do that such an important person eats to no avail. His suits begin to hang on him, soon people might notice that something is wrong, he has already lost thirty-six pounds, and at this critical moment Miss Maria convinces him to try her tea; and see, the cure proves effective—with the help of the tea, four cups a day, Nicolae Ceauşescu is relieved from constant vomiting. Miss Maria has made him healthy again.

She had a bad influence on him, Miss Maria says suddenly.

What she says does not come as a complete surprise. It seems as if she sensed that the constant and intimate consultations in the laboratory, all of her care for the Ceauşescus and her familiar tone with them, risk putting not only her story, but Maria herself, in a doubtful light, in that light that she most wanted to avoid, and I do not believe that this was a sudden insight. It grew slowly as her story neared its end.

A bad influence.

She often heard how the two of them argued. Elena screams: why don't you do as I say? Why don't you grasp anything? And Nicolae screams back: do not forget that I am the president of this country!

Elena used to even spy on her own children, says Miss Maria.

She nods as she says this; as if she still wanted to convince herself that this was just how it once was. Even her own children.

To me she was always friendly because she was afraid of being all alone in the palace, says Miss Maria.

In July of 1989 she goes for the very last time to the palace to massage both Nicolae and Elena Ceauşescu. It is the height of summer. Then everything happened so suddenly in December of that same year. In retrospect Miss Maria has difficulty figuring out whether it was really fair and a fate they had both deserved, though she does not mourn them. But in any case—on this point she is clear—they ought not to have been killed. One cannot kill people in that way. Especially not when the one who is doing the killing is Iliescu, who used to come and go as he wanted at the palace, who for years was like a son to Nicolae and Elena. Many times she heard how Elena asked him to bring up their son Nicu to be a good Communist.

When Miss Maria speaks of Ion Iliescu she becomes agitated; he is an evil man who brought foreign students to the country, Palestinians and others, while Romania's own children are not allowed to study.

SUCH A LONG WAY INTO OUR CONVERSATION THE COFFEE MUST HAVE been gone, but, as I said, if I had been quite certain about the coffee, I probably would have also noticed the thing I did not see.

Instead we look at one another.

I have talked much too much, says Miss Maria. And it was probably not interesting, either.

She is a little embarrassed, perhaps afraid again, too, for the second time this afternoon. But the stains are gone. With her tale she has washed them away, even the invisible ones. On this afternoon she exists not only through the dead bodies that she kneaded for two decades and which no longer exist, but also for the first time it is she, Maria, who is more important than Nicolae Ceaușescu's stomach.

Our leave-taking is hurried; the light outside has already turned to darkness. It is snowing in Bucharest, I watch her disappear out through the garden, she has thrust both of her hands deep into her pockets against the cold

COINCIDENCES

ALMA TELLS ME ON THE TELEPHONE THAT THE SAME EVENING THE two of us had been talking about E. M. Cioran (whom I had not read), he called her up, and for two hours he talked to her without pause on the telephone. Alma does not say what Cioran actually said, only that he thinks that there are way too many books written these days, and especially in France; but I could have told her that myself. And yes, also that he only writes when he is depressed.

"And when you are feeling good?"

"Then I take walks."

He takes walks?

Now he has invited himself to her house for Sunday, and Alma asks me whether she should serve tea or coffee; I have spent so much time in Eastern Europe, I ought to know. Since Cioran is a Romanian, I suggest coffee for him, quite certain that he is a tea drinker. Just to keep myself from being completely deflated by the fact that Alma will soon have a living and breathing Cioran in the same armchair where I sat just last week pontificating about him, I say that I, for my part, think he is a bit too precious, both in his lifestyle and in what he writes. There is an ingratiating and sweetly edge to all of his bitterness, a bright frame that makes all that Cioranian darkness really decorative when one hangs it up on the wall.

But Alma has only heard the word 'coffee,' no more, and when she abruptly hangs up, I discover that I have sliced the sausage and pickle for my sandwich on a page of newspaper that contains an article about Italo Svevo as the employee of a bank in Trieste.

But I, too, have worked in a bank!

Just like Italo Svevo or Witold Gombrowicz, I, too sat in a bank, for half a year in Frankfurt during the beginning of the sixties, and it is strange that I never before connected my adventures in the world of banking with two such important authors. A German bank at that time was still a remarkable institution. The discipline was strict. I never saw any customers, and we had more bosses than employees. My boss was from Stettin; as a child he had "played locomotive" with a raw egg in each fist, which he crashed against two eggs held by one of his friends. That was Herr Baldes. I myself had no duties in the bank, probably because my uncle was one of the Union Bank's three directors. But if the two other bank directors (not to speak of all of the department heads) had known how short his tenure in that position would be, I would certainly have been sent out to run numerous errands.

There I sat at my desk, just like the others, but I cannot recall that I wrote down one single figure. What did I write, anyway? A few years before I had begun a journal. I conceived it as a kind of handbook without knowing exactly for what: in it I wrote mostly ideas, poems, or some particularly successful phrase that I wanted to remember. But in Frankfurt I must have really been playing the role of bank employee. I came on time, supplied myself with an umbrella, and carried myself with a stiff dignity that I have had difficulty getting rid of later in life. In the heat of the summer I wore woven shoes to keep my feet as cool as the bank's offices, shoes that aroused the ridicule of the girls at the newspaper stand, a thin brunette with a few strands of red hair at her forehead and her plumper, black-haired colleague, the only girls I met in Frankfurt who awakened my desire.

For half a year, the two newsstand girls were the only ones I dared approach. But my shoes put me to flight. My conception of business dress also made me the object of ridicule at the place where I ate goulash every day for ninety *pfennig* among the Balkan *Gastarbeiter.* That was my lunch. It was important not to get grease stains on my shirt or tie. No one sat. We all stood at the same high, round table and shoveled in our soup while chewing on a piece of bread; I had hung my umbrella from the edge of the table.

The goulash was a requirement for my entrance into the world of high finance. I saved all the money I had, the apprenticeship money from the bank and the small amounts my father sometimes sent me in an envelope. My plan was to buy stocks. In the bank I had picked up the tip that Neckermann was supposed to be a good investment; it was supposed to rise, and if I stuck to my goulash for half a year, I would be able to afford to buy five—or maybe even six—shares of Neckermann stock in the fall.

And I was really writing, too, but no poems; in light turquoise and yellow folders I was sorting my notes and excerpts from the German stock market and corporate laws, determined to kill two birds with one stone by improving my German with the study of laws and ordinances. I wrote as legibly as possible, convinced that neat handwriting would make the foreign language adhere that much better to my brain. Thanks to my uncle, I had the advantage of being able to devote myself to the planning of my future fortune quite openly.

No one at the bank was interested in what I was writing and arranging in those folders, while at Banco Polacco in Buenos Aires, Gombrowicz must have had a much harder time. It is strange to think that such an important writer must have been forced to stash his own papers, his *real* papers, as soon as the lowest bookkeeper walked by. While the bank existed for me as a possibility of gaining a fortune or at least a future position in the circles of finance, Gombrowicz must have experienced it as a structure just like any other structure, as something hateful and ignominious that kept him from his writing.

Still, it was during his time at the bank that Gombrowicz wrote his journals, which I value more than his novels. And without the bank, I dare say, the journals would never have come into being. Anyone who knows anything about the world of banking knows that it is not exactly a place for experiments or caprices, which is why we should not imagine Gombrowicz's journals as anything other than a pure dividend from the bank, that is, the only literary genre that was available to Gombrowicz when he returned home, exhausted and bored after a long and idiotic day of work. It is the bank and nothing else that forces him into this literary form. Instead of writing a novel or a play, either of which requires a well-conceived structure, in the evenings Gombrowicz empties the strength that the bank did not already claim into his diary. For a page or two, and on some days no pages at all, he pours out all of the immediacy that a bank has no use for whatsoever, an immediacy that would drive it into bankruptcy.

One ought to imagine a bank not only as a discreet business enterprise, but as a activity based exclusively on routine, a conscious limitation of both fantasy and, above all, spontaneity; that is, a bulwark of the fully intentional mediocrity that I had so perceptively adopted my very first week in Frankfurt.

But while I was prepared to lose myself in the world of banking and finance and thus did not write anything, Gombrowicz, in his genius, understood how to use the bank for his own purposes, how to let the bank serve as a godparent to his journals, the works which, along his great intellectual agility, paved the way for his rescue from the bank and his revenge on all of the bookkeepers and their figures. Here I see the decisive difference between Gombrowicz and myself. The bank is indeed a structure to which Gombrowicz was forced to submit for years, a structure he could not immediately crush, but out of which he still managed to slink, while I sat there in Frankfurt and noted the latest stock market figures in my folders in the belief that it was in this way that I would advance in the world.

Neckermann was a department store chain. The owner was a dressage rider and an Olympic gold medalist, and already during the spring the stock rose sharply and put an end to any further plans. Nothing came of my fortune in the stock market. The girls in the newsstand giggled when I showed up in my woven shoes to take a free look at the Swedish newspapers. One day one of the bosses from the trust department walked past on the street as I stood there as usual, shoveling my goulash into my mouth alongside the Serbs and Albanians. I think that he saw me, but as far as I could find out, he never made use of his discovery.

That was Herr Just. Herr Just resembled Cioran in that he liked to walk; instead of eating he often used his lunch break for walking laps around the neighborhood.

But somehow new to me is this connection between "bank" and "walk": both of them seem to destroy the great novelistic literature, both allow only private notes; it makes no difference, really, whether a person is a flaneur here in this life or chooses to sit over columns of figures.

In a bookshop on the Boulevard Raspail the other day I browsed through one of Cioran's latest books—out of purely professional interest—and I found texts in it that were not more than two or three lines long.

Lines, not sentences.

LOLA

OF ALL THE ODIOUS TIMES OF YEAR IN VIENNA, CARNIVAL IS THE MOST odious, when the Viennese disfigure their already ugly faces with even uglier masks, and I knew this all too well, so I would have postponed my visit, if it had not been for what I had to do in Vienna.

Carnival. I could never understand why Lola had settled down in Vienna. Why not in Cracow? Wasn't that where, despite everything, she still had her friends (the ones who were left)? Or near a bank in Switzerland? But Lola had decided on Vienna, and that is why twice already today I have looked for the waitress at Sirk, the redhead, both times in vain, until one of her colleagues in a brown-and-white-striped apron explains that she is working the evening shift, so now I am here for the third time today.

But this time I do not take off my coat.

This evening is the ball at the Opera, and the Viennese have left their masks at home; their faces no longer have anything to hide behind. Some of them are still standing at the bar at Sirk, drinking champagne from tall glasses. Others, dressed for the festival in white tie and tails or long dresses strewn with stars and moons, are on their way across the street to the Opera. On the terrace, now closed, which opens out onto Mahlergasse, the winter's Christmas trees lie in piles; as yet they have not begun to shed their needles. Someone is sitting at Lola's table in the corner looking out onto Mahlergasse; an unknown face.

When Lola died, I was completely inconsolable, and for a long time I did not know what to do with myself. The telephone rang in Paris. Someone called me from Vienna and told me that Lola had died of a heart attack in Copenhagen. Even before the trip she had been worried about having to change trains in Hamburg and about the hours of waiting on the platform. Her death had been instantaneous. She was said to have died painlessly, but all of that distance over the telephone piled up, between Copenhagen and Vienna and then Paris, making me even more inconsolable, and on the telephone the names of the three cities canceled one another out, so that no place on earth seemed to be left for Lola.

I hung up and walked over to the window. Down there the Portuguese doorman, dressed in a green apron, was busily sweeping the courtyard. The broom moved over the paving stones, back and forth, just like yesterday, tomorrow and the day after, just like every day, with the implacable motion of the mute and mechanical works of a clock.

Lola was dead. One Monday in January she had fallen in a street in Copenhagen. During the coldest winter in human memory she had taken the train from Vienna straight through Europe to see her daughter. Lola had died of a heart attack in Copenhagen, with a bottle of wine in a paper bag. Should she buy one or two bottles? Lola had argued with Janka about the wine that morning, and what I had come to Vienna and Lola's favorite café to say to the red-haired waitress was that not even this completely normal death had been of any comfort to me in Paris, though Lola, despite everything, had left the world in a completely different way from the one that had once been decided for her.

Lola was dead instead of the German she had been begging me for years to kill for her. She had settled on me to do it; I was her proxy in this matter. Despite the fact that she usually presented her murderous plot with great seriousness, I always tried to laugh it off, but it was a nervous laugh. Did she want to test me? Still, the contrast between her murderous intentions and her fragile, almost frightened presence was so comical that it undermined most of the threatening aspect of her plan. Only the fantastic and troubling aspects remained. Lola smiled a little herself at her plan, but I could not forget that she still intended for me to be the one to put the plan into action. The assignment was mine, and she acted as if we were out in the country and she was sending me out to behead a chicken for the pot. But I had never had any desire to kill a German, and I began to see it as my duty to prevent this murder.

"You can't be serious," I said.

"What?"

"About killing a German."

"Oh, pooh; just one."

As usual we were sitting together at one of our downtown cafés; at her Sirk, at Landtmann, Tirolerhof, or at my Bräunerhof. She preferred Sirk because the waitresses there were friendly to her, especially the redhead, who Lola was sure came from Poland, despite the fact that she hadn't managed to squeeze a single Polish word out of her. "I'd bet my life on it," Lola used to say, "the redhead is from Poland!" For some reason she had decided that Bräunerhof stank of cooking. She avoided Bräunerhof. Usually I went along with that.

But the murder was never far away, and stubbornly she returned to it: before she herself went into the grave, she wanted to take the life of a German, any German, and the only too apparent absentmindedness with which she returned to the subject again and again embarrassed me, then made me nervous, and Lola noticed it and fell silent.

Every time we met it seemed to me as if she had shrunk, as if she were on the way to removing herself from the world, peacefully and very slowly. Lola was in no hurry. She looked at me searchingly from below; only her brown eyes grew larger every time. Her face was wise and wrinkled. It resembled a walnut. It was unpleasant to realize that I had a much better chance of succeeding at murder than Lola. A murder! I fell silent and hoped that the subject was closed, at least for this time, and that our conversation would soon take another direction. We shared a piece of apple strudel and each drank a glass of wine. Still, I could not help asking her how she thought it should be done, more out of politeness than true interest.

She shrugged her shoulders.

"*Nur so.*"

This calmed me. It was all too obvious that Lola was not concerned about the matter, not its practical side in any case, and therefore could not have begun any preparations. But even if it calmed me to know that she was not carrying around cyanide or a hammer in her purse, it was already bad enough that just any German would satisfy her. If it was the case that she had to kill a German, she ought to have sought out someone worthy of her revenge. But just anybody? Why did she want to leave the victim up to chance when there were still a few Germans left who boldly, without a mask, dared to present themselves like any one of us, but who really deserved Lola's, that is my, hammer? Some of them were still alive.

"Take one of those Germans," I said. "Not an innocent one!"

Otherwise she could just as well leave all the Germans to the mercy of their God or the secular German legal system. My arguments seemed to amuse Lola, and I continued with irritation: wouldn't it be an even grander plan to forgive them all? Each and every one of them?

"That would be another way to take care of things," I said, "without having to involve me or any tools." Surely it would be a better way of improving the world than beginning to kill people once more.

But Lola's interest in improving the world was not especially great. She persisted: a little, obstinate, stubborn lady who wanted me to kill a German for her; Lola looked around where we happened to be sitting, at her Sirk, at Landtmann, Tirolerhof, or my Bräunerhof, as if she hoped that she might be able to find her German right there. To improve the world was not her concern, but maybe her desire for revenge was not of much concern, either. It seemed to me that Lola's own youth interested her more than both the improvement of the world and revenge, which was why the murder she kept pondering seemed even more incomprehensible.

Lola wore provocative makeup, much too excessive for her age. She dressed elegantly and expensively. It was her fall and winter wardrobe that showed her to her best advantage. Lola's colors, too, were autumn colors; the autumn and Lola went together on the color spectrum, where winter was starting to settle in without summer having been driven completely out. The autumn was her time of year. She must have decided to stay put in autumn once and for all, even in the summer, when she took off everything she was wearing to sun herself all day long at the open-air pool in Krapfenwaldl. Without a stitch on, she sunned herself through the summer.

Then came autumn. The doors to the café flew open—her Sirk, Landtmann, Tirolerhof, or my Bräunerhof—and there she stood: bronzed, almost black, in her new autumn outfit.

I was her cavalier. She had chosen me to be her German-killer, but also her very own cavalier, a decision dictated by love and without her ever having asked me. I let her have her way, though her advances embarrassed me. At those times, Lola was the young woman she had never been allowed to be, and about that young woman I knew next to nothing, only that she sat across from me on the other side of the table in a café in Vienna. She painted and powdered herself in front of me. It embarrassed me. But I let her have her way, leafing through a newspaper or two in the meantime, too proud to give her the least reason to suspect that I would allow myself to be fooled by an old woman playing a young one. I was more disturbed by the fact that she provoked ridicule, even if I were the only one who noticed it; everyone else was concerned with their own affairs. But still, it was not appropriate behavior; Lola must have already frightened away the men of her own age.

Where were they now? At her age perhaps no risk was very great anymore, but to try to tie me to her with a sloppily conceived murder plot did not speak well of either her judgment or taste, and I was embarrassed. Lola saw that something was troubling me. I was silent, and this, too, amused her; both the old and the young woman. Lola had the habit of looking at herself in a little pocket mirror. This was another way of courting me. She studied herself in the mirror, and I discovered that I had laid my hand over hers; against the flat of my palm I could feel the veins under her skin. Even in the summer they shone blue-black straight through the sunburn. I kept my hand over hers, and for this lack of caution I paid with pity; I felt sorry for her.

Out of vanity I had laid my hand over hers. Out of arrogance I had kept it there, the arrogance vanity easily grants a younger man in the company of a much older woman.

"*Kochasz mnie?*"

"Yes," I answered.

"Really?"

"Yes, Lola, really. I love you."

With that she was satisfied for a while. But it disturbed me that we should need to take someone's life in a place like a café, an unknown person, too.

One summer evening at my place on Vegagasse I took Lola around the waist and danced with her in the living room until both of us fell down. I had tripped on the rug. We had been at a garden restaurant in Sievering; she was actually on her way home to Taborstrasse, but it was a cool summer evening, and half-way there we had stopped at my place to drink another glass. We fell down, Lola, thank God, on top, and for a moment we lay in one another's arms on the floor like two dead people; I had her breath in my face, and through the thin material of her dress I could feel her heart beat.

The windows were open, outside it was already late in the evening and dark. The evening drew the curtains out into the darkness and slowly blew them into the room again. In my fright I had thrown my arms around her, her already old woman's body, but a body that others had once decided would never get as old as it now was, so that this embrace, in a young man's arms, was a double triumph for Lola. The old woman who clung tightly to me on the floor, afraid to have broken something so that she could not get up, was at the same time the young woman who the old woman had never been allowed to be, and as I held the old woman in my arms, the young woman held me greedily in hers.

I was not blameless. I, too, was guilty of shameless advances that were meant for the young woman the old woman had never been, a young woman who had been where I had not. That she once had been *there* gave everything the old woman said and did—or did not say or do—a special meaning, though the old woman revealed so little of what the young one had experienced; almost nothing, and it was precisely the things that were not revealed that captured my curiosity.

I lay in wait for Lola. With an instinct that was deeper than I probably could have understood, she must have immediately felt this. A great deal of the time I spent together with her was in a state of tense anticipation that she would begin to tell her story. I told myself that it was just a matter of waiting her out. I smoked a cigarette, and then another, but as a pretense, just to get the time to pass. Just what I was waiting for was not clear, and if Lola looked amused as I smoked my cigarettes, it could have been because she knew that I waited in vain.

In my advances there was of course a good deal of presumption. What I hoped was that in her company I could go where she once had been. I wanted Lola to remember and tell what she had given herself pains to forget. I did not want to understand that this was asking too much, that not even the fact that she had not managed to forget anything at all meant that she was planning to tell me about it. She did not tell anything, and when she was reminded against her will of what she did not want to remember, when Lola sat up stiffly in bed, in a cold sweat, surrounded by darkness, I was not there with her; when she might have been able to tell me something, I was sleeping my deepest sleep, the innocent murderer's sleep, a sheep who had no place in Lola's hour of the wolf.

When she was awake, I was asleep. And when I was awake and with her, she was also there, to be sure, but already cool and powdered. Lola made her advances to me again, I was ashamed and looked around, but at her Sirk, Landtmann, Tirolerhof, or my Bräunerhof, no one seemed to notice us.

"*Kochasz mnie?*"

"I love you."

"Really?"

"Yes, Lola, really."

I never did manage to get her to tell me anything of real importance. What Lola sometimes had to say was not more than a handful of sentences in which the words seemed to get in the way of each other, more like a mechanical jingle or a spell than a real tale, like the dark side of the declarations of love she forced from me. The little I was able to find out did not betray any particular intention to humor me. Instead she gave me a sentence or two for quite a different reason: to protect herself from the things she was convinced could not be told, not under any circumstances. What she said to me, I think, was intended to kill all of my hopes to ever get to hear any more. So we ended up at one or another of our Viennese cafés, to retreat there into the innocuous. We told each other jokes without finding them funny, we spoke to each other like a brother and a sister, often without words, as if we were laying out a game of solitaire to kill time, but without any interest in winning.

Actually Lola repelled my advances much more decisively than I repelled hers. Here the German was of help to her. I had turned out to be much too forward, so to protect herself, she had come up with this German and put him between us. I was allowed to lay my hand over hers, but not to get too close to her. At those times, Lola was entirely the young coquettish woman she had never been allowed to be. At Sirk she pulled her legs up under herself and sat in the corner of the sofa; I saw her shoes under the table, they were suddenly empty, and she dispatched the German to keep me in my place.

"Can you kill one for me?"

There stood the as-yet-unmurdered German between us to remind me of the only way to get to the place where Lola had been, and since she did not want to see me killed—for God's sake, anyone but me!—it was my duty to take on the German. A single German, any one, was not a high price. But it was still much too high for me, and only after Lola had died did I understand how important it was for her to make clear to me that I could not afford what she had gone through, and so I ought to leave her in peace.

And why did I want to go where she had been? Her own direction was a different one: Lola did not want to go back there, but *here*, to me; she was still uncertain about whether there was a place for her in the world, whether her place had been forfeited by being where she did not want to send me.

"*Kochasz mnie?*"

"Yes," I answered. I no longer knew how many times I had said it.

"Really?"

Only once did I go home with Lola to Taborstrasse. Her apartment was almost empty. It was furnished with a few simple and cheap objects that had no meaning for her; a table, some chairs, a sofa. There was no cloth on the table. She put a glass of wine on the table in front of me while she took out a box that turned out to contain photographs. The photographs were in black and white, and I was fascinated with some of them that showed a young and rather ugly man with a tennis racket, some young people on skis in a snowdrift, and a girl in profile. They had played tennis before the war broke out. They had gone skiing. All that was left of what they had done was in the old woman's box. The box contained the only images from young Lola's life.

Then the war had broken out, and the images from the war were in Lola's head. There were more of them, and they were more distinct than the ones in the box from before the war. The images in her head belonged to the night. They kept her awake, and at night she was alone with them.

The images in the box, on the other hand, were intended for the day. During the day she was not as alone as she was at night, and Lola tried to make the day last as long as she could; during the day Sirk, Landtmann, Tirolerhof, or Bräunerhof kept her company, so that the cafés became almost like another home, or at least another box.

THEN LOLA'S FORMER EMPLOYER DIED. IT WAS A HARSH BLOW FOR her. We read about it in the newspapers: he had drowned while taking a swim in the sea. It was in every paper, but she doubted it even though I showed her the bold headlines and the articles in such reliable papers as the *Neue Zürcher Zeitung, Le Monde, Frankfurter Allgemeine,* and even in the *Herald Tribune,* though Lola did not understand any English. Together we bent our heads close together to read even the fine print, excerpts from court transcriptions and the dentists' testimony, and reluctantly she came to the same conclusion as the rest of the world: everything indicated that he really had drowned while swimming alone in the sea.

Lola was disappointed. This was not how she had imagined it. Actually, he had been of more use to Lola alive and unpunished than dead in this disappointing way. It was a much too normal, much too banal death, and it did not help matters that I tried to improve on the story for her. "It must have been God Himself who drowned him," I said, "He took him by the heel between His thumb and forefinger and dragged him down under the surface, He held Mengele down there so long that both of his lungs filled with saltwater and he died."

But we were not quite certain that it had happened in just that way. And how were they able to assert that it was he, he alone, and no other? Among all of the murderers and swimmers of the world? Lola did not lay the newspapers in an orderly stack in front of her as she normally did. She no longer looked through them, but let the papers lie as they fell over the marble tabletop, as if they had come to be there by chance, a stream of news that did not really concern her. But she cast quick, stolen glances at them from the side, like a cat eating from its dish.

The same thing was written in *Le Monde* as in the *Frankfurter Allgemeine Zeitung*, and even in the *Volksstimme*, but it was only when he was properly drowned in the *Neue Zürcher Zeitung* that she gave up.

"You see," I said, "Zürich would have been a good city for you. Or Lucerne. All the cows and everything."

There were some days when she did not want to believe anything at all. She had slept badly and she refused to believe that he really had drowned; she was convinced that he was peacefully swimming on in some warm ocean while the newspapers kept writing that he had drowned in a different one. Neither did she want to believe that God had had a hand in the business, the same God who had been absent

where Lola and Mengele had met—that God should suddenly be on
the spot to drag Mengele into the depths off the South American
coast after so many years was one of my worst jokes. It was more
credible that Mengele was a poor swimmer, that he had overestimated
his powers, and that is why he drowned. But she was against such a
rational and flat explanation and wished for Mengele to be alive
again.

"People can not just die any old way."

Two times Lola had stood eye to eye with Mengele. Once she was
forced to do it on her own account, the other time voluntarily, for a
friend. Lola stepped in for her friend. She said "stepped" but it turned
out in fact that all of them had been forced to run, and when she told
me about this at Sirk, the most important thing for her had not been
that her friend was so sick that she could not run, and that Lola had
therefore saved her life, but that Lola had been a different person
then, so young and healthy that she could take such a risk without
thinking about it.

Both times she had tried to look him straight in the eye. Cheekily
she had stared at him, she told me at Sirk, and Lola was frightened
by her own word: cheekily. She giggled, holding her hand in front of
her mouth, as if she were still the young woman who had twice been
forced to run for her life in front of Mengele himself, and it was not
so much the presence of death as her own youth that preoccupied her
in the telling of her tale. Cheekily she had looked him straight in the
eye. She had been young, and it was her past youth that now gave her
the strength to tell me how it had been, speaking with the frivolous
terror or the terrified frivolity that made up the entire difference
between the young woman back then and the old woman on the sofa
in front of me at Sirk.

The newspapers wrote that Mengele was dead. But she had not
imagined it like this. Nor had her old employer kept his word. Work
had not freed them; the ones who had worked were almost all dead,
and the few who had survived, like Lola, were not free. It was true
that she had re-entered the world, but without anyone noticing; in

that way the world was at least the same as it had been, not much different from when she once had been removed from it. But the world went on in the same mute, mechanical way as before, despite the fact that Lola now was back, and it soon became clear to her that it must have gone on the same way while she was absent, and that it would continue to do so tomorrow and the day after, just like every day, so that her place in the world was still just as uncertain as it had been back when she had thought that the world was a safe and secure place.

Guiltily the world had made room for her. But soon it was taken up with itself again, and Lola no longer trusted it. If there had been another world, she would not have had anything against exchanging hers for it.

"*Kochasz mnie?*"

"Lola," I said. "Not again."

But it was precisely those words that were her formula for getting back into the world again. Do you love me? Incessantly she repeated the same question, with a stubbornness that soon became tiresome, and finally irritating even to her, just to convince herself that something like love really still existed. And then there was that short moment of fear—that I would not answer yes, I love you. It was all she had.

A few words and a box.

That is how your loneliness looked, Lola, and I defended myself against it. How often I was bothered by those meetings in cafés that broke up my day, while you did not have a day to break up! How often you insisted on my attention to things that did not interest me and never would interest me; how often I lied to get out of having to meet you at your Sirk, Landtmann, Tirolerhof, or my own Bräunerhof; how often did I hide behind projects at work that did not exist, articles that were not written, people I had to meet who were made up. How predictable everything you said was—and what I really wanted to hear, you did not tell. There I was, forced to listen to your stories until I was exhausted, until I no longer knew if you were grinding them out again out of meanness or forgetfulness. You did not want to remember anything, but you demanded that you have me at your disposal so that you could call me in the morning when I was still asleep, long before breakfast, to tell me that you had not been able to sleep.

As if I could have given you your lost sleep back! You had been reading all night. Until four in the morning you had read a book, not until dawn had you fallen asleep. Did I want to borrow the book?

"What book is it?"

"The book about Wallenberg that you lent me."

"I did not lend you that book. I don't have a book like that. Do you want to lend me a book about Wallenberg?"

"The book about Wallenberg that you lent me. *Kochasz mnie?* What are you doing?"

"I am talking to you on the phone."

"Do you want to borrow it? Can I depend on it?"

"On what?"

"That you love me."

"Yes, Lola. I already said that."

"When did you say it? Do you really think that he is dead?"

"How should I know? Maybe he is dead. Maybe he is sitting in Siberia."

"Not him, I don't mean Wallenberg."

"Lola, I haven't even had my breakfast yet."

"No breakfast? You have to eat a proper breakfast. Promise me that! Will you call me tomorrow for sure?"

"Yes, why do you ask such dumb questions. I promised I would." "Yes."

"Why do you ask, then?"

"*Nur so.* How long will you stay with me?"

"How do you mean?"

"Before breakfast, you will call, do you promise?"

"I promise."

"When do you eat breakfast?"

For Lola it was more difficult to begin the day than to end it, despite the fact that in the morning she had the night behind her, the night, which she feared most of all. Or had the night already taken all of her strength? At night her memories awoke. She struggled to keep them away. She was afraid that they would swell in over her, crash above her head like a black wave, and pull her into the depths, where her old employer, Mengele, was.

Lola called me more and more frequently for help to begin her day. Her voice on the telephone made me see a room with drawn curtains; behind them a solitary person, dragging herself between the unmade bed and the sofa in the living room. On the telephone she was only a voice, an old an confused one. Early in the morning the difference between her night and her day was still not big enough, but in the morning I was there for her to wake up: a person who slept well at night, and who had begun to pack to move away from Vienna.

Lola was against Paris to the end.

She did not want me to move. Lola looked tired under her sunburn; with me in Paris she would be even more lonely in Vienna. We paid. I went and got her coat, and when we had finished getting ready to go, she asked another couple of cautious questions that were formulated to be answered with a "no," "nothing has been decided for sure," or "we'll see," and when I answered just as she had expected, she made one of her wonderful faces. It was already decided that I would move to Paris. Lola knew that, but she did not want to hear it, and I did not tell her. I wanted to believe that a half-truth was better for both of us as long as it was not a complete lie.

So I moved to Paris, and Lola died in January before I had the chance to tell her that on the thirteenth of February I had moved into an apartment at 36, Rue Saint-Louis-en-l'Ile, and that on the door to my apartment was her name, Katz. By pure coincidence; I was renting from a Monsieur Katz. Two small rooms, a kitchen, a bathroom, all very quiet, and on the door was the name Katz in blue and rather small letters, as if Lola and I had not parted at all but continued to be together in Paris, though she was already somewhere else.

What is a journey from one place to another compared to the one we undertake in our hearts? In our hearts not even death can part us, and I see how Lola makes one of her faces, dissatisfied with such a dumb answer.

But then Lola Katz was already dead, and that is what I tell the waitress, the redhead, at Lola's Sirk when she finally begins her evening shift and I already have waited for her more than an hour: that Madame Katz is dead. I say that Lola died of a heart attack in Copenhagen, it was such a cold winter, you know, and that Lola had always spoken warmly of her, the redhead, so that since I happened to be passing by I just wanted to tell her that Lola was not coming back.

The thing about "speaking warmly of her" I had added to make Lola more present, so that she would stay living a little bit longer, though she was already dead. But the rest was true. Around us the last guests are getting ready to leave; they put on their furs to cross the street to the ball at the Opera, the most important and finest ball of the whole season in Vienna. But that does not concern us, each of us has enough to do with our own affairs. We have no part in this departure, and the redhead smiles at me.

"You are moving to Paris, aren't you?"

"I have just come from Paris."

The redhead looks around; there is a cold draft from the door.

"Hadn't you lived there before?"

"No. Never."

"No?" she says.

And I say, "Are you from Vienna?"

"Yes," she says. It is almost certainly a lie. But that doesn't matter, it won't change anything now. Both of us stand still and have nothing more to say to one another, nothing else to do but look at one another. We stand there completely still, and perhaps it is just because she has nothing else to do that she sticks her tongue out and brushes her teeth with its tip. Her front teeth are bared: sticky and red, and between them, a black crack.

I SPENT A LARGE PART OF DECEMBER 1981 IN BED AT THE HOTEL Europejski in Warsaw.

I usually got up just before lunch to make a futile attempt at shaving. Like many other journalists, I was waiting for something to happen, exhausted by what had been happening already day after day, events that seemed to make only a greater tangle of everything. In the last few months the situation had become unbearable. The general, behind his dark glasses and with his little cupid mouth, spoke to the nation without moving his lips. He warned his countrymen. But the nation was not listening, and we journalists reported what the general had to say.

I lay down on the bed. Long afterwards I understood that I had been stricken with depression; I did not realize it at the time, because I imagined that depression was something that could be combated with discipline and a good upbringing; not this limpid listlessness which left you standing in the middle of a room with your pants half pulled on, uncertain as to whether it wouldn't be better to take them off again.

The pants convinced me that depression was a physical condition; it had more to do with shaving than the soul. While I was distracted for a moment it had taken over my body, but no matter how closely I examined myself, I could not find the wound through which this sickness had entered, and without such an opening its presence seemed even more without rhyme or reason. Where was the wound? My body was smooth and unscathed, but my spiritual powers were not strong enough to let me turn over in bed, so at least I did not have to stare at the dirty, yellow-green ceiling in my room. It seemed that this Polish depression was not interested in the soul; it was not interested in anything beyond the body. At most it took its nourishment from the soul and used whatever it could find there to torture and paralyze the body. I could not help thinking about the fact that the two of them, my body and my soul, had once been united and on rather good terms with one another.

Bound to my bed, I continued to search out a cause for my depression. I wanted to place it in a context that could render it comprehensible, something which would perhaps ease the pain, but it was not interested in my wishes; the depression was completely preoccupied with itself, and when it turned to me occasionally it was in order to have a go at me, like whacking a rug with a carpet-beater. It tormented and abused me simply in order to torment and abuse me.

Lying on my back in the hotel bed, I read Max Brod's writings on Kafka. This choice of reading was no premonition, I had not picked the book deliberately; before I left for Warsaw, I had gone to my bookcase at home in Vienna and looked through the books, and I then settled upon the sturdy little German paperback in which Brod, fussily endearing, tries to drive his friend into the arms of God.

I guess I am going to have to try to read this one day, I thought to myself in Vienna.

In my hotel room in Warsaw, the Polish radio woke me every day at seven with the news, preceded by a comical piece of music that went poorly with the mixture of dangers and threats read by the announcer. I put my ear to the radio; was that really music? It sounded like a bird. Every morning it gave its cuckoo call inside the apparatus.

I myself stayed in bed with Brod and his light, soothing voice, which I quickly suspected was just as false as the announcer's, even though it spoke of quite different dangers from the ones on the radio, and of how to save yourself from them. The two voices, the radio's and Brod's, kept grinding away in my hotel room on the second floor without disturbing one another. That was quite all right. A whole world lay between them. I guessed that Brod, too, would have admitted it: what he called "hope" in the book had now shriveled into something that could fit into a handkerchief.

Did tears sometimes run down my cheeks? I did not know why,

but I stayed in bed. Occasionally it happened that I fell asleep with Brod's book lying open on the bedspread. I think that I dreamed. I imagined that many of my friends and family were dead, so that once and for all I had the chance to figure out what I felt for them.

IT SEEMS TO ME THAT DEPRESSION MUST HAVE ITS OWN SET OF LAWS, since every day after waking up I fell back asleep, usually between ten and eleven in the morning, and I knew that at the same moment, the Polish army's honor guard was on its way to the Grave of the Unknown Soldier on Plac Zwycięstwa, and they were going to wake me up with their marching music a few minutes before twelve. Until then, I slept in total security, beyond the reach of depression. When I woke up again I did not even have to look at the clock. I knew that it was shortly before noon, that at that moment the honor guard was coming up Krakowskie Przedmieście and rounding the corner at the Hotel Europejski, past the little shop where you bought cookies and cakes, on the way to the Grave of the Unknown Soldier at Plac Zwycięstwa. Every time it was the brass, not the drums, that awoke me.

I began to appreciate the military. The rhythmic tramping of the honor guard became dear to me, a reminder that there was something that still functioned in Poland, the singular order of the marchers, and I reached out for the open book on the bedspread in which Max Brod's light voice had also awakened and soon began to go on about God and how his friend Franzl was seeking Him.

An excellent institution, a company like that! Men of equal height, a rape of everything civil to the accompaniment of drums and trumpets, a crowd of faces run together into a collective physiognomy, shining with innocence and pride, all of it led by a small baton, something like the lever of a music box. Maybe I fell asleep each time just in order to be awakened by this machinery and its reliable tramp, which gave me back the rhythm that was missing from my own existence. Perhaps it was precisely this marching music which, every day around noon, pulled me back into the world against which I had barricaded myself in the hotel?

I ate breakfast in my room. Why should I, in my condition, show myself to others? I had stopped shaving. Warsaw was in the midst of a deep crisis. There was hardly anything to eat. From one day to the next I was never sure what there might be on the breakfast tray; with indifference I waited to see what would be missing from it each day.

"No milk today," or "Unfortunately no ham." The waiter in his black bow tie and gray vest lingered in my room and looked around carefully. Or there was no more marmalade, butter, or mineral water, and the slice of cheese was something hard and brown that curled at the edges; I saw that it was the same cheese as yesterday, which I had poked to the side of my plate. The waiter made himself at home in my room. Cheese and depression do not go well together. It was best to keep necessities like salt or tea bags in your pocket, but in my room I never wore anything except my underwear; the tea bags and salt were in the pocket of my pants, which were hanging in the closet.

In the afternoons I got dressed with a great deal of effort, and down on Nowy Świat I could sometimes manage to find some apples. I delighted in their colors. They still looked normal, as if normal people would soon bite into them with their normal teeth. On such afternoons I felt almost calm; at least something I did had some meaning.

The waiter had the bad habit of coming in and closing the door behind him. Something was left undone in my room and had to be taken care of immediately; it was as if he were not afraid of the sickness which filled the room. It was only with the greatest difficulty that I got rid of him. I ate alone. I made mincemeat of my table manners, with the feeling that I was performing the sacred duty of the hermit.

Afterwards I opened the door a crack and pushed the tray out into the corridor. Then I locked the door from inside with the security chain. The telephone rang. Occasionally I talked to the outside world over the phone: with my paper in Stockholm, or with Polish friends who breathed heavily into the receiver, excitedly reporting something that I did not understand, only to hang up before I could figure it out. Sometimes I just heard a click. Wrong number. Someone had been connected to the wrong number, or wanted to know if I was still in my room; and in truth, there I was, lying on my back.

BROD'S INTENTION (THIS MUCH I DID UNDERSTAND FROM MY READ-ing) was to attempt to give his friend's life and suffering a higher meaning, posthumously, so to speak. God was the magic word. As a trick it was pretty transparent, but it was human; if only we get the chance, we give people opinions they never had, wishing that they had had them, for the simple reason that they happen to be our own. But in my despair (this, too, I had had the time to learn in bed: despair is the foundation of depression itself) I understood, better than if I had been healthy, the love which, despite everything, rose out of Brod's meddling. Tears came to my eyes. The fussiness of Brod's care and attention no longer bothered me. I no longer stood fully-clothed in front of my bookcase in Vienna, Kafka section, but lay unshaven on my back in a bed in the Hotel Europejski in Warsaw, and the only thing I heard was Brod's voice, which moved me to tears.

So, a love like this was really possible, even when one of the lovers was already dead!

I put the book aside on the bedspread. I wept, I think that I wept, it must have been tears that left the dark stains on the sheets, I wept because I was moved by the heavenly trumpets, by all the brass and drums rising up from Krakowskie Przedmieście, which drove me from my bed, so that I could march, in nothing but my underwear, back and forth in my room, from the door to the window. Outside the military music blared and pounded, and I had to scream to be heard above it, no milk today, I screamed, was forced to scream in order to hear my own voice in my own room, *ingen mjölk idag*, no milk today! In front of the bathroom mirror I repeated those same words, but now silently and to myself, no milk today, I whispered them, like a breath from an angel's mouth, and this phrase ("like a breath from an angel's mouth") I wished that Max Brod had thought of it, so that I could have found it in his book.

Toward afternoon I ventured out for a couple of short hours to do what was expected of me and what I was paid for. I wrote my lines for the paper, but as fast as possible, so that I could rush back to my hotel and lock myself in my room. The words ran out over the paper. I was lying in my bed again. What was it exactly that I had sent to Stockholm? With each day I got sicker. Among my bedclothes, the depression waited for me. It had claws, just as Prague had once had claws which would not let go of Kafka, and they dug themselves into a body which had already passed the border beyond which pain allows nothing but itself, wants nothing but itself, and where anyone who crosses anyway is lost and has to put up with being reduced to nothing but raw material for pain, a pain that will not even show any gratitude.

I tried to think of Brod and about how pain and love must be equally blind, since they come from the same family, and that our greatest pain, death, has the peculiar quality of torturing not so much the one who passes away as the one who is left behind, fit as a fiddle.

Poor Brod, I said half-aloud to myself, my poor little Maxie!

My eyes teared up again, but the tears were not for Franz Kafka's friend but literally for no one, not even for me.

It is certainly true that I was not locked up (I had locked myself up) but I also informed the hotel desk that I was not to be disturbed under any circumstances; anybody who tried to reach me was welcome to think that I was in my room working on my essay, Quo vadis, Polonia? That fall everybody was writing the same essay, but I had already wrapped my typewriter in a towel and shoved it under the bed. On the radio the cuckoos called and reported the news, and I actually opened the window and attempted to air out my sickness. I opened the window as wide as possible. What I was seeking out there was a beach, a cliff, anything at all to hold onto against depression.

Longer than usual I leaned out the window in order to convince myself that the world continued to exist out there.

And there it was! Everything served up like on a breakfast tray: buildings, some trees, people. On the other side of the street, the gray facade of the city garrison, a box made especially for my marching tin soldiers, young lads who occasionally came out onto the steps of the box and were then only themselves, embarrassed and awkward without their usual deafening mechanism; Komenda Garnizonu, guarded by two stone lions with dirty manes and open jaws, ready to swallow me, or were they just yawning, an eternal stone yawn; below the window the hotel's own parking lot with the local alcoholics and their eternal sunburn, thirsty devils who were always ready to wash any car with a German license plate for change; crowds of money changers and black-marketeers, disguised as taxi drivers without meters; a lonely policeman; the hotel doorman, my friend the prisoner-of-war with the watery eyes; the gypsy women who read your palm and made signs in the air; Madame Agatha from the hotel reception; the morning whore; everything was there, nothing was missing.

Everything was in order. Outside, everything was still in its place: stone turned to lions, people turned to shadows, a dismantled music-box, and the pain at being cut off from all of that was even greater than the pain that awaited me in bed.

I CLOSED MY WINDOW AND RETURNED TO BROD'S BOOK. WHAT I needed was a text I could crawl behind, big enough to hide me and my own failure. A text was exactly what was expected from me, but my words had come to an end, no word occurred to me, while Brod poured out quantities of words up and down the pages of his Kafka book, his whole store of sacred words which all had to do with "rescue," "hope," or "salvation," without a single one of them helping me in the slightest, and the tears came again, I began once more to weep.

That same evening my Norwegian friend stepped into my room.

Had I forgotten to lock the door? I lay on my back in the bed. My friend pulled up a chair and sat down on it, right in the middle of the room. I let it happen. I think I suspected what was in store for me. Neither of us said anything. He watched me with curiosity while he drew on his pipe.

"You can't lie around like this much longer," he said.

He kept his pipe in his mouth, and it was true; it couldn't go on like this.

"No."

It surprised me to hear my own voice so suddenly.

I avoided looking him in the eye. On his feet he was wearing his black Romanian dress shoes, manufactured for export to the West, the finest shoes he had ever owned, and he had gotten them as a bribe right in the factor at Cluj. I looked at his shoes. He had already managed to destroy them.

My friend puffed on his pipe.

"You've got to pull yourself together," he said, without taking the pipe from his mouth.

"Yes."

It was completely silent in the room. Even the radio was silent.

"You've got to pull yourself together," he repeated, and pulled on the pipe, rather contentedly, it seemed; after all, he was not the one lying in bed, and I had to admit that he was right. I was the one lying in bed, but I couldn't keep lying there like this for days on end.

"Everything is Brod's fault," I said and felt how the tears were beginning to run down my cheeks again.

Of course it was the truth; I couldn't lie there like this any longer. It couldn't go on like this for days on end, Poland was going to collapse before I managed to pull on my pants. My friend was absolutely right, and he studied me with his pipe in his mouth.

"Hmm," he said.

I had put both hands on the bedspread.

"Max Brod?"

"Yes," I sniffed. "Everything is his fault."

ON THE ELEVENTH OF DECEMBER, IT WAS A THURSDAY, I MANAGED TO pull on my pants and shave for the first time in twelve days. Convinced that nothing more was going to happen, I took the flight to East Berlin. Many of my colleagues did the same. Poland could be left to its own devices a while; the fact that Helmut Schmidt and Erich Honecker were going to have a meeting in the GDR was more important to the solution of the Polish crisis.

Was I healthy again? My head was completely empty. No thoughts turned up there any more, what should have been there was now elsewhere. My body continued to be heavy and immobile. My limbs were stiff; they had nothing special to do and my head just came along for the ride. I tried to lift a hand, then a leg. I had figured that it was only through total physical and mental exhaustion that I could conquer depression, by denying pain the fuel that it needed, and I lifted the other leg, too; it no longer hurt. But what did that mean? Maybe depression had just taken up permanent residence in my body, and even if now, in the middle of December, it seemed to have had its fill and was now keeping quiet, that was nothing I could depend on.

In East Berlin I checked into the Hotel Metropol, and at dusk on the thirteenth of December it was not just some spokesman, but the general himself on the radio. War had broken out in Poland, the general had proclaimed his *stan wojenny*. Polish radio reported the declaration of martial law, the progress of the general's war against the Polish people, and either out of habit or because I still was not well, I listened to Polish instead of German radio; early that Saint Lucy's Day morning, while everyone else was still sleeping, I heard the first reports from the Polish front.

What time could it have been?

I got out of bed and went to the bathroom to wash and shave. It occurred to me that I had left a beefsteak tartare in the closet of my room in the Hotel Europejski. Outside my window the sky was high and clear over Friedrichstrasse. It looked like it was going to be a beautiful day. With my shaving brush, I carefully spread the shaving cream over my face. Did the cuckoo call? I had not finished reading Brod, either. The last two chapters were left.

Some day I will have to read them, I thought, while I began to shave my cheeks clean, first the left one, then the right; I'll have to find out how it turned out with God and Kafka.

Afterwards I rinse the razor carefully under the tap. Somebody is whistling quietly in the room next-door; to my surprise I discover that it is actually me. No one phones. I dry my face with the hand towel. Marching music bounces between the fire walls. I stand on a rug in the middle of the room. Somebody is walking in the corridor outside. Have I cut myself? I grope with my hand behind my left ear, and something white sticks to my fingers, not blood, just lather, just the goddamn shaving cream.